SALESMANSHIP

SALESMANSHIP

Prof. Bholanath Dutta
Asst. Professor
Department of Management Studies
CMR Institute of Technology
Bengaluru - 560 037

Dr. Girish C.
HOD & Asst. Professor
Department of Management Studies
CMR Institute of Technology
Bengaluru - 560 037

FIRST EDITION : 2011

Himalaya Publishing House

MUMBAI • NEW DELHI • NAGPUR • BENGALURU • HYDERABAD • CHENNAI • PUNE • LUCKNOW • AHMEDABAD • ERNAKULAM • BHUBANESWAR • INDORE • KOLKATA • GUWAHATI

First Edition : 2011

Published by	:	Mrs. Meena Pandey for **Himalaya Publishing House Pvt. Ltd.,** "Ramdoot", Dr. Bhalerao Marg, Girgaon, **Mumbai - 400 004.** Phone: 022-23860170/23863863, Fax: 022-23877178 **E-mail: himpub@vsnl.com; Website: www.himpub.com**
Branch Offices	:	
New Delhi	:	"Pooja Apartments", 4-B, Murari Lal Street, Ansari Road, Darya Ganj, New Delhi - 110 002. Phone: 011-23270392, 23278631; Fax: 011-23256286
Nagpur	:	Kundanlal Chandak Industrial Estate, Ghat Road, Nagpur - 440 018. Phone: 0712-2738731, 3296733; Telefax: 0712-2721215
Bengaluru	:	No. 16/1 (Old 12/1), 1st Floor, Next to Hotel Highlands, Madhava Nagar, Race Course Road, Bengaluru - 560 001. Phone: 080-32919385; Telefax: 080-22286611
Hyderabad	:	No. 3-4-184, Lingampally, Besides Raghavendra Swamy Matham, Kachiguda, Hyderabad - 500 027. Phone: 040-27560041, 27550139; Mobile: 09848130433
Chennai	:	No. 85/50, Bazullah Road, T. Nagar, Chennai - 600 017. Phone: 044-28144004/28144005
Pune	:	First Floor, "Laksha" Apartment, No. 527, Mehunpura, Shaniwarpeth (Near Prabhat Theatre), Pune - 411 030. Phone: 020-24496323/24496333
Lucknow	:	Jai Baba Bhavan, Church Road, Near Manas Complex and Dr. Awasthi Clinic, Aliganj, Lucknow - 226 024. Phone: 0522-2339329, 4068914; Mobile: 09305302158, 09415349385, 09389593752
Ahmedabad	:	114, "SHAIL", 1st Floor, Opp. Madhu Sudan House, C.G. Road, Navrang Pura, Ahmedabad - 380 009. Phone: 079-26560126; Mobile: 09327324149, 09314679413
Ernakulam	:	39/104 A, Lakshmi Apartment, Karikkamuri Cross Rd., Ernakulam, Cochin - 622011, Kerala. Phone: 0484-2378012, 2378016; Mobile: 09344199799
Bhubaneswar	:	5 Station Square, Bhubaneswar (Odisha) - 751 001. Mobile: 09861046007
Indore	:	Kesardeep Avenue Extension, 73, Narayan Bagh, Flat No. 302, IIIrd Floor, Near Humpty Dumpty School, Narayan Bagh, Indore - 452 007 (M.P.). Mobile: 09301386468
Kolkata	:	108/4, Beliaghata Main Road, Near ID Hospital, Opp. SBI Bank, Kolkata - 700 010, Phone: 033-32449649; Mobile: 09910440956
Guwahati	:	House No. 15, Behind Pragjyotish College, Near Sharma Printing Press, P.O. Bharalumukh, Guwahati - 781009. (Assam) Mobile: 09883055590, 09883055536
DTP by	:	HPH, Editorial Office, Bhandup (Shilpa Patil).
Printed by	:	A to Z Printer, New Delhi.

Dedication

We dedicate this book to our Parents, Family and all well-wishers.

PREFACE

After having discussed the subject many times with the students, we felt there is a requirement for a customized book on the subject on '*Salesmanship*' as the scope of the subject is very vast and it is very challenging in conceptualizing the ideas.

We are pleased to present this book in order to facilitate the students of MBA, BBA, M.Com. Programme of various Indian and Foreign Universities.

Every care has been taken to ensure 'zero-effect' in the book. But there is always a scope for improvement. And we would request teaching communities and students to suggest in further improvement of the book.

Please reach to author at: bhola_dutta@yahoo.com

Bengaluru
2011

Prof. Bholanath Dutta
Dr. Girish C.

ACKNOWLEDGEMENT

While preparing the manuscript, we have taken the help from some foreign books and inserts the idea, opinion and data, etc., in order to create attractions to the students and clarify critical concepts. We expresse heartiest thanks and gratitude as well as indebtedness to the authors and publishers of those books.

In order to get the book ready for the students, all employees of Himalaya Publishing House have performed such a tremendous job for which no thanks for their contribution will be enough.

We feel great pleasure in expressing our profound gratitude to Dr. K.C. Sabita Ramamurthy – President, CMR Jananadhara Trust (CMRJT) , Shri K.C. Ramamurthy (IPS – Retd Chairman - CMRJT), Shri Jayadeep (CEO — CMRJT), Ms. Tristha Ramamurthy (Vice — President - CMRJT), Dr. K.V.S. Anand Babu – (Principal, CMRIT),Dr. L. Sudarshan Reddy –(Vice-Principal, CMRIT), Dr. DNS Kumar (– Director— CMRIMT), Prof. K. Ravi (– Director, Career Guidance & Placement Bureau, CMRIT), Prof. Sundar Raj Vijaynagar, Prof. MB Lobo and all my esteemed colleagues in CMRIT for their incessant guidance, stimulation and encouragement in my academic endeavor.

Bengaluru
2010

Bholanath Dutta
Dr. Girish C.

CONTENTS

LIST OF FIGURES

LIST OF CASES

LIST OF BOXES

LIST OF TABLE

Chapter 1

Salesmanship

"In the modern world of business, it is useless to be a creative original thinker unless you can also sell what you create. Management cannot be expected to recognize a good idea unless it is presented to them by a good **salesman.**"

- David Ogilvy

Salesmanship – An Introduction - Introduction - Personal Selling - Definition - Nature of Salesmanship - Importance of Salesmanship - Scope of Salesmanship - Salesmanship: Art or Science Origin and Development of Salesmanship - Introduction - Salesmanship in Olden Days - Salesmanship in Modern Says - Competitive Salesmanship - Creative Salesmanship Qualities of a Good Salesman - Introduction - Essential Elements of a Successful Salesman - Qualities of a Good Salesman

OBJECTIVES

At the conclusion of this lesson you should be able to understand:-

- ❖ The concept of Salesmanship
- ❖ Different features of Salesmanship
- ❖ Importance of Salesmanship
- ❖ Scope of Salesmanship
- ❖ Whether Salesmanship is Art or Science
- ❖ Concept of Salesmanship in Olden Days
- ❖ Concept of Salesmanship in Modern Days
- ❖ Attributes of Competitive Salesmanship

- ❖ Attributes of Creative Salesmanship
- ❖ Elements of Salesmanship
- ❖ Qualities of a Salesman
- ❖ The Attributes of a Salesman

CAR SALESMAN : CASE STUDY - I

The Challenge

Selling automobiles is a highly competitive business but when you are a salesman working at just one of six Ford Dealerships, all within a 20-mile radius, the pressure is really on! Customers are increasingly savvy and with six dealerships from which to choose, just getting an opportunity to get in front of a potential buyer is an almost insurmountable challenge.

The Solution

With 80% of all car buyers doing their research and due diligence on the Internet prior to any purchase, it just makes sense that to be competitive a salesman needs to have an effective presence there. Video communications are proven to garner greater results than text or static pictures and the multiple, easy-to-use streaming video products available through **hello**World Studio, offers a cost-effective solution to meeting this need.

The Results

Anthony Williams, salesman at Freeway Ford in Minneapolis, Minnesota, was already actively pursuing potential customers who were searching the web for their ideal car. He realized that 90% of the time these online shoppers were receiving auto-responders from other sales people. Even when they did respond personally, the message was in traditional text format. By using the **hello**World Studio, Anthony was able to respond in a way that was both unique and extremely effective. He began sending video messages that included a few words of introduction and then a video of the car they had expressed interest in. The response was enthusiastic and immediate. He admits that it took him about two weeks to video tape every car they had in inventory but he was always prepared to fire off another video response when the inquiries came in. Sales went through the roof and in no time Anthony became the Number One Ford salesman in the entire region. Freeway Ford owners were so impressed with these results, they became an affiliate and continue to use this innovative way to reach online buyers.

INTRODUCTION

Sale is the pinnacle activity involved in selling products or services in return for money or other compensation. It is an act of completion of a commercial activity. The "deal is closed", means the customer has consented to the proposed product or service by making full or partial payment (as in case of installments) to the seller. Sale is completed by the seller, the owner of the goods. It starts with consent (or agreement) to an acquisition or appropriation or request followed by the passing of title (property or ownership) in the item and the application and due settlement of a price, the obligation for which arises due to the seller's requirement to pass ownership, being a price the seller is happy to part with ownership of or any claim upon the item. The purchaser, though a party to the sale, does not execute the sale, only the seller does that. To be precise the sale completes prior to the payment and gives rise to the obligation of payment. If the seller completes the first two above stages (consent and passing ownership) of the sale prior to settlement of the price the sale is still valid and gives rise to an obligation to pay.

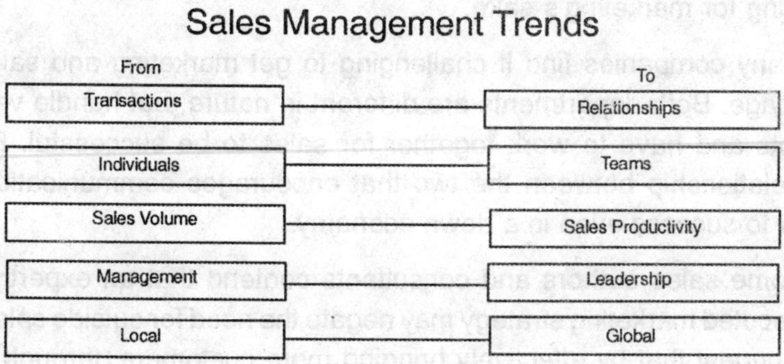

Fig. 1.1. Sales management trends

Marketing and sales are very different, but have the same goal. Marketing improves the selling environment and plays a very important role in sales. If the marketing department generates a potential customers list, it can be beneficial for sales. The marketing department's goal is to increase the number of interactions between potential customers and the sales team using promotional techniques such as advertising, sales promotion, publicity, and public relations, creating new sales channels, or creating new products (new product development), among other things.

In most large corporations, the marketing department is structured in a similar fashion to the sales department and the managers of these teams must coordinate efforts in order to drive profits and business success. For example, an "inbound" focused campaign seeks to drive more customers "through the door" giving the sales department a better chance of selling their product to the consumer. A good marketing program would address any potential downsides as well.

The Sales department's goal would be to improve the interaction between the customer and the sales facility or mechanism (example, web site) and/or salesperson. Sales management would break down the selling process and then increase the effectiveness of the discreet processes as well as the interaction between processes. For example, in many out-bound sales environments, the typical process is out bound calling, the sales pitch, handling objections, opportunity identification, and the close. Each step of the process has sales-related issues, skills, and training needs as well as marketing solutions to improve each discrete step, as well as the whole process.

One further common complication of marketing involves the inability to measure results for a great deal of marketing initiatives. In essence, many marketing and advertising executives often lose sight of the objective of sales/revenue/profit, as they focus on establishing a creative/innovative program, without concern for the top or bottom lines. Such is a fundamental pitfall of marketing for marketing's sake.

Many companies find it challenging to get marketing and sales on the same page. Both departments are different in nature, but handle very similar concepts and have to work together for sales to be successful. Building a good relationship between the two that encourages communication can be the key to success even in a down economy.

Some sales authors and consultants contend that an expertly planned and executed marketing strategy may negate the need for outside sales entirely. They suggest that by effectively bringing more customers "through the door" and enticing them to contact you, sales organizations can dramatically improve their results, efficiency, profitability, and allow salespeople to provide a drastically higher level of customer service and satisfaction, instead of spending the majority of their working hours searching for someone to sell to.

While this theory is present in a few marketing consulting companies the practical and realistic application of this principle has not been widely proven in the market and sales forces worldwide continue to be responsible for developing business as well as closing it.

Some marketing consulting firms postulate that each selling opportunity at each enterprise lies on a continuum of numbers of people involved, necessary degree of face-to-face interaction, overhead, and through-put time, to name a few dimensions. The number of people involved in actual face-to-face selling at, say, a clothing store is probably vastly different than at an online book-seller.

Another key area of conversation that has arisen is the need for alignment and integration between corporate sales and marketing functions. According to a report from the Chief Marketing Officer (CMO) Council, only 40 per cent of companies have formal programs, systems or processes in place to align and integration between the two critical functions. Traditionally, these two functions, as referenced above, has been largely segmented and left in siloed areas of tactical responsibility. Internet applications, commonly referred to as Sales 2.0 tools, have also increasingly been created to help align the goals and responsibilities of marketing and sales departments.

To make effective sales, salesmen must have certain desirable attributes and drive, which is known as salesmanship. Basically, salesmanship is the knack of selling a product or service. Salesmanship is an important method of selling. It is the process of assisting and persuading a prospective buyer to buy a product in a face-to-face situation. It involves direct and personal contact between the seller and his representative with the prospective buyer. It provides feedback and performs the complete job of selling.

Salesmanship today covers a wide range of activities and constitutes an integral part of management. It also offers wide scope for development in future. In fact, modern salesmanship is growing on scientific lines, day by day. Time is not far when a salesman will be in a position to dictate to the producers of goods and services, what, when and how much to produce for sale in the market. This lesson will help you to understand meaning of salesmanship, its feature, importance and scope.

Fig.1.2. Sales management hierarchy

PERSONAL SELLING

Personal selling is a promotional method in which one party (e.g., salesperson) uses skills and techniques for building personal relationships with another party (e.g., those involved in a purchase decision) that results in both parties obtaining value. In most cases the "value" for the salesperson is realized through the financial rewards of the sale while the customer's "value" is realized from the benefits obtained by consuming the product. However, getting a customer to purchase a product is not always the objective of personal selling. For instance, selling may be used for the purpose of simply delivering information.

Because selling involves personal contact, this promotional method often occurs through face-to-face meetings or via a telephone conversation, though newer technologies allow contact to take place over the Internet including using video conferencing or text messaging (e.g., online chat).

Concept

- ❖ It's a part of product mix.
- ❖ It's a personal (face-to-face, telephone, or internet chat) presentation for the purpose of making sales and building relationships.
- ❖ Oral presentation.
- ❖ Salesmanship.
- ❖ Perceive and persuade buyers.

The effort of sales people go far beyond simply making transactions, they also include following:

- ❖ Explaining product benefits.
- ❖ Demonstrating the proper operation of the product.
- ❖ Educating customers about the new product.
- ❖ Answering questions and responding to the objections.
- ❖ Organizing and implementing point of purchase promotion.
- ❖ Arranging the terms of purchase.

Following up the purchase to ensure that customers are satisfied

- ❖ Developing the relationship with the buyers.

Collecting market and competitive information to improve marketing strategies.

Personal selling is mostly used when:

- ❖ The market is concentrated either geographically, in a few industries or a few large customers.
- ❖ The product has a high unit value, quite technical in nature or requires demonstration.
- ❖ The product must be fitted to the individual customer needs as in case of insurance or investments.
- ❖ The product is in the introductory stage of its life cycle.
- ❖ The organization does not have enough money for an adequate advertising.

Features

- ❖ More specific communication aimed at one or more persons.
- ❖ Effective at buyers' preferences, convictions and actions.
- ❖ Cost per person is high and is the most expensive promotional tool.
- ❖ Greater impact on the consumers.
- ❖ Provides immediate feedback.
- ❖ Allow the marketer to adjust message quickly to improve communication.
- ❖ Buyer feels a great need to listen & respond.
- ❖ Long term commitments is needed to develop a sales force.
- ❖ Advantages of personal selling.
- ❖ Personal selling is a face-to-face activity; customers therefore obtain a relatively high degree of personal attention.
- ❖ The sales message can be customized to meet the needs of the customer.
- ❖ The two-way nature of the sales process allows the sales team to respond directly and promptly to the customers'questions and concern.
- ❖ Personal selling is a good way of getting across large amounts of technical or other complex production information.
- ❖ Frequent meetings between the sales force and the customers provide an opportunity to build good long-term relationships.

Exhibit 1.1. Success factors in selling

Sales managers	**Sucess Factors in Selling**	**Mean**	**S.D.**
importance ratings	***Highest level of importance***		
of sucess factors	Listening skills	6.5.2	0.683
for professional	Follow-up skills	6.358	0.772
salespeople	Ability to adapt sales style from situation to situation	6.321	0.687
Source:Greg W.Marshal,	Tenacity—sticking with a task	6.107	0.924
Daniel J. Goebel, and	Well organized	6.084	0.889
Willam C.Moncrief, "Hiring	Verbal communication skills	6.047	0.808
for Sucess at the Buyer-Seller Interface". Journal of	Proficiency in interacting with people at all levels of a customer's organization	6.000	0.991
Business Research 56(2003),	Demonstrated ability to overcome	5.981	1.085
pp. 247-55. Copyright 2003,	objections Closing skills	5.944	1.109
reprinted with permission from Elsevier	Personal planning and time management skills	5.944	0.946
	Proficiency in interacting with people at all levels of your organization	5.912	0.994
	Negotiation skills	5.827	0.975
	Dresses in appropriate attire	5.791	1.063
	Empathy with the customer	5.723	1.074
	Planning skills	5.685	0.966
	Prospecting skills	5.673	1.209
	Creativity	5.670	0.936
	Ability to empathize with others	5.549	1.105
	Skills in preparing for a sales call	5.526	1.219
	Decision making ability	5.502	1.023

Note:All items were scaled as follows: 1 = of no importance at all in hiring decision, 7= of the utmost importance in hiring decisions.

S.D = Standard leviation

FUNDAMENTALS OF SUCCESSFUL PERSONAL SELLING

- ❖ Sales people must have greater flexibility; he must tailor sales presentations to fit the needs and behavior of the individual customers.
- ❖ He must have the potential of explaining the product benefits,answer questions of his customers.
- ❖ He must be truthful.
- ❖ He must behave in a reliable manner.
- ❖ Must seek similarity of personality between you and the customer and the commodity interest and goals.
- ❖ Sales person must see whether the person or his prospect has the potential to pay for the product or not.

Two way form of communication

In selling situations the message sender (e.g., salesperson) can adjust the message as they gain feedback from message receivers (e.g., customer). So if a customer does not understand the initial message (e.g., doesn't fully understand how the product works) the salesperson can make adjustments to address questions or concerns. Many non-personal forms of promotion, such as a radio advertisement, are inflexible, at least in the short-term, and cannot be easily adjusted to address audience questions.

The interactive nature of personal selling also makes it the most effective promotional method for building relationships with customers, particularly in the business-to-business market. This is especially important for companies that either sell expensive products or sell lower cost but high volume products (i.e., buyer must purchase in large quantities) that rely heavily on customers making repeat purchases. Because such purchases may take a considerable amount of time to complete and may involve the input of many people at the purchasing company (i.e., buying center), sales success often requires the marketer develop and maintain strong relationships with members of the purchasing company.

Finally, personal selling is the most practical promotional option for reaching customers who are not easily reached through other methods. The best example is in selling to the business market where, compared to the consumer market, advertising, public relations and sales promotions are often not well received.

Disadvantages of personal selling

Possibly the biggest disadvantage of selling is the degree to which this promotional method is misunderstood. Most people have had some bad experiences with salespeople who they perceived were overly aggressive or even downright annoying. While there are certainly many salespeople who fall into this category, the truth is salespeople are most successful when they focus their efforts on satisfying customers over the long-term and not focusing on their own selfish interests.

A second disadvantage of personal selling is the high cost in maintaining this type of promotional effort. Costs incurred in personal selling include : -

High cost-per-action

Since personal selling involves person-to-person contact, the money spent to support a sales staff (i.e., sales force) can be steep. For instance, in some industries it costs well over (US) $300 each time a salesperson contacts a potential customer. This cost is incurred whether a sale is made or not!

These costs include compensation (e.g., salary, commission, and bonus), providing sales support materials, allowances for entertainment spending, office supplies, telecommunication and much more. With such high cost for maintaining a sales force, selling is often not a practical option for selling products that do not generate a large amount of revenue.

Training Costs

Most forms of personal selling require the sales staff be extensively trained on product knowledge, industry information and selling skills. For companies that require their salespeople to attend formal training programs, the cost of training can be quite high and include such expenses as travel, hotel, meals, and training equipment while also paying the trainees' salaries while they attend.

A third disadvantage is that personal selling is not for everyone. Job turnover in sales is often much higher than other marketing positions. For companies that assign salespeople to handle certain customer groups (e.g., geographic territory), turnover may leave a company without representation in a customer group for an extended period of time while the company recruits and trains a replacement.

OBJECTIVES

Personal selling is used to meet the five objectives of promotion in the following ways:

Building Product Awareness

A common task of salespeople, especially when selling in business markets, is to educate customers on new product offerings.But building awareness using personal selling is also important in consumer markets. Word-of-mouth marketing is leading to personal selling — a useful mechanism for introducing consumers to new products.

Creating Interest

The fact that personal selling involves person-to-person communication makes it a natural method for getting customers to experience a product for the first time. In fact, creating interest goes hand-in-hand with building product awareness as sales professionals can often accomplish both objectives during the first encounter with a potential customer.

Providing Information

When salespeople engage customers a large part of the conversation focuses on product information. Marketing organizations provide their sales staff with large amounts of sales support including brochures, research reports, computer programs and many other forms of informational material.

Stimulating Demand

By far, the most important objective of personal selling is to convince customers to make a purchase. Salespeople accomplish this when they offer detailed coverage of the selling process used to gain customer orders.

Reinforcing the Brand

Most personal selling is intended to build long-term relationships with customers. A strong relationship can only be built over time and requires regular communication with a customer. Meeting with customers on a regular basis allows salespeople to repeatedly discuss their company's products and by doing so helps strengthen customers' knowledge of what the company has to offer.

SCOPE OF PERSONAL SELLING

In the business there are two types of personal selling activities

- Inside selling
- Outside selling

Inside selling

It involves retail stores. In this group we include the sales person in the stores and the sales people at the catalog retailers who take telephone orders. Also included are telephone order takers at manufacturers and wholesalers, most of whom take existing customers' routine orders over the telephone.

Outside selling

Sales people go to the consumer. They make contact by telephone or in person. Most outside sales force usually represents producers or wholesalers, middleman, selling to the business users and not to the household consumers. In outside selling, we also include

1. Producers whose representatives sell directly to the household consumers (e.g.) insurance companies.

2. Representatives of retail organizations who go to the consumer's house to demonstrate a product, give advice, or provide an estimate such as sales people for some furniture stores, home heating and air-conditioning retailers.
3. Representative of non profitable organizations (e.g.) charity fund raisers, workers for political candidate.

DIFFERENT TYPES OF SALESMAN

ORDER GETTERS

The role most synonymous with selling is a position in which the salesperson is actively engaged in using their skills to obtain orders from customers. Such roles can be further divided into :-

New Business Development

A highly challenging yet potentially lucrative sales position is one where the main objective is to find new customers. Sales jobs in this category are often in fields that are very competitive, but offer high rewards for those that are successful. The key distinguishing factor of these positions is that once a sale is made new business salespeople pass customers on to others in their organization who handle account maintenance.These positions include:

Business Equipment Sales

These salespeople are often found in industries where a company's main profits come from the sale of supplies and services that come after an initial equipment purchase. The key objective of business equipment salespeople is to get buyers to purchase the main piece of equipment for which supplies and service are needed in order for the equipment to function. For instance, in the photocopier industry certain salespeople only seek out new accounts and once a photocopier sale is made they pass along the account to other sales personnel who handle the sales of maintenance and supply products.

Telemarketing

This category includes product sales over the phone, whether aimed at business or consumer. While in the US, laws restrict unsolicited phone selling, the practice is still widely used in the business market.

Consumer Selling

Certain companies are very aggressive in their use of salespeople to build new consumer business. These include: retailers selling certain high priced consumer products including furniture, electronics and clothing; housing products including real estate, security services, building replacement products (e.g., windows); and in-home product sellers including those selling door-to-door and products sold at "home party" events such as cosmetics, kitchenware and decorative products.

ACCOUNT MANAGEMENT

Most people engaged in sales are not only involved in gaining the initial order, but work to build and maintain relationships with clients that are intended to last a long time. Salespeople involved in account management are found across a broad range of industries. Their responsibilities involve all aspects of building customer relationships from initial sale to follow-up account servicing. These include:

Business-to-Business Selling

These salespeople sell products for business use with an emphasis on follow-up sales. In many cases, business-to-business salespeople have many different items available for sale (i.e., broad and/or deep product line) rather than a single product. So while the initial sale may only result in the buyer purchasing a few products, the potential exists for the buyer to purchase many other products as the buyer-seller relationship grows.

Trade Selling

Sales professionals working for consumer product companies normally do not sell to the final user (i.e., consumer). Instead their role is focused on first getting distributors, such as wholesalers and retailers, to handle their products and once this is accomplished, helping distributors to sell their products to by offering ideas for product advertising, in-store display and sales promotions.

ORDER TAKERS

Selling does not always require a salesperson use methods designed to encourage customers to make a purchase. In fact, the greatest number of people engaged in selling are not order getters, rather they are considered order takers. In this role, salespeople primarily assist customers with a purchase in ways that are much less assertive than order getters. As might be expected, compensation for order takers is generally lower than that of order getters. Among those serving as an order taker roles are :

Retail Clerks

While some retail salespeople are involved in new business selling, the vast majority of retail employees handle order taking tasks, which range from directing customers to products to handling customer checkout.

Industrial Distributor Clerks

Industrial purchase situations, such as distributors of building products, will also have clerks to handle customer purchases.

Customer Service

Order taking is also handled in non face-to-face ways through customer service personnel. Usually this occurs via phone conversations, though newer technologies are allowing for these tasks to be handled through electronic means such as online chat.

ORDER INFLUENCERS

Some salespeople are not engaged in direct selling activities at all. That is, they do not sell directly to the person who is the ultimate purchaser for their product. Instead these salespeople concentrate on selling activity that targets those who influence purchases made by the final customer. The primary example of an order influencer is the missionary salesperson:-

Missionary

These salespeople are used in industries where customers make purchases based on the advice or requirements of others. Two industries in which missionary selling is commonly found are pharmaceuticals, where salespeople, known as product detailers, discuss products with doctors (influencers) who then write prescriptions for their patients (final customer) and higher education, where salespeople call on college professors (influencers) who make requirements to students (final customer) for specific textbooks

SALES SUPPORT

A final group involved in selling mostly assist with the selling activities of other sales professionals. These include:

Technical Specialists

When dealing with the sale of technical products, particularly in business markets, salespeople may need to draw on the expertise of others to assist with the process. This is particularly the case when the buying party consists of a buying center. In business selling many people from different functional areas may be involved in the purchase decision. If this buying center includes technical people, such as scientists and engineers, a salesperson may seek assistance from members of their own technical staff, who can help address specific questions.

Office Support

Salespeople also may receive assistance from their company's office staff in the form of creating promotional materials; setting up sales appointments, finding sales leads, arranging meeting space or organizing trade show exhibits.

PLACE OF PERSONAL SALESMANSHIP IN THE FIELD OF MARKETING

In the distribution of any product or service there are two coordinate and complementary sets of considerations; those of advertising which aims to influence sales in the masses; and those of personal salesmanship which seeks to influence the individual. Back of these is another more fundamental than either, having to do with Marketing, a term denoting the whole plan of distribution and inclusive of every phase of it.

It includes the selection of marketing channels, trademarking, packaging, pricing, discounts, credits and the many other considerations which must be gone into and decided upon before the first salesman can be employed or the first piece of advertising copy written.

Personal salesmanship takes its place and has its setting in this broader field of marketing. It carries the message of the product and the marketing campaign to the middlemen along the channel of distribution, or to the final consumer, or both. Ordinarily it is the activity which brings in the cash and makes effective, finally the aims and objects of the marketing campaign as a whole.

While at one time very much of an individualist, and selling in his own way and on his own plan, the salesman today finds himself becoming more and more an integral part of a broad marketing plan that involves the necessity of handling and understanding advertising, discounts, credit policies, dealer helps and the numerous other marketing considerations which now play a large part in making the product itself attractive to the customer.

Because a large part of the salesman's work deals with the uncertainties of human nature, he will always remain something of an individualist. He finds himself today compelled to assume the proportions of a broad-gauged business man if he would continue to be an effective salesman.

It is with a statement of the principles and practices of personal salesmanship—with ways and means of developing and increasing personal selling ability—that this Text is concerned. Throughout, we keep constantly in mind this requirement of business knowledge running along with selling effectiveness.

DEFINITION OF A SALE

Legally, a sale is a transaction in which one person persuades another to purchase something at an agreed price. From a business point of view, the sale should result in a profit to the seller. As a legitimate phase of commerce, it should convey an advantage or a profit to the buyer.

As a practical matter, the salesman should keep the last two parts of this definition constantly in mind. He will want to gauge the effectiveness of his selling in terms of profit to his house. And recognition of benefit to the buyer kept constantly before him will prevent an apologetic attitude, not uncommon to salesmen, which, if allowed to develop, tends to lower sales morale.

As a practical matter also, it must be recognized that this mutual advantage may not always materialize. The price of sugar may go up or down and result in a loss either to the buyer or the seller. The price of a security, sincerely recommended, may go off, either temporarily or permanently, sometimes from causes quite aside from its intrinsic value.

Trends in a neighbourhood, changes in the plans of a municipality, or some existing condition, unknown to buyer or seller at the time of sale, may cause real estate to deteriorate in value. But these are ordinary risks to which all business is subjected. The salesman who has acted in good faith is not called upon to assume a personal responsibility for these occasional happenings.

Salesmanship has been defined by different people in different ways: Some people say salesmanship is "Practice of investigating and satisfying customer needs through a process that is efficient, fair, sincere, mutually beneficial, and aimed at long-term productive relationship."

"The art of successfully persuading prospects or customers to buy products or services from which they can derive suitable benefits, thereby increasing their total satisfaction."

- I.J. Sapiro

Professor Stephenson defines salesmanship as: "a concise effort on the part of the seller to induce a prospective buyer to buy even if he had not thought of it favorably."

Gauss, Weightman and Bates observe: "salesmanship consists of persuading people to buy what you have for sale, in making them want it, in helping to make their minds."

E.F. Schumaker defined selling as "the process affecting the transfer with a profit to buyer and seller of goods and services that give them lasting satisfaction that the buyer is predisposed to come back to the seller for more of the same."

According to American Marketing Association, "salesmanship is an oral presentation in a conversation with one or more prospective customers for the purpose of making sales."

According to C.A. Paderson, "salesmanship is the process whereby a seller ascertains and activates the needs or wants of the buyer and satisfies these needs and wants to the mutual continuous advantage of both the buyer and seller."

According to National Association of Marketing Teachers of America "Salesmanship is the ability to persuade people to buy goods or services at a profit to the seller and benefit to the buyers."

Hence, salesmanship can be defined as an art of influencing another person for the object of persuading him to buy a specific product. It may be regarded as the process of winning the confidence of consumer. According to Whitehead "It is a method in regard to the desirability of some article, service or idea." Salesmanship may also refer to convincing a customer by certain technique and he is really persuaded in buying the particular product.

If we closely observe the above definitions, we find certain essential features of salesmanship. They can be summarized as follows:-

1 Salesmanship is the ability to persuade.

2 Salesmanship benefits both the buyers and seller.

3 Salesmanship stands for commercial honesty.

4 Salesmanship aims at winning the buyers' confidence.

5 Ideal salesmanship aims at serving the producer, distributor and consumer.

6 Salesman acts as a link between the seller and the consumer.

7 Salesmanship is an educative process.

8 Salesmanship creates satisfied customers.

NATURE OF SALESMANSHIP

The basic features of salesmanship are as follows:-

a. Salesmanship involves persuasion of customers

A salesman has the ability to convince the people to buy his product. It essentially involves the ability to influence or persuade people to buy a product or service. In fact, persuasion is the soul of modern salesmanship. Gone are the days when a sale was forced on the customers. Modern salesmanship does not rely on pressure tactics or compulsion to clinch a sale. The customer is led to a favourable buying decision through careful and imaginative handling. The salesman necessarily creates a favourable impression on the prospective buyer's mind by presenting the benefits associated with the product or service being offered for sale.

b. Salesmanship involves winning buyer's confidence

Modern salesmanship aims at educating the customer and providing a solution to his problems. This helps in winning his confidence. It aims at winning the confidence of the buyers by persuading and educating them about the availability of products and services, their special features and their utility in satisfying their respective needs.

c. Salesmanship involves providing information

Salesmanship is an educative process. It tells customer the ways in which they can satisfy their needs. Salesman provides information about products available, their broad features and their uses and utility to the customers.

d. Salesmanship aims at mutual benefit

Salesmanship is a two way process. It results in benefits not only to the sellers but also to the buyers. It helps in solving the problems of the buyers and satisfying their needs. Customer satisfaction leads to increase in profitable sales volume for the salesman.

e. Salesmanship creates satisfied customers

Salesmanship in modern days aims at creating satisfied customers, rather than just profit-generating sales. In any marketing transaction, a sale once made would indicate the end of the process. However, once there is a satisfied customer, it is the beginning of long lasting relationship which can create man more sales in future. Therefore, modern salesmanship always aims at creating satisfied customers who will most likely purchase his goods and services as and when necessary.

IMPORTANCE OF SALESMANSHIP

Salesmanship is an indispensable technique of promotion. The importance of personal selling may be described under the following heads:

a. Benefits to consumers

A salesman acts as a friend and guide to consumers. He informs them of new products and new uses of existing products. He helps them in choosing products, which match their needs and incomes. A salesman guides the customers in buying products that will provide maximum satisfaction.

b. Benefits to businessman

They help in the creation of demand for new products and in the extension of markets for existing ones. Through personal selling, a businessman can not only inform customers of his products but can know their tastes, attitudes and behaviour. Such information is helpful in the design and development of products that match market demand. By creating large scale and regular demand, salesmanship makes planned and regular mass production possible. Salesmen help to build up a favourable corporate image necessary to secure repeat sales.

c. Benefits to society

Salesmanship helps to expand employment and income of a country through large and rapid sales turnover. Salesmen provide marketing information to producers so that consumers can get new and better products.

Salesmen perform several non-selling tasks, e.g., after sale service, meeting complaints, conducting marketing research, providing credit information, delivering goods, collecting payments, etc. Salesmen help minimize price fluctuations and trade cycles by matching demand and supply.

Some of the importance can be summarized as follows

1. Salesmanship helps to create demand for new products or new brands. It influences to change in patronage from one source of supply to another which results concentration of purchases of specific product.
2. As it wins the buyer's confidence so it helps to make regular and permanent customers.
3. The person who is engaged in convincing the public about the desirability of a specific product is called a salesman. He informs the customers about the usefulness of commodity with a view to inducing him to buy the goods.
4. He establishes the goodwill of firm in the market. So the sales volume may easily be increased.
5. He constantly observes the fashion, taste, like and dislike of customers and informs the producer about their choice.
6. He helps to establish close relationship between the manufacturer and consumer.

SCOPE OF SALESMANSHIP

Salesmanship has become an indispensable part of business activity. Today everybody is a seller, selling something or the other. It has been rightly pointed out that sales are the life blood of business. The job of today's salesman is not confined to selling consumer goods. He also has to sell industrial and agricultural goods and services like transport, repairing, teaching, painting, banking, legal consultancy, medicine, insurance, and so on. Thus, the scope of salesmanship is vast and varied with the advancement of science and technology, the scope of salesmanship has become unlimited. It is a skill which is essential in every sphere of human activity. Everyone of us, in one sense or the other is a salesman. The job of a lawyer pleading his case, a teacher teaching his ideas, an applicant applying for a job, resembles the job of a salesman. In each of these cases, skill and ability of a salesman is very much necessary in order to be successful. Thus, we observe that the skill of salesmanship is not restricted to selling goods and services but is applicable in several other fields.

A modern salesman occupies a pivotal position in the structure of an organisation. Modern sales managers take decisions about recruitment, selection, training and controlling of sales force. Similarly, the activities of production and sales are also considerably regulated by the sales manager of an organisation.

Salesmanship today covers a wide range of activities and constitutes an integral part of management. It also offers wide scope for development in future. In fact, modern salesmanship is going on scientific lines, day by day. Time is not far when salesmanship will be in a position to dictate to the producers of goods and services, what, when and how much to produce for sale in the market.

The scope of the salesman's activities will, of course, depend to a considerable extent upon the line he is selling and the channels of distribution used. However, it is possible to present an outline, part or all of which will apply to the average salesman. First and foremost, his main activity is to sell an adequate volume at satisfactory profit.

As a matter of fact, all of the rest of the rather wide range of his activities should and does contribute in one way or another, directly or indirectly, to this main objective. This will be found to require a working knowledge of his industry, a fairly definite knowledge of his company, its history and its organization, an even more detailed acquaintance with his sales department and its every activity, and a most thorough knowledge of the product or offering to be sold and how best to sell it.

He must study his territory, analyse it and know it, thoroughly organize it, build a list of prospects in it on which he can keep profitably busy, and create in it a personal goodwill for himself and business goodwill toward his company.

His is the duty of cooperating with the credit manager through his intimate knowledge of local conditions and detailed knowledge of the individual customer. Many times, of course, he must lend personal assistance in the collection of accounts. He will also, whenever possible, cooperate with the production end of the business by reporting the reaction upon the trade and upon the consuming public of the company's product and production policy and let the home office know of competing articles and the reception accorded them.

He will cooperate with the advertising manager by coordinating his activities with the general marketing and advertising plan, sell his company's advertising policies to the customer, assist him in availing himself of advertising helps and encourage him in every way to tie in with the company's advertising. It is not at all unusual today for a salesman actually to sell the customer the entire marketing and advertising plan rather than the goods alone.

Likewise, he is responsible for carrying out, so far as his territory is concerned, the instructions, policies and ideas of his sales manager. One of his most important duties frequently will be to assist his customer by constructive suggestion and assistance in stock display, improved merchandising methods, advertising, and window trim, as well as by instruction and suggestion to clerks, to move the goods he has sold.

For it is generally understood today that goods are not truly sold when they are placed upon the shelves of the dealer. They are not really sold until they have moved off the shelves of the dealer into the hands of the final consumer, for then and only then can a new order find its way back through the channels of trade.

In addition, the salesman must present a detailed report of his daily activities and any changes in trade conditions, and should take a personal pride in submitting any personal sales methods which have been effective with him and which he believes will be helpful to other men in the sales organization. He has a moral obligation constantly to improve his salesmanship by reading and study, consulting the latest books and keeping in close touch with his trade journals.

In the foregoing outline, we have assumed a salesman selling "to the trade." Some of these activities will not apply to the speciality salesman who sells to users or consumers, but some of these duties devolve upon all salesmen; and the principle involved—thorough preparedness from every angle—applies to all. It will be seen that the scope of personal salesmanship is a broad one.

SELLING ABILITY IS NOT INHERENT

Business man had been arguing that "Salesmanship cannot be taught. It must be born in a man." As he talked, he had been watching one of his men in the front part of his store demonstrate a mechanical device. When the customer had gone, he stepped quickly forward. "Bill," said he, "I noticed that you did all the demonstrating and all the talking.

Why didn't you let your prospect handle the machine—operate it? By doing that you would have held his interest and created in him a desire to own the machine. Instead of that, he walked out on you.".

He had laid down a definite principle of salesmanship. He had endeavoured to do that which he had just finished stating could not be done—teach salesmanship. This illustrates how little thought a man is giving to the subject when he says that salesmen are born and not made.

It is undoubtedly true that some men are "born" salesmen in the sense that they have selling instinct more highly developed than most men. It is also true that many such men succeed in selling work without any special training other than that afforded by their personal experience.

It is also true, however, that probably a majority of men have latent in them real selling ability which requires nothing but sound instruction and training to bring it out and get it into action. There are "born" salesmen in the same sense that there are "born" musicians or "born" artists.

It cannot be gainsaid, however, that musical or artistic ability must be developed by training. Almost any man of ordinary intelligence, provided there is not present in him some obvious drawback of temperament or physical ability, can be developed into a sales producer satisfactory both to himself and to his house.

CAN SALESMANSHIP BE TAUGHT?

Not so long ago, it was not at all unusual for a sales executive to decry the necessity for any extended formal training for recruits to the selling organization. A man of more or less apparent selling ability was hired, given a day or so around the plant or office, handed a sample case and started for his territory with a few parting instructions—to sink or swim.

Only one out of ten breasted the tide. This method has long been recognized as inefficient and wasteful of the company's money, of territory, and of good sales material. The leading organizations of the country have long since demonstrated conclusively that adequate sales training, both before the salesman actually enters upon his selling work and after he is in the territory, greatly reduces the percentage of salesmanship mortality, makes satisfactory producers out of mediocre men who would otherwise inevitably fail, and gets good men into profitable production sooner than would otherwise be possible.

Furthermore, competition becomes constantly keener and the salesman must be more thoroughly prepared for the job than before. It is no longer enough that he be a genial mixer and a persuasive talker. He must have business instruction and business training. Business executives are giving more serious attention than ever today to the development of good salesmanship through adequate instruction and training.

It goes without saying that marketing, sales, and advertising executives should possess a detailed and thoroughgoing knowledge of every phase of personal salesmanship and every detail of the salesman's work.

It is equally true that every other executive in business, no matter in what department his work may lie, should have a knowledge of this, one of his company's most important activities. In determining the general business policies of the company—credit terms, discounts, brands, sizes, containers, advertising and distribution policies—a sympathetic knowledge of the salesman, his needs and his problems is necessary.

After all, the main purpose of the organization is to sell the product. The executive working in fields more or less removed from the keen competitive battle on the firing line of business is all too likely to lose sight of, or never to know, the details of the salesman's duties, activities and responsibilities. His intelligent and sympathetic cooperation is of vital importance.

Furthermore, selling in its broader sense consists in bringing another to your point of view and inducing him to take a desired action. This is a matter of personal influence and persuasion—in other words, of personal salesmanship. The highest type of executive is one who leads rather than drives his subordinates. He secures voluntary action rather than compulsory action. He sells ideas.

The principles and methods of personal salesmanship are inherent in his work. The financial executive, production manager, advertising manager, all must sell their plans to the general manager, president, or board of directors —and sell, too, the necessity of appropriations for carrying them out. The corporation treasurer, when he goes to borrow funds for the business, sells the banker on his proposition.

The general manager must sell his plans to his department heads if he is to secure whole-hearted cooperation. The great lawyer pleading for a life before a jury is in essence simply trying to sell that jury a point of view. Every man then has a vital interest in that knowledge of the human mind and that practice of persuasion in which lie the essence of salesmanship.

SALESMANSHIP: ART OR SCIENCE

The Art of Salesmanship

As Art is a science applied, it involves actual doing. It is the practical application of knowledge or natural ability. One might have a broad knowledge of the science of medicine and possess, or develop, but indifferent ability in applying it. It may be said, speaking generally, that knowledge of a science is gained by study; proficiency in an art by practice.

Knowledge of selling principles alone is not sufficient. Actual practice in their application is necessary. But knowledge of principles will enable one to get his selling ability into action more quickly and make of him a better salesman than he otherwise could hope to be. The art of salesmanship may be defined as the 'ability to apply fundamental selling principles to the circumstances of the individual selling situation'.

The Science of Salesmanship

Selling is definitely an Art. But Art is an applied Science. It is the practical application of knowledge or natural ability. It is possible to make a study of the sales process and the experience and methods of successful salesmen. Because of the many immeasurable human elements involved, it will always remain, to some degree, an inexact science.

Mathematics, physics, chemistry are regarded as science. Salesmanship may also be considered as science on the basis that salesmanship is a specialised knowledge that has its own standards, principles and theories. It has already developed a systematized knowledge of its own like the other subjects of science. However, these rules and principles cannot be applied to each and every one in the world since all human beings are not equal. No doubt, although a majority of the customers can be convinced by a particular line of approach and behaviour of the salesman, the same cannot be applied to all customers and it may not be successful in each and every case. This is so because the process of handling customers can never be reduced to unchangeable laws and rigid principles. Thus, salesmanship is not exact science like physics or mathematics. It is science based on human psychology. It can be considered as science like sociology or economics.

Therefore, the term Salesmanship includes both knowledge of fundamental selling principles and the ability to apply them in the actual making of sales. It comprehends both the science and the art.

Salesmanship: A Profession

According to the Concise Oxford Dictionary, 'a profession is a "vocation, especially one that involves any branch of learning or science". Profession may be defined as an employment mechanical but requiring some degree of skill.

Most often the question is raised whether salesmanship is a profession or not. In order to ascertain the same, the basic characteristics of profession should be discussed in detail. A profession has the following characteristics:

- It is an organized body of knowledge.
- It must possess a formal structure of specialized knowledge.
- It must possess an organised plan of individual training for the people who prefer to enter the profession.

- It must possess an established and accepted code of ethics.
- It must possess a set of standards for admission and disqualification.
- Service to others before self interest must be the prime motto. In other words, principle of service first and profit last, must exist.

If the above characteristics of profession are examined for salesmanship, it can be seen that it has yet to become a true profession like law, medicine, etc. Salesmanship, like other professions, is yet to have a ready-made knowledge for application in each and every situation. Skill and technique applied by a salesman to clinch a sale varies from person to person and with place and time. A particular selling method and technique cannot claim to have a command over all possible selling methods and techniques. Therefore, salesmanship cannot unhesitantly be called a profession. A great deal of effort and perfection is needed before salesmanship achieves the status of true profession. It is, however, capable of growing into a profession with substantial development of knowledge.

IMPORTANCE AND UTILITY OF SALESMANSHIP

In the modern day world, distribution system is a complex as well as difficult process. With the vast expansion of business and commerce and increasing competition, establishment of link between the manufacturer and the consumers has become very essential. Successful and profitable operations of business enterprises depend to a great extent on the creation of such a connection. In the process of maintaining the link between the manufacturer, seller and the consumers, salesmanship plays a vital and significant role.

In the earlier days, manufacturing activities were undertaken relatively on a small scale and accordingly distribution network was spread over a small area. Goods were produced either only after receiving the orders or for which sufficient demand existed. Such a high demand, less supply situation was quite convenient to the manufacturers to sell their goods and services. Further, there existed little or no competition in those days. Therefore, salesmanship during those days was of little use for the manufacturers and sellers.

After industrial revolution, production activities started being undertaken on a fairly large scale and mostly in anticipation of demand. Consequently, greater efforts became essential on the part of the sellers to create demand. With the substantial increase in the volume, the business territory also expanded and spread to national and international levels. Distribution also became quite complicated because of stiff competition among producers of similar and identical products. Therefore, the producers and the distributors needed the skill and persuasive ability of efficient sales force in order to sell their products and services in the market. In fact, distribution of products and services in today's competitive as well as ever expanding market is impossible without modern salesmanship and publicity.

Today salesmanship holds a key position in the business world of manufacturing and distribution. As facts stand today, salesmanship is universally accepted as an essential today, might not have been there but for the efforts of the salesman. One can easily examine the utility of salesmanship to producers, society, consumers, government and the salesmen himself.

Producers and manufacturers

In the earlier days, goods were mostly manufactured whenever orders were placed for them. Manufacturing in anticipation of demand was a rare phenomenon during those days. As a result, the process of selling was quite easy and never considered as an important function. When mass production became the order of the day, production of goods started being undertaken on a large scale in anticipation of demand. Consequently, the essentials of selling efforts were keenly felt by the manufacturers. As a matter of fact, efficient salesmen are able to sell whatever the producers produce, in a competitive market. Thus, they help the manufacturer to continue and expand production, thereby, expanding the overall capacity of the industry. Therefore, producers of manufacturers are significantly benefited by salesmanship in an economy.

Society

Salesmanship is also of considerable importance to the society. Besides helping the producers to produce more, sell the same and earn high profits, salesmanship also benefits the shareholders by way of higher dividends and the middlemen to make more profits and the benefits arising out of salesmanship. The sales force of an organisation always contributes to increased sales as well as profits. A portion of such profits is distributed among shareholders and employees in the form of dividends and wages respectively, thereby, increasing the per capita income and also the living standard of the people. The remaining balance is further invested in the business which is popularly known as 'ploughing back of profit'. Such activities contribute to the growth and development of an economy. Further, salesmanship enriches the life of society. It is through persuasive techniques of salesmanship which enriches the life of society. It is through persuasive techniques of salesmen that we have started using many items like refrigerators, vacuum-cleaners, washing machines, etc. These products, once considered luxuries, have become necessities in our daily lives gradually. Thus, salesmanship has helped in raising the standard of living of people in the society.

Salesman

Salesmanship also benefits the Salesmen considerably. It is now viewed as a lucrative career and an attractive source of employment for many people. Salesmanship as a career is highly remunerative. Generally a salesman is paid monthly salary and commission which is linked with sales volume. Any increase in sales ultimately increases the commission of the salesman. A sincere and hardworking salesman therefore can increase his commission by incremental sales. The salesman has the opportunity of learning business methods and practices from close quarters. Later, if he wishes, he can set up a business of his own on the basis of his experience in selling and knowledge of the business. A travelling salesman enjoys the opportunity of the outside world, resulting in developing one's personality. It makes an individual dynamic, resourceful, self-confident, social, cheerful and broadens his outlook. Salesmanship is a skill which is in continuous demand throughout the world. Thus, salesmanship skills are universally acceptable.

SALESMANSHIP IN OLDEN DAYS

Earlier days, selling was not regarded as noble profession by the general public. Seller faced very tough time during those days. Nobody was ready to listen to a salesperson. But over the period of time, salesman has become highly educated professional and gained lot of respect in the society. The concept of selling has undergone a lot of change over the years. It is quite different from the earlier concept. In the past, the salesman, used to take orders in his job which was more or less routine and mechanical. But, modern selling, on the other hand is more creative.

The Roman equivalent of salesman meant cheat. It was true that many of the commercial adventurers were pirates who would attack a merchant vessel, kill the crew, seize the cargo and scuttle the vessel to remove the traces of their crime.

It was the responsibility of the buyers to satisfy themselves whether the goods they purchased were upto the mark or not. The seller neither disclosed the defects nor gave any assurance about the quality of the goods they were selling. The main idea of the salesman was to sell goods by any means. Different prices were charged from different customers. High prices were charged invariably for all the goods.

Further, selling was not regarded as an honorable profession by the general public. During those days, the society looked at selling with contempt and disrespect. Sellers hardly expected repeat orders from the customers, since most of them cheated and deceived customers in the selling transaction. Societal status of the salesman was the lowest; both in terms of earnings as well as mobility and people took up sales jobs only as the last resort.

Most of the commodities in those days were sold in small general stores. There were also a few travelling salesman. Advertising and publicity was rare.

SALESMANSHIP IN MODERN DAYS

The industrial revolution of the 18th century gradually swept off the earlier concept of production and distribution. Manufacturing activities started in a big way. This time transportation system like railways, roadways, sea routes also expanded rapidly. This development boosted the commercial activities. Mass production started and competition also became intense. This led to the emergence and development of modern day salesmanship which aimed at winning the confidence of the prospective consumers through persuasion.

Gradually, producers started improving the quality of products and providing guarantee and warranty against defective products so as to win the confidence of potentials consumers. The theory of *'caveat emptor'* gradually lost its significance. Sellers started offering several freebies, benefits, concessions to attract the customers in order to sell in the competitive market.

Sellers gradually realised that in the long run honesty proved to be the best policy. As a result, they followed the principle of commercial honesty, creating permanent and satisfied customers by selling genuine goods and offering dependable services at reasonable prices through honest means.

With the passage of time, travelling salesman was appointed by the manufacturers for canvassing their products and services. These travelling salesmen were given the responsibility of contacting prospective buyers and dealers, explaining the merits and usefulness of goods and services, terms of sale etc. At present, manufacturers and distributors of medicine, stationery, luxury goods, books and journals engage such travelling salesmen who travel from place to place canvassing their products and services to the prospective buyers and dealers.

The stigma of sales profession being dishonest has changed long since. The career of a salesman is no longer considered to be the job of last resort. In fact today, salesman is a very sought after career. Modern selling is very creative. The salesman always attempts to create needs, makes the prospective buyers aware of such needs and uses his resourcefulness and imagination to persuade them to buy products and services in order to satisfy their needs. Modern day salesmanship is a skill set to persuade the customers and make a sale which fulfils their requirement.

Another significant aspect of modern day salesmanship is the emergence and growth of selling services. They are basically intangible or impersonal activities which are offered for sale or in connection with sale of goods. Services may be either consumer related or industry related. Consumer services include hotel, personal care like beauty parlour, hair care, entertainment, transport, warehousing, insurance, banking, advertising, engineering, sales promotion, consultancy like legal , health etc. thus as we see, individuals as well as industries and business houses require these services. Professionals rendering these services require high level of knowledge and skill of salesmanship since they have to sell intangibles or impersonal activities. These service salesmen usually form firms and companies for enlarging their scope of selling.

Thus, the concept of selling has undergone a lot of change over the years. It is quite different from the earlier concept. In the past, salesman, used to take orders and his job was more or less routine and mechanical. He used to show goods, wait for an order and receive payment. He made little attempt to guide, help or persuade the customer in the process of selling.

Exhibit 1.2. B.J. Hughes' Checklist of Dos and Don'ts Help It to be a Customer-oriented Company

Salesperson's Checklist of Dos	Salesperson's Checklist of Don'ts
1. Known the current products/services and their applications in your area. Look for the new techniques/services your customers want.	1. Never bluff: If you don't know, find out.
2. Maintain an up to date personal call list.	2. Never compromise your's or anyone else's, morals or principles.
3. Listen attentively to the customers.	3. Don't be presumptuous–never with friends.
4. Seek out specific problems and the improvements your customers want.	4. Never criticise a competitor–especially to a customer.
5. Keep calls under five minutes unless invited to stay.	5. Do not take criticisms or turndowns personally–they're seldom meant that way
6. Leave a calling card if the customer is not in.	6. Do not worry or agonize over what you cannot control or influence. Be concerned about what you can affect.
7. Identify the individual who makes or influences decisions and concentrate on that person.	7. Do not offend others with profanity.

8. Entertain selectively; your time and your expense account are investments.	8. Do not allow idle conversation to dominate your sales call. Concentrate on your purpose.
9. Make written notes as reminders.	9. Don't try to match the customer drink-for-drink when entertaining. Drink only if you want to and in moderation.
10. Plan work by the week, not by the clock. Plan use of available time, Plan sales persentation. Have a purpose.	10. Don't be so gung ho that you use high-pressure tactics.
11. Ask for business on every sales call.	11. Never talk your company down– especially to customers. Be proud of it and yourself.
12. Follow through with appropriate action.	12. If you smoke, never do so in the customer's office unless invited to smoke.

COMPETITIVE SALESMANSHIP

A distinction should also be made between creative salesmanship and competitive salesmanship. The selling of fountain pens and typewriters in earlier days when they were newly introduced in the market was an example of creative salesmanship. Here the pioneer salesman had to sell the "idea" that the use of fountain pens or typewriters was a better method of conducting business correspondence than the earlier ones. However, these articles are today considered a matter of course and bought automatically. Yesterday's novelty thus become today's necessity and the salesmanship involved which was once "creative" has become "competitive" in this type of products.

Competitive salesmanship aims at increasing the sales of the existing products or services, no matter how the sales have increased. Here, the main motive is to clear the stocks of the manufacturer in the competitive market. In order to increase the sales, the salesman must make all possible efforts. Most often credit is offered to the prospective customers to boost sales. Sometimes, goods are offered at a cheaper price by the salesman.

The main motive of the competitive salesman is to outwit the competitors in the market by increased sales volume. Competitive salesmanship aims chiefly at increasing the sales of the existing product or services, by adopting traditional methods and rarely uses new and innovative methods in the selling process.

CREATIVE SALESMANSHIP

Creative salesmanship hardly aims to increase sales. Rather, his job is to motivate customers and make them satisfied with the sale. Basically, creative salesmanship aims at creating sales for new and novel products or services.

Even in specific cases, producers or sellers resort to creative salesmanship aims chiefly at increasing the sales of the existing product or services, by adopting traditional methods and rarely uses new and innovative methods in the selling process.

Creative salesman generally provides more emphasis on the utility and services of the products offered for sale. Such salesmen do not aim at cheap sales and rarely adopt pressure tactics in selling. Instead, emphasis is given to the ultimate satisfaction that the product or service would provide. A close look at the history of marketing clearly indicates that it is only through creative salesmanship that most of the products or services we see today have been introduced successfully in the market. Many of the products or services might not have seen the light of the day but for the creative salesmanship.

Creative salesmanship requires adequate technical knowledge of the product. The more he knows about the product, the more appeals or benefits for the customer will the salesman be able to think up creatively. This means that the salesman who works harder will make more appeals and sell more creatively. The quality of his salesmanship will determine to a large extent how creatively he can sell. More important perhaps than how much the salesman knows. How well he has organised such knowledge in his sales talk on presentation. Basically the salesman has to sell the "need" for his product to the customer. Creative selling is not "high pressure" selling or "trick" it is the result of creative thinking on the salesman's part and requires imagination and resourcefulness. It consists of making customer realize the need through dramatizing it where required, arousing his curiosity, making him buy more in his own interest and above all making him buy now.

Whether you sell a product, provide a service or are a politician - your success depends on how well you understand and implement the dynamics of Creative Selling. There are basically three types of selling . . . charismatic, classical and creative.

In charismatic selling, you become part of the value along with the product or service. A person buys because he/she likes you. The exact same product or service may be had from many sources but because the individual connects with you, they will purchase from you. You become an important part of the sale as you add worth and assurance.

Classical selling is selling benefits, value, uniqueness, product or service as a problem solver. The buyer sees the product or service as filling a need and buys that resolve. They will hardly remember the salesperson. The buyers objective is in fulfilling their need no matter who the sales person is.

Creative selling is simply the art of allowing the prospect to sell himself/herself. You just act as a guide in the process. Pointing out those things that the prospect finds most stimulating. You help the prospect build a mental picture so he/she can see himself/herself using, and enjoying its benefits. Help the prospect to focus on the product so he/she may experience the feeling of ownership. Give the prospect an awareness of the relationship between your product and the "good life" that he/she longs for. Turn the product into a living, breathing vital thing.

Creative selling is more than a few words. It's a continuous process of letting the prospect know that his/her welfare is very important to you. No matter what you sell, you must be less concerned with the product than you are with the prospect. Forget about how much you are going to make on the sale, that's a result of you doing your job right. The only thing of importance is the prospect — and the filling of his/her desires.

A few simple rules can guide you toward the goal of creative salesmanship and do wonders for your pocket book.

1 Know the product – the better you know the product the better you can relay its benefits and engage the prospect in it.

2 Know your market – where can you find new markets for your product? Are there any new uses for it? Are you selling to the right demographics?

3 Know your prospects – are you filling the prospects needs? Are you addressing his/her concerns?

4 Know what you are going to say – before you talk to the prospect, prepare your presentation and know just how you're going to present it. Know the answers for every stall or objection the prospect will bring up. Great athletes practice and practice and practice, until they master the game. You must commit yourself to be a master of salesmanship.

5 Know you're going to close the sale – feel in your mind that the prospect needs what you are offering and that he/she will buy it. See yourself fulfilling the customer's needs. Embrace the customer and his/her desires as your own. Be thankful and happy you are part of their buying experience.

ATTRIBUTES OF A CREATIVE SALESPERSON

In addition to having a person who understand and apply the creative selling process, an organization should try to have salespeople who possess certain attributes that can make them more effective in their jobs. These attributes, which can be grouped into mental and physical categories, merit further discussion.

Judgment, common sense, maturity, intelligence—these and other terms are used interchangeably with judgment. A salesperson knows that it does not pay to argue with a customer. The salesperson also knows that the firm should never be "cut" in front of customers. These situations reflect the use of good judgment on the part of the employee. Please note that the term maturity is sometimes used in place of judgment but that it is not necessarily a function of age. Many older people do not use good judgment while some young employees will have a high level of commonsense.

Be Tactful

If an employee has a keen sense of what to say and do, many problems can be overcome before they are created. Many employees give little thought to the impact of their actions. A child playing with toys in the toy store is told in a blunt manner to "quit playing with the toys and go find your mother." While all this is going on, the mother is standing behind the salesperson. Was a confrontation with the child necessary? No. Could it have been handled differently? Yes. How does the child and mother feel about the store? The feeling is not good. This salesperson lacked the ability to know what to do and say in order to maintain good customer relations.

Attitude

A good salesperson will have a positive attitude toward customers, merchandise, services, and the business. A good attitude means that an employee is willing to accept suggestions, to learn and to apply the steps in the creative selling process, and to not be afraid of work. A salesperson with a bad attitude can create unnecessary problems. A bad attitude is contagious. If any employee is otherwise competent, management should work with the employee to develop a positive attitude. Positive attitudes can result in sales.

Selected Physical Attributes

To be a success, the salesperson must physically belong in the firm's particular environment. Personal appearance and personal hygiene are important in the selling environment. In terms of personal appearance, a slim salesperson would be more appropriate than a larger person in a sales position at a health spa. Equally important in terms of personal appearance is a clothing salesman who wears last years clothing. He will have difficulty in selling the latest fashions to his customers. Personal appearance does count in the selling equation.

As for personal hygiene—body odor, bad breath, dirty hair, soiled clothes, scruffed shoes, and unkempt hands are all reasons why a sale may be lost.

Obviously, be tactful when handling the problem of personal hygiene. An observant owner manager should keep a watchful eye out for hygiene problems among the staff when necessary, counsel the offending employee in private about improving his or her appearance. If you do not feel physical attributes are important, ask yourself if you would buy low-calorie health foods from an overweight salesperson with body odor. Sounds funny? It is not! Your customers will usually react unfavourably to this and similar inappropriate selling situations.

Word of caution, mental and physical attributes of salespersons are important. Management must continue to observe sales personnel in regard to the desired traits. Either mental or physical attributes of individuals may change over time relative to desired attributes. Management must be aware of this possibility and attempt to correct any deviations from desired norms before problems are created. A business can greatly enhance its probability of success by stressing the creative selling process, giving special attention to the desired mental and physical attributes of a creative salesperson. Good creative selling can provide the competitive edge

Creative Selling Process

The creative selling process consists of eight steps, none of which is less important than any other if the process is to be effective. It should be emphasized to all employees that all steps are vital to the achievement of effective selling.

1. Pre-Customer Contact

A smart builder would not attempt to build a house without a good foundation. Likewise, a businessperson should not place people on the sales floor or telephone until these people know the business, merchandise, services, and customers. Before any contact is made with the customer, every salesperson should know:

1. Policies, Procedures and Rules: Have these in writing for all employees to see and know.
2. Operation of Equipment: No matter whether the register is electronic or mechanical, the time to learn how to work it is not after a sale while the customer waits for change.
3. Target Market Knowledge: The better salesperson knows something of the likes and dislikes of the firm's primary customers. The business operator should tell all sales personnel about the business's customers and their lifestyles. Tell the salespeople about customer's interests and ability to buy.

4. Product Knowledge: A salesperson gains confidence by knowing about the products and services he or she is selling. If a person sells shoes, it helps to know the merchandise as well as how to fit them. If a person sells building materials, the selling job is probably more effective if the salesperson can also help answer questions about home repairs. It helps the person who sells clothes to know something about fabrics and current fashions. If the person is in the lawn service business, that person should know about lawn care. Most sales personnel will not take the initiative to acquire product knowledge on their own. It is management's responsibility to encourage employees to gain product and service knowledge. Management should make such knowledge available to them.

2. Prospecting

Although not appropriate to every selling situation, prospecting should be used whenever possible. Essentially, prospecting involves not waiting for the customer to show up at a store or phone about a service. It is concerned with taking the initiative by going to the customer with a product or service idea. Prospecting may be of two types: new or regular customer prospecting.

New Customer Prospecting

A salesperson sees that a person is getting married. Action is taken on this knowledge by contacting the person and telling her about appropriate items (or services) that might be of assistance to a new bride. By using newspapers and personal contacts, a salesperson can take the initiative to contact and create new customers.

Regular Customer Prospecting

A firm's best prospects are its current customers. A salesperson should make a practice of calling regular customers on a periodic basis to tell them about products or services. "Hello, Mrs. Anderson, I just wanted to tell you about the new shipment of dresses we received today. As I unpacked them I saw several that made me think of you." Prospecting with regular customers works! All salespeople should be encouraged to prospect by phone and in-person whenever they see regular customers. A word of caution must be emphasized. Do not go to the well too often. Prospecting with the same regular customer on a frequent basis can make prospecting lose the special feeling that it can create in customers. Do not overuse it.

3. Initial Contact

The most effective way to close a sale is to open it on a positive note.

Unfortunately, most sales do not open this way. The typical initial store contact begins in this manner:

Clerk: "May I help You?

Customer: "No thank you, I'm just looking."

This ritual leaves much to be desired. Why? It is an automatic statement that shows no creativity on part of the salesperson. Also, because the customer has heard the statement many times, his or her response is usually given without thinking what was said. Every salesperson should be challenged to treat each customer as an individual by responding differently to each customer.

Initial contact also means responding to customers when they enter the sales areas even when they cannot be waited on immediately. Salespeople should be instructed to tell waiting customers that, "I'll be with you in a moment." Such actions will reduce the number of customers who leave without being served. When the employee is free to help the waiting customer, the initial comment should be, "Thank you for waiting." A courteous, creative initial contact with the customer can go a long way to promote sales.

3. Presentation of Merchandise

In presenting merchandise (or services) to the customer, the salesperson should use product knowledge to best advantage. How? Although it is good to talk about the lawnmower's 3.5 horsepower mower, customers may be more interested in hearing about how fast the lawnmower will cut the grass. Product knowledge is important but the salesperson must remember what makes the customer buy. Clothes may be made of durable fabrics but it is also important to stress the implied benefits that they will also appeal to the opposite sex. Sell benefits!

4. Customer Involvement

Product knowledge can be used to get customer involvement. Show the customer several features of the digital watch and then have the customer put it on and work it. If the interest is there, it will be hard for the customer to take off the watch so that the salesperson can put it back into the case. The best way to present many products is to get involvement. Want to sell dance lessons? Get the customer on the dance floor and let the fun of dancing do some of the selling. The same is true with clothes, perfume, sports equipment, and almost anything else. Limit the choices If during the sales presentation more than three items are in front of the customer, the chances of a sale is reduced while the possibility of shoplifting is increased. If, for example, the salesperson continues to carry dresses into the fitting room for the customer to try without removing any for consideration, the customer will likely not buy any because of the inability to decide among so many choices.

Also, with so many items under study, the clerk may lose track of how many items are in the fitting room. It is possible that some may be put on under customer's clothing while the clerk is not present, thereby resulting in an expensive experience for the store. Likewise, if a travel agency attempts to sell a customer a Caribbean cruise, the chances of making the sale will diminish if too many trip options are presented.

Unless there is a definite reason for an exception, the rule of three (never show more than three choices at one time) should be followed whenever merchandise is presented. Limited choices have been found to promote sales

(a) Use of Showmanship

In presenting merchandise to the customer, encourage all personnel to be creative. Be enthusiastic about the merchandise. Hold the necklace up for the customer to see it. Make the portable baby crib "look" easy to work. Lay the different pieces of the cookware set before the customer in an attractive, easy to-see everything manner. Ask your salespeople to think like a customer. If I were a customer, what would I like to see?

(b) Message Adaption

A knowledgeable salesperson should know about the products being sold. Message adaptation involves deciding what information is needed to sell to a particular customer and how that information should be presented to that customer. Canned sales presentations do not allow for adaptation. The effective salesperson will make an effort to adjust the presentation to the customer. If the customer knows about gardens and lawns, the person selling a lawn service should adapt the sales presentation to the level of the customer's expertise. Do not bore the customer with known facts. It could lose a sale.

5. Handling Objections

Remember, if objections are present, progress is probably being made on the sale. Most salespeople are afraid of objections. Stress to all employees that objections are a natural part of the selling process. That does not mean that the sale is lost. In most cases, all that is required to overcome an objection is more selling on the part of the salesperson.

Common types of customer objections that are faced by a salesperson are:

Product: "That dress looks out of date."

Store: "You never have the right merchandise."

Service: "If I believe what I hear, I cannot get good service from you."

Price: "It is just too expensive."

Salesperson: "Are you sure these shoes fit right?"

These and other objections can be met by the salesperson in several ways. Using the above product objection as an example, these methods include:

Yes-But "Yes, it does look out-of-date, but it is the latest." This approach begins on a positive note by agreeing with the customer and then moves on to answer the objection.

Counter question "Why do you feel it's out-of-date?" The counter question puts the ball back in the customer's court. By asking "Why?" the real reason for the objection may become known.

Restate Question "You feel that the dress looks out-of-date." By restating the objection, the customer may respond by saying, "No, I mean it just does not look good on me," or something of a similar nature. This approach tends to reduce the magnitude of the objection in the eyes of the customer.

Direct Response "The dress you have on was first shown at the market this season.It is the latest thing." Although offensive to some, this approach may be necessary if the customer is not going to buy unless the lie is corrected. Tact is important when using this approach.

These four approaches for handling objections are not meant to be all-inclusive. These and other approaches do point out, however, those objections should and can be answered by the salesperson. Unless objections are overcome to the satisfaction of the customer, it is questionable that the sale will be made.

6. Closing the Sale

In various ways, the salesperson can assist the customer by helping him or her to make the buying decision. Closing techniques that can aid in this effort include:

1. Offer a Service "Let us deliver it to you this afternoon." A "yes" implies purchase.
2. Give a Choice "Do you want the five-piece or eight-piece cooking set?" Either choice implies purchase. Note that "No" was not one of the choices.
3. Offer an Incentive "If you buy now, you can get 10% off the already low price." If you wait, you don't get the 10% discount.
4. Better Not Wait "If you want this refrigerator, better get it now. It's the last in stock."

5. Note, it pays to be honest. If the customer buys and then comes by the store the next day and sees that the store did have another one, this closing technique may have made the sale but it could lose the customer.

7. Suggestion

Selling the customer has made a purchase. Now what? Encourage your sales personnel to make a definite suggestion for a possible additional sale. For many businesses, sales can be increased by 25 percent through positive suggestion selling. Please note that statements such as: "Will there be something else?" or "Can I get you something else?" are not suggestion selling. They do not make a positive suggestion. When a customer buys a lamp, what about a light bulb to go with it? If a picture is purchased, what about the necessary hardware to hang it? If a suit is bought, what about a new blouse or shirt that goes well with the color?

Where appropriate, the creative salesperson will actually get the suggested item and show it to the customer. Or if a person brings in a watch to be repaired, why not clean it while it is taken apart? This type of initiative usually results in more sales. It should be emphasized that most customers like to receive a valid suggestion. In some cases, suggestions may even permit the customer to avoid another shopping trip to pick up the needed item that they had not thought about. Good suggestion selling makes sales and builds confidence in the firm's business.

8. Sales follow-Up

Although not apparent to many salespeople, follow-up is a part of every sale. The closing statement, "Thank you for shopping at (name of store)," is a form of sales follow-up if done with enthusiasm. Unfortunately, just making the statement in an automatic manner is about as effective as that other "worn out phrase, "may I help you?" If done correctly, however, it allows the customer to leave on a positive note.

SALESMANSHIP

Selling is a vital function of business. The purpose of all marketing activities is to sell the products of the business enterprise. Selling enables the business to achieve its objectives by satisfying the needs of the customers. To perform selling activities efficiently, certain qualifications among salesman is desirable.

Good Salesmanship is not about never loosing a sale. It's about learning from every lost sale and never letting history repeat itself in that arena! Everyone cannot be a good salesman. It requires a great deal of competence or excellence. Following are a few qualities that a master salesman must develop.

Deliver more than you promise

For instance, if your customer is promised a good quality product on a particular date but the product reaches him before time and the quality too is better than expected, you have acquired a loyal customer for life! This is how a super-salesman works! He pursues the practice of rendering service that is greater in quantity and finer in quality than he is expected to deliver, thereby bringing profit not just for himself.

Make mistakes, but learn to profit from them

For a good salesman, no effort is ever lost. A good salesman not only never repeats his sales blunders, but learns from them. A good observation is a plus point. Learning from others mistakes helps prevent business gaffes too! Also, any mistake made is thoroughly analyzed to look for a solution. Good is sure to come out of it!

A Good salesman understands that a **coordination of different minds** for the attainment of a single purpose is sure to produce positive results.

Have an aim

Another attribute of a good salesman or quality he must aim at the attainment of a particular goal or quota, within delineated time. A good salesman never goes with an intention of selling all he can. There has to be a specific objective to be attained.

A good salesman before making his sales pitch always tries to **put himself in the customer's shoes.**This provides a much better understanding of the customers' needs and how those requirements can be amply fulfilled.

The most important attribute of a salesman is his passion and his keenness to complete a sale. This infectious enthusiasm is immediately picked up by the prospective clients, which makes it easier to build a relationship of mutual trust. Good Salesmanship is a combination of the elements of persuasion, creativity, education and the ideal of mutual benefits.

This section will deal with the essential elements and qualification required for successful selling.

ESSENTIAL ELEMENTS OF A SUCCESSFUL SALESMAN

(i) Element of persuasion

Personal selling is the art of winning the confidence of the customers and thereby convincing them to accept the proposal. It is through powerful suggestions and tactful handling of situation that the salesmen are able to make the people agree to the sales proposals.

(ii) Element of creativity

It is the creative thinking of the salesmen that arouses interest for the product. It creates and maintains demands for the product. It tends to satisfy the individual needs of the customer.

(iii) Element of education

Personal selling helps the customers to increase their satisfaction by educating them about the uses of new products and new uses of old products. It educates people about the availability of products, their features, uses, etc.

(iv) Element of mutual benefits

The main aim of personal selling is not to make high profits. It is beneficial both to consumers and sellers. It not only increases the profit of the businessman but also provides full satisfaction to the consumers.

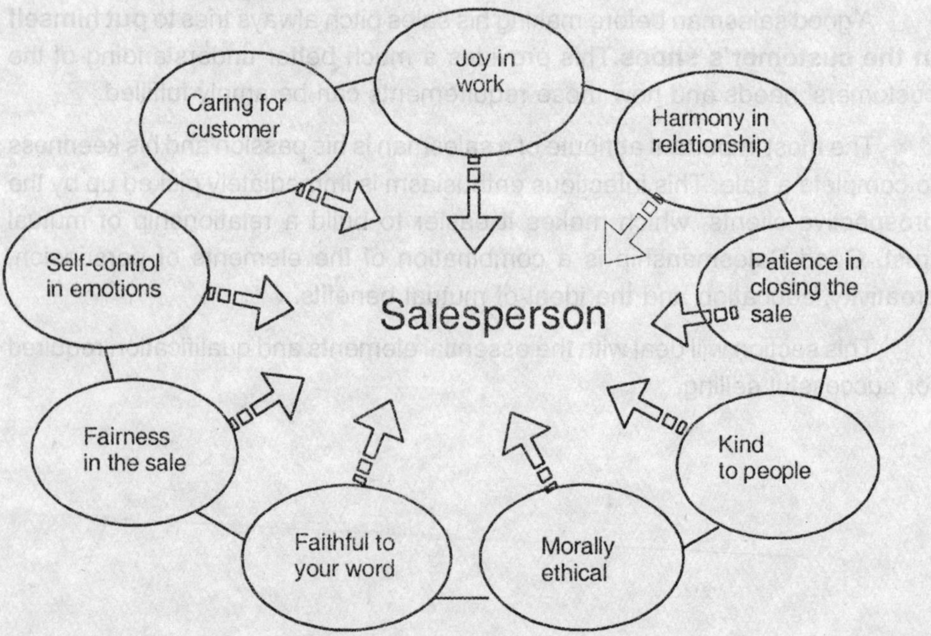

Fig.1.3. Personal Characteristics Needed to Sell for Building Long-term Relationships

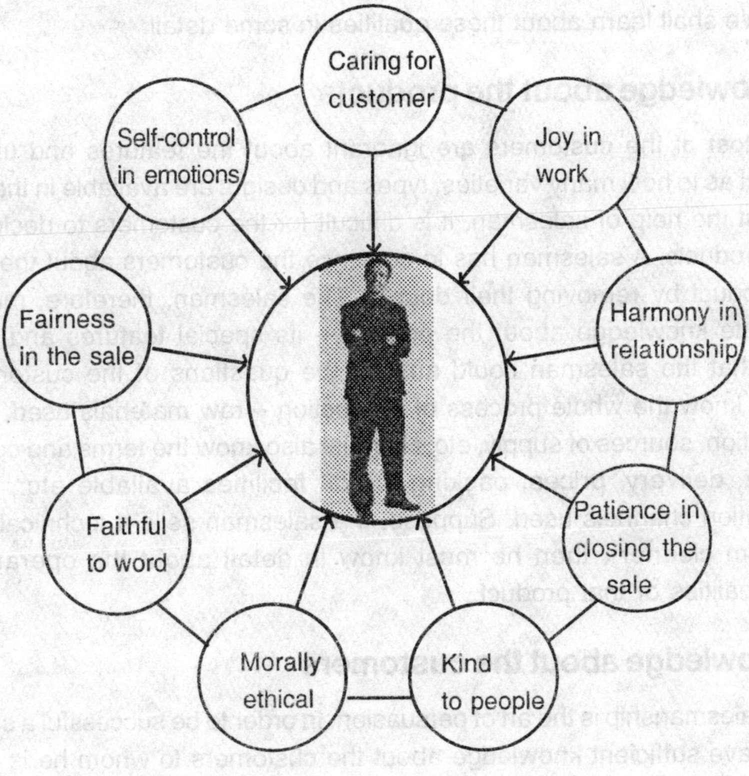

Fig.1.4. Qualities of a good salesman

QUALITIES OF A GOOD SALESMAN

In order to become a successful salesman, a person should possess some qualities. These qualities may be:

(i) Knowledge about the products.

(ii) Knowledge about the customers.

(iii) Knowledge about the techniques of selling.

(iv) Personal qualities

- Personality
- Mental qualities
- Social qualities
- Character qualities

We shall learn about these qualities in some detail:

1. Knowledge about the products

Most of the customers are ignorant about the features and utility of a product as to how many varieties, types and design, are available in the market. Without the help of salesman, it is difficult for the customers to decide about their products. A salesman has to convince the customers about the utility of the product by removing their doubts. The salesman, therefore, must have complete knowledge about the product – its special features and uses. In order that the salesman could answer the questions of the customers, he should know the whole process of production – raw materials used, place of production, sources of supply, etc. He must also know the terms and conditions of sale, delivery, prices, packing, credit facilities available etc., and the distribution channels used. Suppose, if a salesman sells a technical product (vacuum cleaner), then he must know in detail about the operation and functionalities of that product.

2. Knowledge about the customers

Salesmanship is the art of persuasion. In order to be successful a salesman must have sufficient knowledge about the customers to whom he is going to sell. He must try to understand their nature, types, habits and buying motives (considerations that compel a customer to buy). It is only then that he wins permanent customers. Salesman selling vacuum cleaner must identify the target customers for their product. Like for this product customers generally will be high income group urbanites.

3. Knowledge about the selling techniques

All the above knowledge is of no use unless salesman learns some techniques of selling and uses them. For example, firstly, he should see that the prospect line customer is well attended to. Secondly, he should try to understand his requirements. Thirdly, he should always be prepared to help him in order to win his confidence. Fourthly, he should ensure that the need of the customer is suitably met. If salesman follows these steps then selling vacuum cleaner won't be a problem to target customers (potential customers)

4. Personal qualities

Some of the personal qualities are:

a. Personality

A successful salesman must have sound health and pleasing personality, good appearance, good tastes, good habits, impressive voice, etc. First impression is the last impression. A pleasing and charming personality boosts self-confidence. It plays an important role in selling. The good appearance has a far reaching impact on the customers.

b. Mental qualities

An effective successful salesman must possess certain mental qualities intelligence, presence of mind, imagination, confidence, observation, sharp memory, foresightedness and above all the power to take quick decisions, etc.

c. Social qualities

A successful salesman should be co-operative, courteous, well mannered, have a liking for people, etc. He should always be ready to help his customers, remove their grievances and give new suggestions. He should be friendly and ready to mix with his customers. He must have the power to lead the people.

d. Character qualities

A successful salesman should have moral qualities like honesty, integrity, loyalty, etc. A salesman should be such that his tasks, promises, gestures and behaviours can be trusted, respected and honoured. He should be honest in his dealings. He should be loyal both to the customers and business.

ATTRIBUTES OF A GOOD SALESMAN!

Good Salesmanship is not about never loosing a sale. It's about learning from every lost sale and never letting history repeat itself in that arena! Everyone can't be a good salesman. It requires a great deal of competence or excellence. Following are a few qualities that a master salesman must develop.

Deliver more than you promise

For instance, if your customer is promised a good quality product on a particular date but the product reaches him before time and the quality too is better than expected, you have acquired a loyal customer for life! This is how a super-salesman works! He pursues the practice of rendering service that is greater in quantity and finer in quality than he is expected to deliver, thereby bringing profit not just for himself.

Make mistakes, but learn to profit from them

For a good salesman, no effort is ever lost. A good salesman not only never repeats his sales blunders, but learns from them. A good observation is a plus point. Learning from others mistakes helps prevent business gaffes too! Also, any mistake made is thoroughly analyzed to look for a solution. Good is sure to come out of it!

A Good salesman understands that a coordination of different minds for the attainment of a single purpose is sure to produce positive results.

Have an aim

Another attribute of a good salesman or quality he must develop is his working towards the attainment of a particular goal or quota, within delineated time. A good salesman never goes with an intention of selling all he can. There has to be a specific objective to be attained.

A good sales man before making his sales pitch always tries to put himself in the customer's shoes. This provides a much better understanding of the customers? Needs and how those requirements can be amply fulfilled.

The most important attribute of a salesman is his passion and his keenness to complete a sale. This infectious enthusiasm is immediately picked up by the prospective clients, which makes it easier to build a relationship of mutual trust. Good Salesmanship is a combination of the elements of persuasion, creativity, education and the ideal of mutual benefits.

A quality salesman must have a good knowledge of products (special features and uses), knowledge about customers (nature, types, habits and buying motives),

- The technique of selling and terms and conditions of the sale - delivery, prices, packing, credit facilities available etc.
- Also, he must have ample familiarity with sales promotion activities such as distribution of samples, coupons, premiums, exhibitions and clearance sales.
- At the same time the objectives must remain to properly introduce new products, win new customers, and to improve public image of the company.
- Besides, personal and moral qualities of honesty, integrity, loyalty are a must! A successful salesman should be co-operative, courteous, well mannered, and outgoing. He should be intelligent with a presence of mind, imagination, confidence, observation, sharp memory, foresightedness and above all the power to take quick decisions. A pleasing personality only adds to the selling process. A good appearance, good tastes, good habits and impressive voice are sure to make a lasting impression.
- A good salesman is one who proves beneficial to both the sellers and the buyers. While ensuring that the need of the customer is suitably met, a good salesman ascertains a profit!

- ❖ The ability to quickly develop rapport with their prospective customers. Without rapport, your prospects won't trust you enough to feel comfortable doing business with you. What makes a good salesman is either an innate ability to bond with people, or more likely, working hard to study and acquire this ability.

- ❖ A desire to truly help their customers. People can sense when the only thing you care about is your commission. What makes a good salesman is putting the customer's needs and desires first.

- ❖ The habit of asking questions to gather information before making a pitch. The average salesman will just start right in with every reason they can think of why someone might want their product and hope that the customer will pick up on something and decide to buy. What makes a good salesman is their knack for finding out what is most important to each individual customer and showing them a product that gives them exactly what they said they wanted.

- ❖ Sticking to a consistent, proven sales process. Good sales people don't just show up and "wing it". They know that even though they make some sales that way, in the long run their closing ration is much higher when they follow a step-by-step process that consistently results in more sales. What makes a good salesman is his discipline in sticking to that process every time.

- ❖ A never ending desire to learn more about how to sell more effectively. Most salespeople never take it upon themselves to further their own education in the profession of selling. What makes a good salesman is his drive to keep learning, keep improving even when he is already at the top of his game.

STARTING DELL COMPUTERS:CASE STUDY- II STUDY

The creation of Dell Computers by Michael Dell is a good case study of entrepreneurship.

Dell showed skills in salesmanship early on in his youth. While in college, he built a desktop computer by buying parts from local dealers. He then started making and selling computers to his college classmates. Business was so good that he quit school to start up his computer business.

Interests and skills

When Michael Dell was 15, he showed a fascination of the inner workings of a computer by breaking down his brand new Apple II computer and then rebuilding it.

Dell did not excel academically while attending Memorial High School in Houston, Texas. However, he exhibited great business instincts while selling subscriptions for the Houston Post. He was able to sell $18,000 in subscriptions by focusing on selling to newlyweds, thus earning himself a BMW automobile.

Part-time business

Dell realized that the IBM and IBM-compatible personal computers were not made of IBM parts, but rather stock parts from various vendors.

In 1984, while a student at the University of Texas at Austin, Dell got the great idea of making IBM-compatible computers to sell to fellow students at a price much lower than they would have to pay in a computer store.

With capital of only $1000, Dell started a part-time business, working out of his off-campus dorm room.

Started Dell Computers

By 1985, the demand for his computers motivated Dell to focus full-time on his business.

Funding

He dropped out of school. His grandparents had enough faith in his idea and determination that they provided him with $300,000 so that he could expand his business into a full-scale company.

Marketing

He advertised his computers—which were custom-made according to a selection of options—through popular computer magazines. His prices were lower than retail stores and were sold and shipped directly to the customers.

Business model

This business model—which was the first of its kind in the computer business—and his reputation for quality and customer service resulted in an astounding $73 million gross in the company's first year.

Questions

(i) How did he get the idea for his business?

(ii) How did he start Dell Computers?

CHECK YOUR PROGRESS

(A) True or False

(i) Personal selling and salesmanship are the same.

(ii) Salesmanship is the ability to persuade customers.

(iii) Salesmanship is an art and not science.

(B) Fill in the blanks

(i) The Roman equivalent of salesman meant ....

(ii) The industrial revolution occurred in the ....century

(iii) Creative salesmanship aims at creating sales for.....................

(C) True/False

(i) Personal selling helps manufacturers to improve their products based on suggestions made by sellers.

(ii) Customers do not have immediate solution of their problems regarding a product from the salesman.

(iii) Personal selling leads to creation of new customers only for the existing products.

LET US SUM UP

Salesmanship is the skill and the ability of a person in convincing the other about the proposition of goods or services so that the latter is automatically induced to desire and buy them at a price which is profitable to both. Salesmanship is the skill of creating an attitude in the mind of the buyer to buy a product of service. As a matter of fact, it is not an effort to sell; it is the effort to make the buyer buy a product or service. Salesmanship is the skill of creating an attitude in the mind of the buyer to buy a product or services.

The salesman always attempts to create needs, makes the prospective buyers aware of such needs and uses his resourcefulness and imagination to persuade them to buy products and services in order to satisfy their needs. A modern day sale does not simply mean getting rid of a product or a service. Salesmanship is not an effort to sell; it is making the customer buy a product or service. In fact, it is a service that is serving the cause of human civilization better.

Earlier days, selling was not regarded as noble profession by the general public. Seller faced very tough time during those days. Nobody was ready to listen a sale person. But over the period of time, sales man become highly educated, professional and gained lot of respects in the society. The career progression of a salesman is also very high and regarded as very prestigious. Salesman today can earn huge amount of commission apart from their regular salary.

In order to become a successful salesman, a person should possess some qualities. These qualities may be:

(i) Knowledge about the products.

(ii) Knowledge about the customers.

(iii) Knowledge about the techniques of selling.

(iv) Personal qualities

- Personality
- Mental qualities
- Social qualities
- Character qualities

Good Salesmanship is not about never losing a sale. It's about learning from every lost sale and never letting history repeat itself in that arena! Everyone cannot be a good salesman. It requires a great deal of competence or excellence. A salesman must possess the above mentioned attributes and qualities to become successful.

LESSON END ACTIVITY

1. We said that today's professional sales representative is a marketing consultant and a manager of a market – his or her territory. Explain how a sales representative can be a marketing consultant and a manager.
2. Interview a marketing or product manager. Ask him or her to identify the primary sales objective for one of the company's products. Ask a sales manager and a sales representative at that company the same question for the same product. Compare and contrast the three viewpoints.
3. While buying any goods and services, carefully notice the behaviour of the salespersons and note down the various qualities he/she possess.

KEY WORDS

Salesmanship:

A concise effort on the part of the seller to induce a prospective buyer to buy even if he had not thought of it favorably.

Personal Selling:

It refers to oral presentation in conversation (by a sales rep) with one or more prospective customers for the purpose of making sales.

Sales Management:

The planning, direction and control of personal selling, including recruiting selecting, equipping, assigning, routing, supervising, paying and motivating as these tasks apply to the personal sales force.

Salesmanship:

A concise effort on the part of the seller to induce a prospective buyer to buy even if he had not thought of it favourably.

Competitive Salesmanship:

S/he aims at increasing the sales of the existing products or services, no matter how the sales are increased.

Creative Salesmanship:

S/he aims to increase sales. Rather, his job is to motivate customers and make them satisfied with the sale.

Advertising:

Paid for communication to increase the saleability of the product.

Publicity:

Unpaid communication.

Product:

Anything that can be sold in the market place including services, ideas, brand ambassador etc.

Services:

An act or performances that does not result into ownership of anything.

Personal Qualities:

It includes personality, mental qualities, social qualities and character qualities.

Personality:

Psychological traits and attributes.

Mental Qualities:

Intelligence, presence of mind, imagination, confidence, observation, sharp memory, foresightedness.

REVIEW QUESTIONS

1. Explain the concept of salesmanship?
2. Is there any difference between personal selling and salesmanship? Explain.
3. Define salesmanship?
4. Explain the nature and scope of salesmanship?
5. Salesmanship is an art or science? Explain.
6. Explain the importance of salesmanship.
7. "Salesmanship" is an educative process- Explain.
8. How society is benefited from salesmanship? Explain in your own words.
9. Define sales management.
10. What do you understand by personal selling? Mention its characteristics.
11. Explain the different types of salespeople briefly.
12. Explain the concept of salesmanship in olden days.
13. Explain the concept of salesmanship in modern days.
14. Write short notes on (i) Competitive salesmanship (ii) Creative salesmanship.
15. Compare the concept of salesmanship in modern days with respect to olden days.
16. "Job of a salesman is very prestigious now" – explain in your own words..
17. How 18th century industrial revolution had changed the business scenario across the world- write briefly.

18. Describe the importance of personal selling form the point of customers.

19. Explain the importance of personal selling from the point of view of manufacturers.

20. State the physical and mental qualities of sales persons engaged in personal selling.

21. State the social qualities of sales persons engaged in personal selling.

22. What are the occupational qualities of salespersons engaged in personal selling?

23. Do you think that to be a successful salesperson only personal and mental qualities are sufficient? Give reasons in support of your answer.

24. Describe the different qualities of sales persons engaged in personal selling.

25. A salesman need not possess any quality if the product is good. Do you agree with the Statement? Give reason.

CHECK YOUR PROGRESS: MODEL ANSWER

(A)

(i) False

(ii) True

(iii) False

(B)

(i) Cheat

(ii) 18th

(iii) New and novel products or services

(C)

(i) True

(ii) False

(iii) False

SUGGESTED READINGS

PK Sahu & KC Raut: *Salesmanship and Sales Management,* Vikas Publishing House Pvt Ltd, New Delhi, 2003.

S A Chunawalla: *Sales Management,* Himalaya Publishing House, Mumbai, 2005.

Spiro, Stanton, Rich: *Management of a Sales Force,* Tata McGraw Hill, New Delhi, 2008.

⊠⊠⊠

Chapter

2

Understanding Consumer Behaviour

"If consumers are asked to make greater sacrifices than industry, this country is going to have the greatest shortage of all–consumers"

– Betty Furness

Introduction – Selected consumer behaviour roles – Model of consumer behaviour – Major factors influencing consumer behaviour – Buying behaviour pattern – Buyer's motivation – Post purchase behaviour – Buyer decision making process – Consumer behaviour in e-commerce – Organization buying behaviour.

OBJECTIVES

At the conclusion of this lesson you should be able to understand:

- ❖ Different consumer behaviour models
- ❖ Major factors influencing CB
- ❖ Different buying behaviour pattern
- ❖ Buyer's motivation
- ❖ Post-purchase behaviour
- ❖ Buyer decision making process
- ❖ Consumer behaviour on e-commerce
- ❖ Organisation buying behaviour

GOOD PACKAGING CAN CHANGE CONSUMER PERCEPTION: CASE STUDY - III

Good packaging can change consumer perception. Smaller manufacturing companies, that include private labels, have taken to innovative packaging to hit their target consumers. Dadima's Magic mango pickle, ITS fruit tomato ketchup, Mehek Dehradoon Basmati, 24 Letter Mantra and Bread & More are some of the products available in shops with good packaging motifs.

Most of these companies have an advertising budget of Rs 2-5 crore, of which a good amount is invested in packaging the product. "If I am asked to do only packaging and the rest of the communication is outsourced, I'd say give me the entire kitty. Jokes apart, it's prudent to assign 5-7% for packaging alone," said Tarun Das of Oxygen.

Agrees Rajshekhar Reddy of Sresta Bio Products: "Most companies end up spending more in packaging than the product itself as packaging is an important aspect nowadays. Unless the goods stand out from the clutter, it is not sold out. We tend to review our packaging every two years." The company has launched an organic food store chain brand called '24 Letter Mantra' based out of Hyderabad. "We are doubling revenues on a Y-o-Y basis and I think a significant part can be attributed to good packaging," adds Mr Reddy.

This was not so a few years back as packaging was not given much emphasis by the smaller companies. Technology upgradation, awareness and increased competition has helped smaller brands establish themselves in a little time. This, backed by innovative communication ideas, promotions and packaging, has helped these companies grow.

Sresta created innovative packaging for the kids meal segment with a tiffin box. "Packaging has changed in the last few years with innovative technology chipping in. The standards of packing has changed as there are no restrictions in terms of use of colour, shape and even material," adds Mr Das of Oxygen that looks after the entire communication of the company.

The retail boom has also helped these companies as they get a platform to showcase their products in multi-brand outlets. "The consumer buying behaviour is very impulsive and it is the pricing, colour scheme, offers and packaging that attract them to buy a product if that is not an important item," adds Mr Das. Agrees Asheesh Sethi of Noshe Oceanic: "A well-packaged product gives an edge over other products because the consumer might find it attractive if there is not much of a difference in the quality of the product." "Groverson's Paris Beauty, a lingerie brand, is a good example of packaging.

While all other brands were concentrating on the same package style, we thought of changing it. Instead of a picture of single women on the packet, we did seven different poses of a single girl wearing different designs of lingerie. This was done to fight back the intrusion of foreign brands in India," added Mr Sethi.

"The consumer can now have a visual impact of the various product lines available at one go. The consumer behaviour has also changed, adds Sethi. Bread & More from the Kwality Group is another example of good packaging. "The recent trend is to constantly evolve the packaging. No one continues with the same look for too long. Most brands that have identified the importance of packaging constantly evolve to cater to the evolving needs of the consumer," says Creative land Asia MD Sajan Rajkurup.

For Aureole Inspecs' new eyewear brand Mayhem, Innocean has developed key brand visuals and packaging formats to illustrate the brand's cool attitude and appeal. "Sometime, even additions like a branded carry-bag help in enlarging the brand idea," says Innocean Worldwide India joint MD Vivek Srivastava.

INTRODUCTION

Consumer behaviour is comparatively a new field of study which evolved just after the Second World War. The sellers market has disappeared and buyers market has come up. This led to paradigm shift of the manufacturer's attention from product to consumer and specially focused on the consumer behaviour. The evaluation of marketing concept from mere selling concept to consumer-oriented marketing has resulted in buyer behaviour becoming an independent discipline. The growth of consumerism and consumer legislation emphasizes the importance that is given to the consumer. Consumer behaviour is a study of how individuals make decision to spend their available resources (time, money and effort) or consumption related aspects (What they buy? When they buy? How they buy? etc.).

The heterogeneity among people makes understanding consumer behaviour a challenging task to marketers. Hence, marketers felt the need to obtain an in-depth knowledge of consumers buying behaviour. Finally this knowledge acted as an imperative tool in the hands of marketers to forecast the future buying behaviour of customers and devise four marketing strategies in order to create long-term customer relationship.

Businesses stay in business by attracting and retaining customers. They do this by engaging in exchanges of resources including information, money, goods, services, status, and emotions with consumers, exchanges that both businesses and customers perceive to be beneficial. When companies ask, who are our customers? How do we reach them? What should we sell to them? What will motivate them to buy? What makes them satisfied? They are asking questions that require sophisticated understanding of consumer behaviour. This unit provides a brief insight into the meaning and perspective of consumer behaviour as well as understanding why it is important to study consumers.

DEFINITION

"CB behaviour refers to the actions and decision processes of people who purchase goods and services for personal consumption."-

James F. Engel, Roger D. Blackwell and Paul Miniard.

"The mental and emotional processes and the physical activities of people who purchase and use goods and services to satisfy particular needs and wants"-

Bearden *et. al.*

"The behaviour that consumers display in searching for, purchasing, using, evaluating and disposing of, if products and services that they expect will satisfy their needs."-

Leon G. Schiffman and Leslie Lazar Kanuk

SELECTED CONSUMER BEHAVIOUR ROLES

Table.2.1. Selected Consumer Behaviour Roles

Role	Description
Initiator	Initiator is the individual who determines that some need or want is not being fulfilled and authorizes a purchase to rectify the situation.
Gatekeeper	Influences the family's processing of information. The gatekeeper has the greatest expertise in acquiring and evaluating the information.
Influencer	Influencer is a person who, by some intentional or unintentional word or action, influences the buying decision, actual purchase and/or the use of product or service.
Decider	The person or persons who actually determine which product or service will be chosen.
Buyer	Buyer is an individual who actually makes the purchase transaction.
User	User is a person most directly involved in the use or consumption of the purchased product.

THE DIVERSITY OF CB

Human being differs from one to another. It is not easy to predict the human behaviour. Human being differs in their taste, needs, wants and preferences. But one constant thing is that we all are consumers. CB is a vast and complex subject. Understanding CB and "knowing consumers" are not that simple. It is almost impossible to predict with one hundred per cent accuracy, how consumer(s) will behave in a given situation. Marketers are interested in watching people shopping, flirting, parading, playing, and entertaining, as they are keenly interested in the wide variety of behaviours they display. The efforts of all marketers are to influence the behaviour of consumers in a desired manner. The success or failure in this pursuit determines the difference between success and failure of marketing efforts or even the business itself.

MODEL OF CONSUMER BEHAVIOUR

OUTSIDE STIMULUS		BUYER'S BLACK BOX		BUYER'S DECISION
Mktg Stimuli	Other Stimuli	Buyer's characteristics	Buyer's Decision Process	
Product	Economical	Cultural	Problem Recognition	Product Choice
Price	Technological	Social	Information Search	Brand Choice
Place	Political	Personal	Evaluation	Dealer Choice
Promotion	Cultural	Psychological	Decision	Purchase Timing
			Post Purchase Behaviour	Purchase Amount

Fig.2.1. Model of Consumer Behaviour

This is a simple model of consumer behaviour. Consumers when makes a decision for purchase, they do not just go to shop and purchase, above-mentioned factors influence the decision of the buyer. There are some outside stimulus, as well as internal factors, which influence the decision. Internal factors and process is known as Buyers Black Box as it cannot be seen.

MAJOR FACTORS INFLUENCING CONSUMER BEHAVIOUR

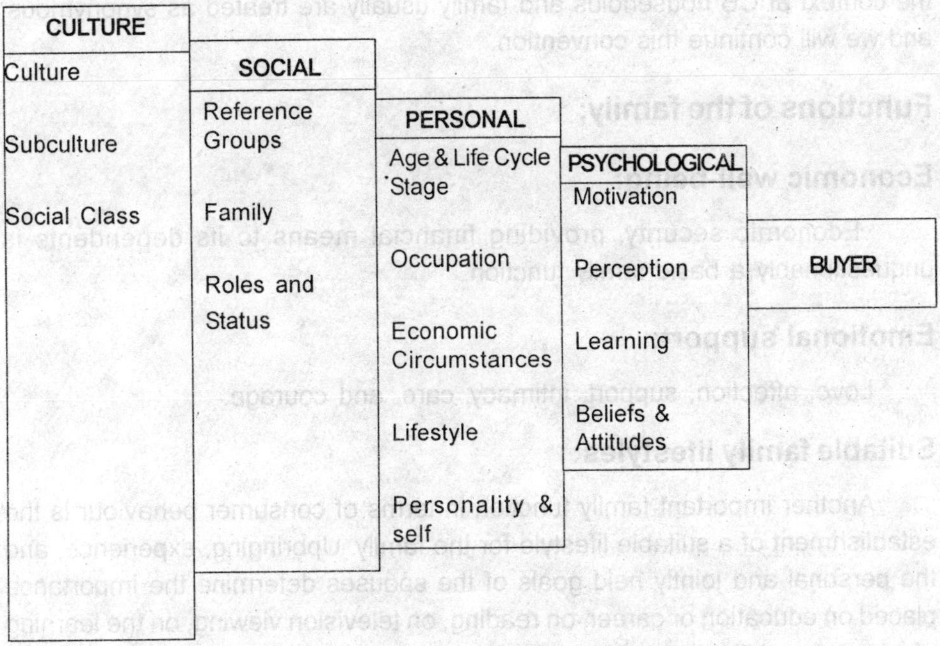

Fig.2.2.Major Factors Influencing Consumer Behavior

Culture:

Values and beliefs in which one is born and grown up.

Subculture:

Differences in lifestyle, food-habit between different parts of India. India as whole has one culture and again it has different subculture in different parts of India. Even a particular age group, male, female segments, etc., is also known as subculture.

Social Class:

Economic, Caste, Profession.

Reference group:

The group of people whom one consults before purchasing something; family, friend, etc.

Family:

It is defined as two or more persons related by blood, marriages or adoption who reside together. Although families are sometimes referred to as households, not all households are families. For example, a household might include individuals who are not related by blood, marriage or adoption, such as unmarried couples, family friends, roommates, or boarders. However, within the context of CB households and family usually are treated as synonymous, and we will continue this convention.

Functions of the family:

Economic well-being:

Economic security, providing financial means to its dependents is unquestionably a basic family function.

Emotional support:

Love, affection, support, intimacy, care, and courage.

Suitable family lifestyles:

Another important family function in terms of consumer behaviour is the establishment of a suitable lifestyle for the family. Upbringing, experience, and the personal and jointly held goals of the spouses determine the importance placed on education or career, on reading, on television viewing, on the learning of computer skills, on the frequency and quality of dining out, and on the selection of other entertainment and recreational activities.

Socialization of family members:

It encompasses from young children to adults, is a central function. In the case of young children, this process includes imparting to children the basic values and modes of behaviour consistent with the culture. These generally include moral and religious principles, interpersonal skills, dress and grooming standards, appropriate manner and speech and the selection of suitable educational and occupational or career goals.

(a) Traditional FLC:

Stage-I: Bachelorhood — young single adult living apart from parents.

Stage-II: Honeymooners — young married couple.

Stage-III: Parenthood — married couple with at least one child living at home.

Stage-IV: Post parenthood — an older married couple with no children living at home.

Stage-V: Dissolution — one surviving spouse.

(b) Non-traditional FLC stages:

Childless Couple: It is increasingly acceptable for married couples to elect not to have children. Contributing forces are more career oriented married woman and delayed marriages.

Couples who marry late in life (in their late 30s or later): More career oriented men and women and greater occurrence of couples living together. Likely to have fewer or even no children.

Couples who have first child late in life (in their late 30s or later): Fewer children. Emphasis on lifestyles.

Single Parent–I: High divorce rates contribute to a portion of single parent households.

Single Parent–II: Young man and woman who have one or more children out of wedlock.

Single Parent–III: A single parent who adopts one or more children.

Extended family:

Young single adult children who return home to avoid the expenses of living alone while establishing their careers. Divorced daughter and son return home. Newly-weds living with in-laws.

(c) Non-family households:

Unmarried couples: Increased acceptance of heterosexual and homosexual couples.

Divorced person (No Children): High divorce rate contributes to dissolution of households before children are born.

Single person (most are young): Men and women who never marry.

Widowed person (Most are elderly): Longer life expectancy, especially for women, means more over 75, single person households.

BUYING BEHAVIOUR

Significant differences between brands	COMPLES BUYING BEHAVIOUR	VARIETY SEEKING BUYING BEHAVIOUR
Few differences between brands	DISSONANCE REDUCING BUYING BEHAVIOUR	HABITUAL BUYING BEHAVIOUR

Fig. 2.3. Buying Behaviour

Complex Buying Behaviour:

Consumers are highly involved in a purchase and aware of significant differences among brands. This is usually the case when the product is expensive, bought infrequently, risk and highly self-expressive. Typically the consumers do not know much about the product category and has much to learn. Example: Personal Computer.

Dissonance-reducing:

Sometimes, the consumer is highly involved in a purchase but sees little differences in the brands. The high involvement is based on fact that the purchase is expensive, infrequent and risky. Example: Carpet. After purchase consumer might experience dissonance that stems from noticing certain disquieting features of the carpet or hearing favourable things about other carpets.

Habitual Buying Behaviour:

Many products are bought under conditions of low consumer involvement and the absence of significant brand differences. Consider salt. Consumers have little involvement in this product category. They go to the store and reach for the brand. If they keep reaching for the same brand, it is out of habit, not strong brand loyalty.

Variety-seeking Buying:

Some buying situations are characterized by low consumer involvement but significant brand differences. Here consumers often do a lot of brand switching. Consumers do the brand switching for the sake of variety rather than dissatisfaction. Example: Wafer potato chips.

BUYER MOTIVATIONS AND MASLOW'S THEORY

What motivates a buyer? The earliest understanding of the rationale of buyer behaviour was provided by the well-known economist Adam Smith. According to him, a human being is a *rational individual.* He or she evaluates various alternatives and will buy or select alternatives where the marginal utility is more than the marginal price he or she paid for it.

Consider the case of Priti, a housewife. After spending a few hours on her shopping she is tired and walks over to a nearby restaurant. She has the choice of either buying a fruit juice, a soft drink, a tea or coffee. A glass of fresh fruit juice costs her Rs 7.50, a soft drink also costs her Rs. 7.50, and tea or coffee costs Rs 3.50. Now if she decides to buy a soft drink, then the utility of this soft drink is more than the marginal price she is paying to get it. In this case she is paying almost Rs 4.00 more than a cup of tea or coffee. The utility of soft drink to her at this time is more than tea or coffee or fruit juice.

The assumption in the economic version of buyer behaviour is that the lowest priced product will sell, as its marginal utility will always be higher than others. Price therefore is the critical factor in determining customer choice. Another assumption is that all products are alike and no differentiation is possible between them. Finally, the customer is aware of the alternatives available to him or her.

The economic model can explain human behaviour to a limited extent only because humans are not always rational beings. We are all known to indulge in acts and shopping behaviour which are not necessarily rational. For example, a young man who loves his wife very dearly, and works in a different town away from his wife and family may make a long distance call almost every day not caring for the cost. The economist would like us to believe that this young man will consider the marginal cost and utility of making a long distance call and writing a letter (buying postage and stationery).

Besides, rarely or rather never is the information on alternatives complete. Marketers create differentiation in their products. Branding is common in manufactured consumer goods. And each brand communicates a different image.

However, the limits to product differentiation through technology, features, packaging, intangibles like guarantee or warranties are soon reached. In today's world of technology standardization there is hardly any differentiation between two brands of the same product on a feature-to-feature basis. Price then becomes important yet not the crucial factor. Hence the economic model does provide limited but useful insight into buyer behaviour.

PSYCHOLOGICAL FACTORS

To get a better understanding of consumer behaviour, we need to examine three major psychological factors. These are:

(a) Motivation
(b) Learning
(c) Perception

Motivation

The well-known psychoanalyst, Sigmund Freud, provided the earliest explanation of human motivation. According to him man learns from his environment. Taking a cue from a child, Freud said that a child is uninhibited in his behaviour until the time he or she is taught the worldly ways by his or her parents. Gradually as the child grows, he starts behaving in a manner, which is socially acceptable. This obviously means that his basic urges and instincts get suppressed and what we see is the socially approved behaviour pattern. Freud says that the human psyche could be understood as comprising of Id, Ego and Superego. Id is the reservoir of all the basic instincts and urges whereas the Superego consists of socially approved behaviour patterns. Ego is the conscious self and often acts as a balancing wheel between the Id and the Superego. Freud also believed that the most basic instinct that gets suppressed is sex and he traces much of human behaviour to this motive. Like the way a person dresses is often to attract the opposite sex. Cars have always had a feminine image and most men take care of their car the same way as they would of their wives, mistresses or girl friends.

The problem with Freudian theory is that it is too much focussed on sexual need. Not all-human behaviour is sex motivated. Often, the need to influence or need for power is an important need guiding human behaviour. Some products tend to give this power to individuals. Credit cards, for example, give the individual the ability to influence others as in most cases it gives to him/her a higher social status.

Another understanding and more comprehensive view, was provided by Abraham Maslow. According to Maslow, all individuals have needs, which are placed in a hierarchy as shown below:

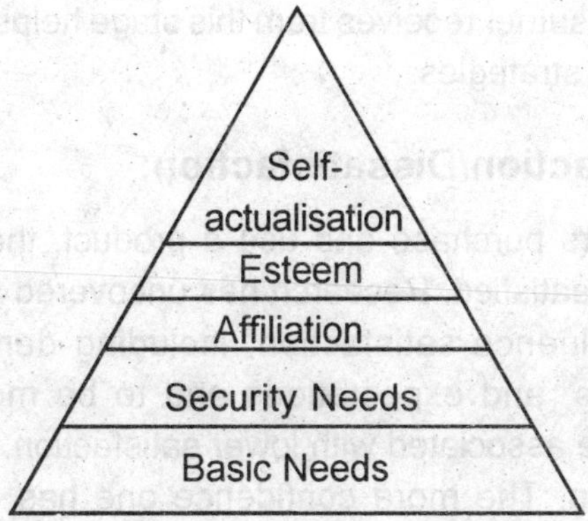

Fig.2.4. Maslow's Hierarchy of Needs

According to Maslow, human beings first satisfy their lower order needs, i.e., basic and security needs before moving up the hierarchy to satisfy esteem and self-actualisation. Applying Maslow's theory, we find that we can have different groups of customers with different needs buying products. Consider for example, the case of toilet soap.

An individual, motivated by basic need, may just buy any soap so long as it serves the core need of his, *viz.*, cleaning. Maybe to him at this point, price is important. But an individual high on belonging or affiliation or esteem may look for a premium priced soap. He or she would look for fragrance, shape, packaging, brand name, lathering effect and the like, before selecting the brand. Modern cars, do-it-yourself kits, or learn-by-yourself are some of the products that satisfy esteem and self-actualisation needs.

It may be recalled that esteem need is a learned psychological need while security is a learned physiological need. Marketers often tend to invoke the esteem need of the customer. Nothing better illustrates this than the Onida campaign, which is centered around the envy concept.

The contribution of Maslow's theory is that it helps the marketer segment his market and develop product-marketing strategies accordingly.

CONSUMPTION AND POST-PURCHASE BEHAVIOUR

Post-purchase Evaluation:

After purchase, the consumer also engages in an evaluation of the purchase decision. Because the consumer is uncertain of the wisdom of his decision, he rethinks this decision in the post purchase stage. There are several functions, which this stage serves. First, it serves to broaden the consumer's set of experiences stored in memory. Second, it provides a check on how well he is doing as a consumer in selecting products, stores, and so on. Third, the feedback that the consumer receives from this stage helps to make adjustments in future purchasing strategies.

Consumer Satisfaction/Dissatisfaction:

Once consumers purchase and use a product, they may then become either satisfied or dissatisfied. Research has uncovered several determinants, which appear to influence satisfaction, including demographic variables, personality variables, and expectations and to be more satisfied. Higher education tends to be associated with lower satisfaction. Men tend to be more satisfied than women. The more confidence one has in purchase decision making and the more competence in a given product area, the greater one's satisfaction tends to be. There is also greater satisfaction when relevant others are perceived to be more satisfied. Persons who are more satisfied with their lives as a whole, and that is by persons with more favourable attitudes toward the consumer domain, the market-place, business firms and consumerism also indicate higher levels of product satisfaction.

The interaction between expectations and actual product performance produces either satisfaction or dissatisfaction. However, there does not appear to be merely a direct relationship between the level of expectations and the level of satisfaction. Instead, a modifying variable known as "disconfirmation of expectations" is thought to be a significant mediator of this situation. When a consumer does not get what is expected, the situation is one of disconfirmation. Such disconfirmation can be of two varieties: a positive disconfirmation occurs when what is received is better than expected, and a negative disconfirmation occurs when things turn out worse than anticipated. Thus, any situation in which the consumer's judgement is proven wrong is a disconfirmation. Confirmation occurs if the expectations of performance are met.

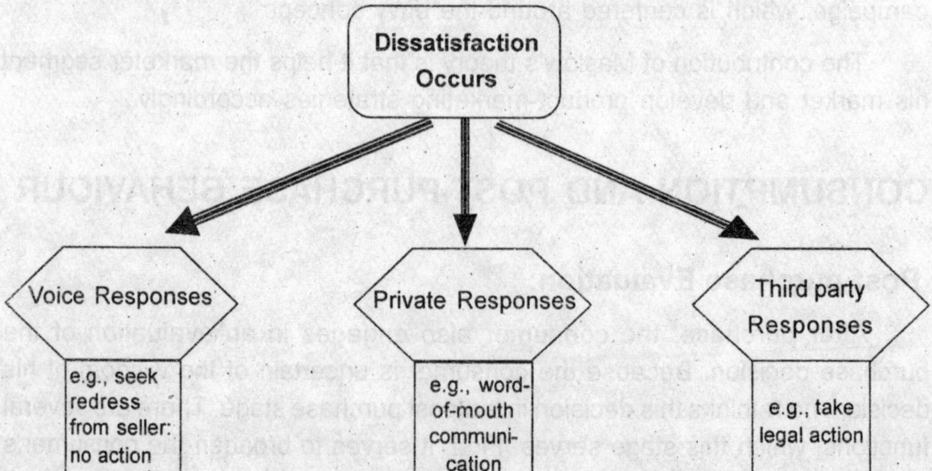

Fig. 2.5. Consumer Complaint Behaviour

POST PURCHASE DISSONANCE

Cognitive dissonance occurs as a result of a discrepancy between a consumer's decision and the consumer's prior evaluation. From a review of research findings on cognitive dissonance, it appears that dissonance is likely to occur under the following conditions.

- ❖ Once a minimum threshold of dissonance tolerance is passed. That is, consumers may tolerate a certain level of inconsistency in their lives until this point is reached.
- ❖ The action is irrevocable. For instance, when the consumer purchases a new car, there is little likelihood that he will be able to reverse his decision and get his money back.
- ❖ Unselected alternatives have desirable features.
- ❖ There are several desirable alternatives. Today's car buyer, for example, has an abundance of choices among similar attractive models. In fact, research indicates that those consumers who experience greater difficulty in making purchase decisions, or who consider a wider range of store and brand options, are more likely to experience greater magnitudes of post-purchase dissonance.
- ❖ Available alternatives are quite dissimilar in their qualities. For instance, although there are many automobile models, each one may have some unique characteristics.
- ❖ The buyer is committed to his decision because it has psychological significance. A large and important living room furniture purchase is likely to have great psychological significance to the buyer because of its dramatic reflection of one's decorating tastes, philosophy, and lifestyle. Ego involvement will be quite high.
- ❖ There is no pressure applied to the consumer to make the decision. if the consumer is subjected to outside pressure, he will do what he is forced to do without letting his own viewpoint or preference to be challenged.

It is clear that dissonance is likely to be strongest for the purchase of durables, although it can exist for almost every purchase.

DISSONANCE REDUCTION

(i) Changing product evaluation:

One of the ways consumers seek to reduce dissonance is to reevaluate product alternatives. This is accomplished by the consumers' enhancing the attributes of the products selected while decreasing the importance of the unselected products' attributes. That is, consumers seek to polarize alternatives in order to reduce their dissonance.

(ii) Seeking new information:

A second way consumers may reduce dissonance is by seeking additional information in order to confirm the wisdom of their product choice. According to dissonance theory, dissonant individuals would be expected to actively avoid information that would tend to increase their dissonance and seek information supporting their decision. It seems reasonable to assume that consumers would seek out advertisements for products they have purchased and tend to avoid competing ads.

(iii) Changing attitude:

As a result of dissonance, the consumer may change his attitudes to make them consonant with his behaviour.

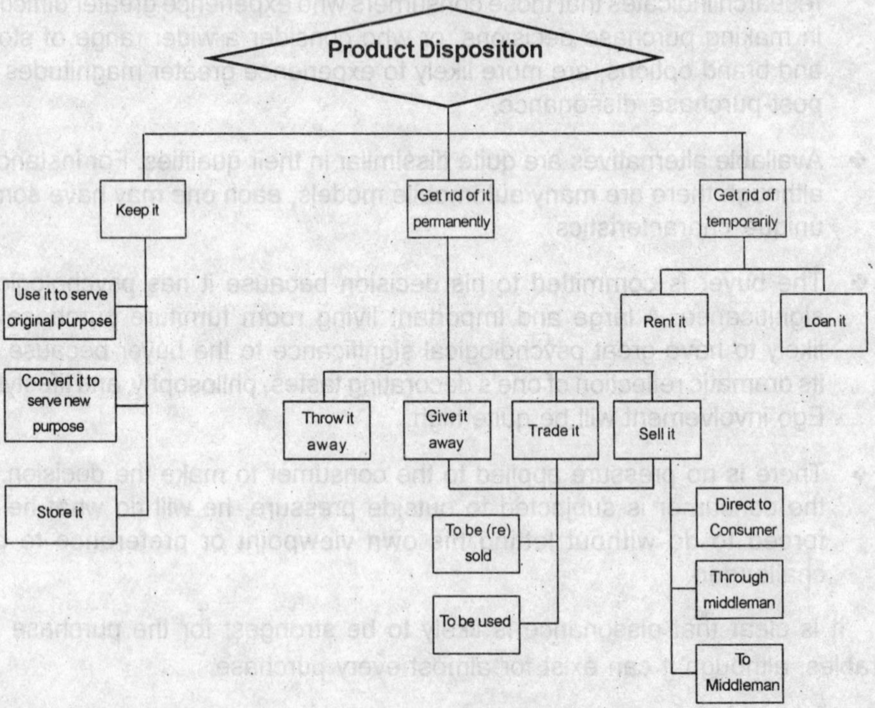

Fig.2.6. Product Disposition

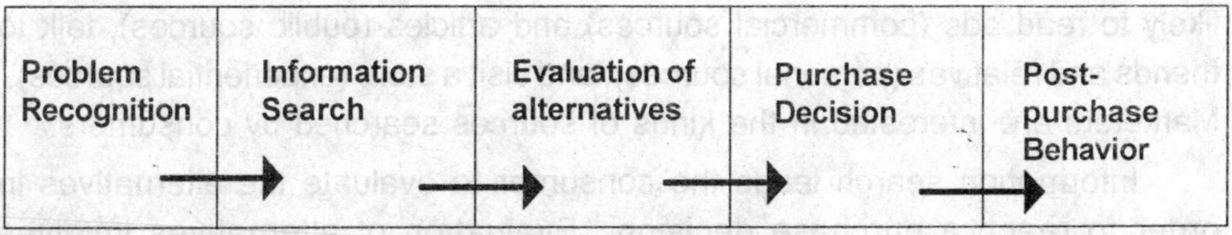

Fig. 2.7. Consumer Buying Process

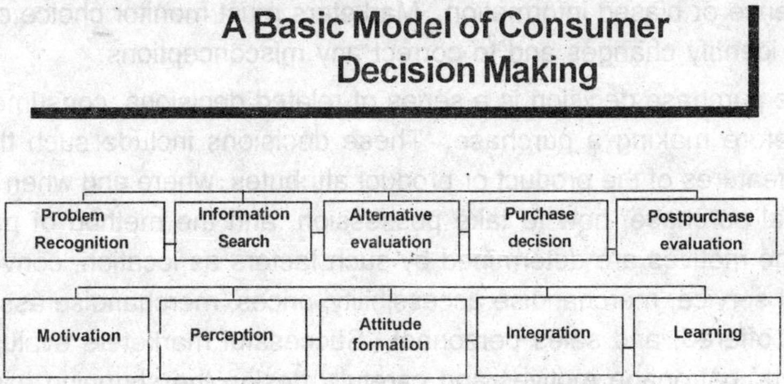

Fig.2.8. Model of Consumer Decision Making

Consumers go through a five-stage buying decision process: (1) need recognition, (2) information search, (3) evaluation of alternatives, (4) purchase decision, and (5) Post-purchase behaviour. The consumer selects an involvement level or how much effort to exert in satisfying a need. The more effort exerted the higher the involvement. For some purchases, consumers may go through these stages very quickly or may actually even skip stages or reverse some of the steps. Most buying decisions for products sold in supermarkets, drugstores, and discount stores are low involvement. These products have close substitutes and are relatively low-priced. The consumer will be more involved when he or she lacks information about the purchase, views the product as important, thinks the product has considerable social importance, and sees the product as having a potential for providing significant benefits.

Need recognition occurs when buyers perceive a significant difference between their actual state and their desired state. Marketers are very interested in the factors that trigger a conscious recognition of a need.

After the need is triggered, consumers search for information that will satisfy the need. This may be as simple as a memory scan or as complex as an extensive search. In other words, the information search may be internal (the consumer scans his or her memory for alternatives that would satisfy the need) or external (the consumer actively engages in a search for information that would assist in the decision). In an active search, consumers are very likely to read ads (commercial sources) and articles (public sources), talk to friends and relatives (personal sources), and visit a store (experiential sources). Marketers are interested in the kinds of sources searched by consumers.

Information search leads the consumer to evaluate the alternatives in order to reach a purchase decision. Evaluation of alternatives involves establishing criteria with which to evaluate each alternative before making a purchase decision. Often a consumer's evaluation may be incorrect due to inexperience or biased information. Marketers must monitor choice criteria in order to identify changes and to correct any misconceptions.

The purchase decision is a series of related decisions, consumers must make before making a purchase. These decisions include such things as specific features of the product or product attributes, where and when to make the actual purchase, how to take possession, and the method of payment. Patronage motives are determined by such factors as location, convenience, speed of service, merchandise accessibility, prices, merchandise assortment, services offered, and sales personnel. Successful marketers evaluate their customers' patronage motives and carefully design the shopping experience accordingly.

The purchase process does not end with the purchase. Post-purchase behaviour can influence future purchases and what the buyers tell others about the product. You may recommend the brand to everyone who asks you about your purchase. Or, you may tell everyone about your unhappy experience with the product. In many purchases, consumers may experience anxieties, known as cognitive dissonance. This occurs anytime there is inconsistency in a person's cognitions such as knowledge, attitudes, beliefs, and values. Each product considered by the consumer has both advantages and disadvantages. Thus, the purchased product has both advantages and disadvantages. The rejected products have some advantages. Given the importance of post-purchase behaviour in influencing future purchases, marketers want to help reduce dissonance. They can reassure buyers through their advertising and personal selling, while giving quality service after the sale.

ONLINE DECISION MAKING IN CONSUMER PURCHASE PROCESS

Consumers keep making decisions to buy the products of their choice. The steps included in the decision making are same as discussed earlier.

1. Problem recognition
2. Information search

3. Evaluation of alternatives
4. Purchase
5. Post-purchase behaviour.

The decision making as we have seen earlier is influenced by the internal determinants, which include learning, memory, personality, self-concepts, attitude, motivation and involvement. The external determinants consist of cultural and subcultural influences, social group influences, family influences, social influences and other influences. External and internal influences thus, together influence the decision making process and most customers follow these steps in a logical manner.

E-business enhances this process, and saves time of the consumer by providing all relevant information on the Internet that is required.

Problem Recognition:

A problem is recognised when there is a gap between the existing and the desired position in the use of a product by the consumer. This gap may be caused by a number of factors, and it has to be reduced for satisfaction of the consumer. E-Business provides the customer with more information regarding products and services. The customer, therefore, has a better understanding of the solving of these problems and starts demanding products, which were earlier not available locally. He has higher aspirations and fulfils his needs in a better way.

For example, microwave oven and automatic dishwashers, which were not available locally, are now made available to the Indian consumer.

Information search and Evaluation of alternatives:

Once the problem is recognised, the customer can find the alternatives to solve the problem on the computer. It gives enough and sufficient information to a consumer to choose. It provides many alternatives which can also be evaluated by mathematical models in the case of extensive problem solving, where more money and time is at stake. The evaluation of alternatives can be done speedily, and the advantages and disadvantages of various brands and products can be recognised. This also depends on the weightage given to different desired attributes in a product and making assumptions on a comparative scale. Internet can give comparative charts for making evaluation easier and rational.

The computer can also help in deciding about the choice heuristics (rule that guides the decision in areas of high probability). Information processing becomes eásier and the area of information is enlarged greatly.

Purchase:

E-consumer is a fully informed consumer and is aware of various product offerings by all competitors. His purchase decision cannot be influenced easily. He take's rational decisions and usually decides to go for a product that offers good value for money. He also knows the advantages and disadvantages of when to buy, how to buy, from where to buy, what to buy, and from whom to buy.

Post-purchase behaviour:

After using the product/service consumers can electronically interact with the manufacture or marketer giving valuable feedback. The critical feedback to the company regarding the improvement of the product. If the customer is dissatisfied, he may communicate his anger against the company to lakhs of people worldwide instantly. This may affect the reputation and goodwill of the company and tarnish its image. A satisfied customer acts as a best advertising and promotional means of worldwide publicity at no cost.

The theoretical study of consumer behaviour cannot be overlooked and remains an important aspect, in spite of the development of E-business. The theoretical framework of consumer behaviour has to be understood and applied in the application of E-business for proper marketing results. E-business does not replace, but supplements the theoretical foundation of consumer behaviour.

BUSINESS MARKET

Organizational buying behaviour and consumer buying behavior are similar. Organizations, after all, are made up of people. However, differences exist between organizational and consumer markets. Organizational markets have fewer customers. Those customers make larger purchases (both in volume and dollars). Many organizational products are more complex than consumer products and must be tailored to exacting technical standards. Service components, such as delivery and technical advice, are important to the total value package marketed to organizational customers.

CHARACTERISTICS:

- Fewer buyers
- Larger buyers
- Close supplier-customer relationship
- Geographically concentrated buyers

- Derived demand
- Inelastic demand
- Professional purchasing
- Several buying influences
- Direct purchasing
- Leasing

Participants in the business buying process:

- Initiator
- User
- Influencer
- Decider
- Approver
- Buyer
- Gatekeeper

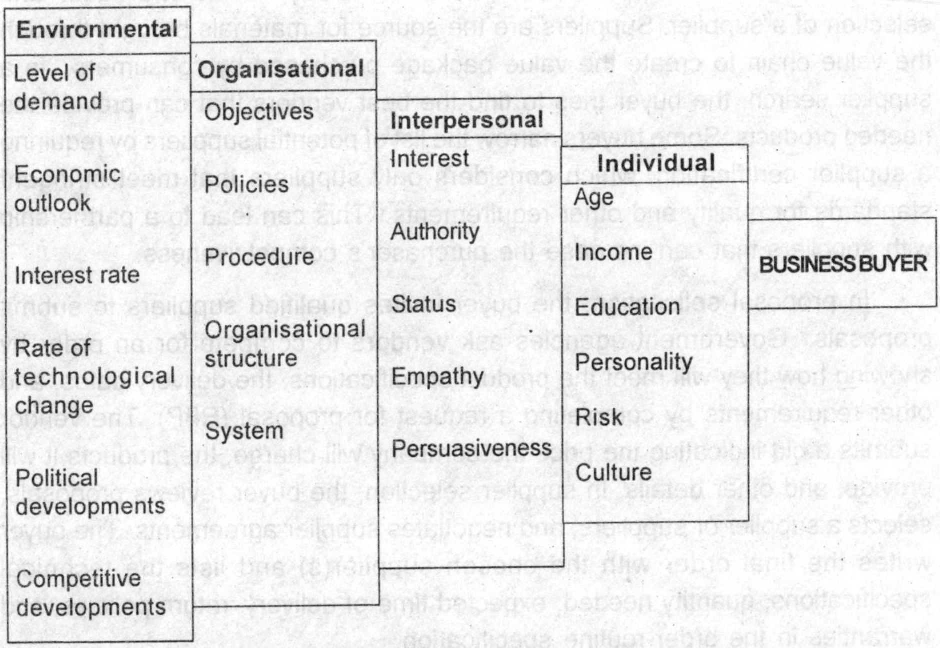

Fig. 2.9. Major Influences on Industrial Buying Behaviour

ORGANIZATIONAL BUYING DECISION PROCESS

Just like consumers, organizational buyers go through a process of decision making. Unlike ultimate consumers, organizational buyers are expected to follow a set of formal procedures to place orders. Organizations go through a multistage buying decision process: (1) problem recognition, (2) identification of alternatives, (3) evaluation of alternatives, (4) purchase decision, and (5) post-purchase behaviour.

Problem recognition begins when someone realizes that a product can solve a problem. This can result internally (low inventory report) or externally (salesperson has a new product that can lower costs).

Identification of alternatives includes a description of the general characteristics and quantity of a needed item. In product specification, the buying organization specifies the exact requirements for a needed item. Alternative brands, models, and sources of supply that meet these specifications are identified.

Evaluation of alternatives includes examining each supplier's value package (product performance, price, delivery, and quality). A value analysis examines the balance between a product's cost and its design, quality and performance.

Purchase decision includes to buy or not to buy, choice of product, and selection of a supplier. Suppliers are the source for materials brought through the value chain to create the value package purchased by consumers. In a supplier search, the buyer tries to find the best vendors that can provide the needed products. Some buyers narrow the list of potential suppliers by requiring a supplier certification, which considers only suppliers that meet stringent standards for quality and other requirements. This can lead to a partnership with suppliers that can increase the purchaser's competitiveness.

In proposal solicitation, the buyer invites qualified suppliers to submit proposals. Government agencies ask vendors to compete for an order by showing how they will meet the product specifications, the delivery dates, and other requirements by completing a request for proposal (RFP). The vendor submits a bid indicating the price the company will charge, the products it will provide, and other details. In supplier selection, the buyer reviews proposals, selects a supplier or suppliers, and negotiates supplier agreements. The buyer writes the final order with the chosen supplier(s) and lists the technical specifications, quantity needed, expected time of delivery, return policies, and warranties in the order-routine specification.

Post-purchase behaviour evaluates whether the product and its supplier met or exceeded the organization's expectations. In a performance review, a formal vendor analysis, the buyer rates its satisfaction with supplier's performance, deciding whether to continue, modify, or drop them.

ORGANIZATIONAL RELATIONSHIPS

Marketers take a broad view of the exchange process and form relationships at all levels of the exchange. Suppliers, producers, and distributors are part of the value chain. Marketers are better serving customers by benchmarking world-class standards in areas such as delivery time, order fulfillment, quality, and purchasing costs. Partnerships are formed on a customer-by-customer basis. Marketers collaborating with customers to tackle issues that are important to both parties can strengthen relationships. In addition, they can get together with another marketer to supply what organizational customers need rather than going it alone. They can form strategic alliances and joint ventures for the benefit of the customer. Another way to build strong value-chain relationships is to cross-functional borders within organizations or geographical boundaries.

Reciprocity and reverse marketing arrangements may be used. Suppliers may voluntarily buy from customers to show commitment to the relationship. Reciprocity is the practice of buying from suppliers that are also customers. It is legal in the U.S. as long as it is not enforced through coercion or does not harm competition. In reverse marketing, customers use marketing to build stronger relationships with suppliers. Customers want loyal suppliers that will satisfy very specific needs and also anticipate and react to changed needs.

An Electronic Data Interchange (EDI) is the computer-to-computer exchange of common business documents over telephone lines using a standardized electronic format. The use of EDI replaces the very costly labor and time intensive process of typing and retyping paper forms and mailing them to partners. There are no forms to type and nothing to mail since every exchange between the two partners can be accomplished through EDI except the actual delivery of the products. Some ma,keters use the Internet, while others dial into their customers' computers. An internal database can be used to track the purchase and product usage behavior of the organizations that buy an organization's products. EDI cuts paperwork and speeds information exchange.

Value added networks (VAN) are an integral part of the EDI system and without them a large-scale EDI program is virtually impossible. VAN acts as a postal system for EDI. It is a third-party service provider that furnishes clients with electronic mailboxes, storage and forwarding services, tracking capabilities, and translation services that are not offered by normal public networks.

APEX ELECTRICAL COMPANY LTD. – CASE STUDY– VI

Mr. Nathan, sales manager of Apex Electrical Co. Ltd., received a proposal from his regional manager at Bengaluru for opening a sub-office in Chennai and was considering what the best decision would be in the company's short-run as well as long-run interests. The company was in the business of manufacturing and marketing electric motors of a wide range of horse powers that could be used as a prime mover in numerous applications.

The company's factory and head office were situated in Mumbai and it had branch offices at New Delhi, Kolkata and Bengaluru: each headed by a regional manager. The regional office at Bengaluru was responsible for sales in Karnataka, Tamil Nadu and Kerala. The company also maintained a godown at Bengaluru, which, was used as the stocking center for feeding sales to the entire region. The company's distribution network had grown over several years and as such there was no one rule by which the arrangements could be explained. In Karnataka, due to the proximity of the regional headquarters, the distribution network was closely controlled by the regional office. The company had several dealers covering sales and they all purchased goods directly from the regional office. All the dealers got a fixed discount. The ultimate prices for the customers were fixed by the company. Each dealer covered a specific area, which was generally one to several districts and the company discouraged the interference of one dealer in another's territory. However, in the cities of Bengaluru and Mysore, there was more than one dealer. They collectively covered the sales in the city. The company salesmen regularly contacted the dealers and the office maintained good marketing information.

In the states of Tamil Nadu and Kerala, however, the arrangement was quite different. Due to some historical reasons, all the sales in this territory were channelled through one distributor. This distributor in turn had appointed his own dealers to cover the cities of Chennai and Kochi and other districts in these 2 states. The regional office, therefore, had very little information on the exact marketing set-up in this territory and the distributor operated almost independently. On several occasion, the regional manager had attempted to bring the distributor under closer control. He had the impression that the company was not able to exploit the full potential of the regional due to the authoritarian rule of the distributor.

He occasionally received reports that the distributor was not even aware of certain important tenders floated in the region and that on other occasions he had not bothered to submit quotations in time. There were also complaints from dealers that they did not get a fair deal and would instead prefer to deal with the company directly. The sales and service personnel of the regional office used to visit the states of Tamil Nadu and Kerala only when requested specifically by the distributor. Their independent visits were generally objected to by the distributor, as it would mean by-passing him. The real problem behind this was that the distributor had, in the initial states, given consider able financial help to the company. He was also important that did not mean, however, that the top management was prepared to sacrifice the company's interests. But at the same time they preferred to leave the distributor undisturbed.

The regional manager felt that the little pieces of negative feedback he had received could be the tip of the iceberg. However, in the absence of any information, he could not put up a convincing case against the distributor. He had always been helpless whenever some dealer working under the distributor complained to him. He felt it would seriously affect their morale if they realized that the company could not control the distributor.

He had discussed this matter at length with the sales manager, Mr Nathan realized that some tightrope walking was needed if he had to steer and clear this problem. Mr. Nathan was, however, anxious to do something about it and one idea was to open an office at Chennai, the headquarters of the distributor. While this would be for the declared purpose of helping the distributor in his marketing effort, it would also put an automatic check on undesirable practices. Moreover, the sub-office could collect more factual information that could be used to put up a convincing case against the distributor, if such a need arose. Accordingly, the regional manager had now submitted a detailed proposal for opening a sub-office at Chennai, which would look after Tamil Nadu to start with.

The company had a strict policy of insisting on the regional office to achieve a fixed ratio of sales per rupee of expense. For the Bengaluru office this ratio was 50 in the previous year when the sales were Rs. 2 crore and expensed Rs. 4 lakh. Of this, the sales in Tamil Nadu were Rs. 50 lakh. The proposal stated that a sales forecast of Rs. 60 lakh could be expected in Tamil Nadu next year and estimated expenses of Chennai sub-office at Rs. 1.2 lakh, thus achieving a ratio of Rs. 50 sales per rupee of expense. Among other things, the details of the proposal stated the following splitting up of the expenses–Rs. 40,000 towards salaries and Rs. 30,000 towards travelling expenses of 2 sales personnel who would be transferred from Bengaluru to Chennai.

Questions

1. What decision would you take if you were in place of Mr. Nathan?
2. Do you feel the proposal of new sub-office is economically justified against the stated policy of the company? If yes, why? If no, then how could it be made justifiable?

CHECK YOUR PROGRESS

True or False

(i) Customer = Consumer

(ii) Gatekeeper means security personnel.

(iii) Organisation buying behaviour is based on derived demand.

LET US SUM UP

Businesses stay in business by attracting and retaining customers. They do this by engaging in exchange of resources including information, money, goods, services, status, and emotions with consumers, exchanges that both businesses and customers perceive to be beneficial. When companies ask, who are our customers? How do we reach them? What should we sell to them? What will motivate them to buy? What makes them satisfied? They are asking questions that require sophisticated understanding of consumer behaviour. This unit provides a brief insight into the meaning and perspective of Consumer behaviour as well as understanding why it is important to study consumers.

"CB behaviour refers to the actions and decision processes of people who purchase goods and services for personal consumption."— James F. Engel, Roger D. Blackwell and Paul Miniard. Organizational buying behaviour and consumer buying behaviour are similar. Organizations, after all, are made up of people. However, differences exist between organizational and consumer markets. Organizational markets have fewer customers. Those customers make larger purchases (both in volume and dollars). Many organizational products are more complex than consumer products and must be tailored to exacting technical standards. Service components, such as delivery and technical advice, are important to the total value package marketed to organizational customers.

KEYWORDS

Consumer Behaviour: "CB behaviour refers to the actions and decision processes of people who purchase goods and services for personal consumption."

Culture: Values and beliefs in which one is born and grown up.

Subculture: Differencs in lifestyle, food-habit between different parts of India. India as whole has one culture and again it has different subculture in different parts of India. Even a particular age group, male, female segments etc. also known as subculture.

Social Class: Economic, Caste, Profession.

Reference group: The group of people to whom one consults before purchasing something; family, friend etc.

Family: It is defined as two or more persons related by blood, marriages or adoption who reside together.

LESSON AND ACTIVITY

Find out 5 product advertisement in TV and write brief about the types of consumer behaviour the advertisements have been targeted.

REVIEW QUESTIONS

1. Define consumer behaviour. Discuss the different types of buying behaviour?
2. What is Buyer's Black Box? Explain.
3. Explain the consumer buying decision process.
4. What is business market? What are the characteristics of Business Market? Differentiate between consumer market and business market.
5. Briefly explain the organizational buying process.

ANSWER FOR CHECK YOUR PROGRESS

(i) False

(ii) False

(iii) True

SUGGESTED READING

1. Bholanath Dutta: *Marketing Management*, 2nd Edition, Parshva Publisher, New Delhi, 2010.
2. Bholanath Dutta: *Consumer Behaviour,* 1st Edition, Kalyani Publisher, 2010.

☒☒☒

Chapter 3

Knowledge of Products, Competition and Methods of Acquiring Product Knowledge

I am the world's worst salesman; therefore, I must make it easy for people to buy."

— ***Gene Fowler***

Knowledge of products - Introduction - Knowledge- salesman should have - Importance of product knowledge - Knowledge about the product - Methods of acquiring product knowledge – understanding government policy.

Buying motives - Introduction - Understanding consumer behaviour - Product buying motives- Emotional - Rational product buying motives - Product buying motives- Patronage - Importance of buying motives

OBJECTIVES

At the conclusion of this lesson you should be able to understand :-

- Importance of knowledge about the product.
- What are the products, knowledge salesmen should have?
- Methods of acquiring product knowledge.
- Importance of buying motives.
- The concept of emotional buying motives.
- Patronage buying motives

PRODUCT KNOWLEDGE - AN EXAMPLE — CASE STUDY-V

The Marketing of Instant Coffee

Retail marketing through supermarkets is an intensely competitive business, based on large volumes and thin margins. If we take instant coffee as an example, it has attributes of:

Weight - 200g jar

Taste or Quality - powder, freeze dried, granulated

Brand - Maxwell House, Nestles

A distributor anxiously watches the small blips in sales from week to week, eager to ascertain any change in consumer behaviour. The distributor wants to know how their brand is faring, and how each particular product is faring against its competition.

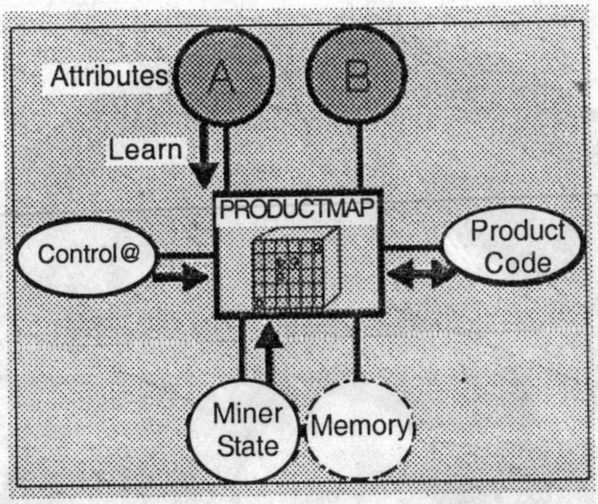

A product map can be used to link a product and its attributes. Then specifying a brand will result in a set of products, while specifying a product will result in a set of attributes. Competing products can be found by specifying the product, remembering the attributes, then using those attributes to produce a set of products.

The retail marketing model will contain at least two product maps - one to represent products, the other to represent stores and their attributes. Brands could also be treated as objects rather than just names - they have attributes of value, market dominance, mindshare.

The constrainable sets of products and stores coming from the product maps are used to extract sales information.

INTRODUCTION

The salesperson should have the knowledge about the products he is selling. Sales person without technical knowledge about the product would be a danger to the customer. Naturally he cannot explain something prospective to the customers, which he himself does not understand. If the salesman has the knowledge about the product he would be able answer all the queries raised by the customers. Even if a single answer were not given clearly, the customer would doubt about the quality of the product. Besides by having the knowledge it will become easier to make the customer understand about the product.

The extent of the knowledge required of a salesman depends on whether he is selling high cost products or low priced products. The salesperson should acquire information as to the policies behind the products as these are reflected in the products. Knowledge of the production methods can be used by the salesman to justify the cost of the product, he should also know about the law affecting the sales and selling, knowledge about the firm, knowledge about tariffs delivery conditions also.

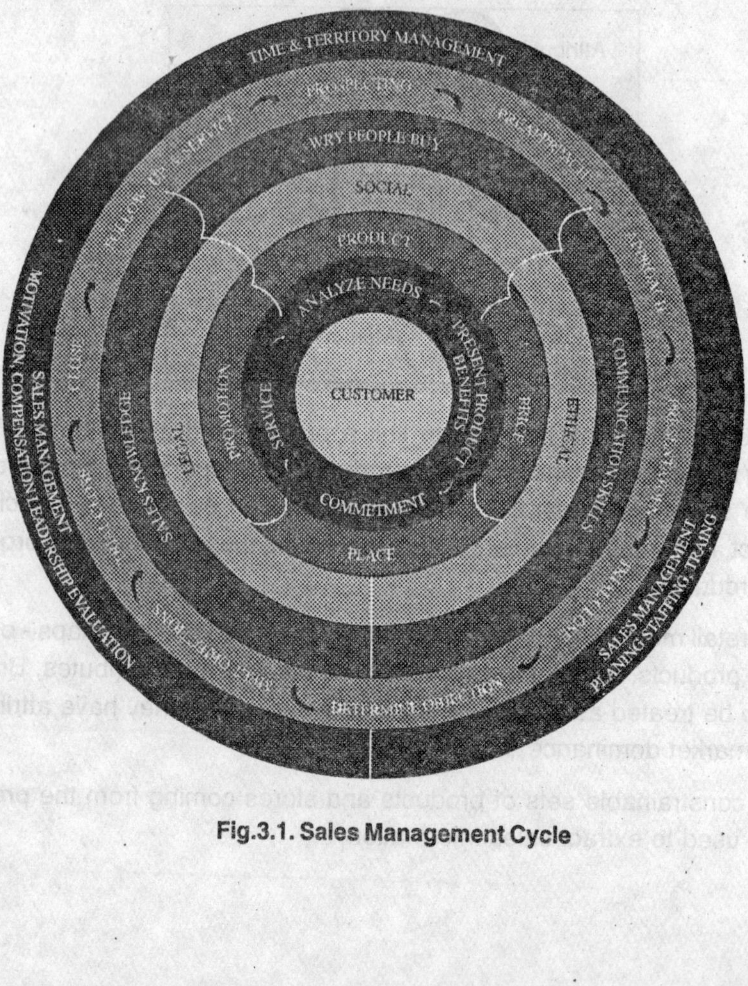

Fig.3.1. Sales Management Cycle

KNOWELDGE SALESMAN SHOULD HAVE

Knowledge of self

He should be able to make the best use of his personality by continuously assessing himself and analysing his qualities in the light of the requirements of his job. This will help him to improve upon his strengths and overcome his weaknesses through training and experience.

Knowledge of Firm

He should be fully conversant with the history of the firm. He should have a thorough knowledge of the objectives, policies, standing and organizational structure of his firm. Such knowledge will help him to utilize the strong points of the firm in personal selling.

Knowledge of product

He should be able to convince customers about the features and utility of the product by removing their doubts and objections. Thus, he should have full knowledge about the nature of the product, manufacturing details, terms and conditions of sale, distribution channels used and promotional activities.

Knowledge of competitors

In order to prove the superiority of his product, he must have full knowledge about the competitive products, their positive and negative features. Knowledge of competitors' sales policies, their brands and prices, etc., is also helpful. In all companies, marketing department has an additional sub-department known as MkIS (Marketing Intelligence System); its function is to collect competitor's information on marketing techniques, product modification, sales techniques, promotional strategy etc. Salesman can have enough information from the department as well.

Knowledge of customers

In order to be successful, he must use the right appeal and approach. He should be able to understand the prospects correctly and quickly and to motivate and win them permanently. He should, therefore, have complete knowledge of the nature and type of customers (their age, location, sex, income, education, etc.) and their buying motives (low price, convenience, prestige, fashion, etc).

Knowledge of selling techniques

Above all, he should be well-versed in the principles and techniques of salesmanship. He should pay undivided attention to the customer, be courteous and sympathetic towards customers, never loose patience, consider customer as the king, aim to build permanent customers and goodwill, serve the customer in the best possible manner, etc.

Government Policy

Government policy with regard to production and distribution changes frequently. Success in selling, therefore, depends to a great extent on the knowledge of the current government policies. The salesman should have the latest information about sales tax, surcharge, octroi duties, which vary from product to product. Government policy regarding price control and distribution policy also affects sales. Therefore, on the basis of a thorough and up to date knowledge of taxation and other government policies, the salesman can reply to the complaints and objections raised by the customers efficiently and thereby, sell the products with least difficulty.

Knowledge of competition

Competition is an essential feature of the modern marketing environment. It also poses a serious challenge to the very survival of the business. Therefore, the salesman should have an up to date knowledge of his competitive position in the market. He should also have knowledge about the strong and the weak points of his products in comparison with those of the competitors. He should also have information about the price and utility of products of similar nature and having identical use. Awareness of competition enables the salesman to compare his product with those of the rivals. This helps an effective tool in the competitive market.

IMPORTANCE OF PRODUCT KNOWLEDGE

Personality is not enough

Personality matters a lot in the initial stage of selling process but itself can not make a sale. Product knowledge is very important. Personality is like a body without soul, if the salesman does not have product knowledge.

Ensures better sales

In the selling process customers ask many questions regarding the product benefits, its usage, risk factors. Until salesman knows about the product in details he/she fails in handling the customer queries and ultimately fails to make a sale. Thus better product knowledge ensures faster and better sale of products and services.

Strengthens self-confidence

A through knowledge of the product or service he is selling helps the salesman to speak with self-confidence and courage. It makes sales much easier.

Makes selling a pleasant task

If salesman has indepth product knowledge then it becomes easier for him to and further he also enjoys his work as a salesman. It gives lot of satisfaction to the salesman.

Ensures satisfactory meeting of objections or enquiries

The salesman should be well equipped with all the technical as well as non-technical knowledge of the products and services in order to satisfy them. This enables the salesmen to meet queries from the buyers and convince them.

Enables to withstand competition

Modern era is the age of competition. A number of manufacturers compete with one another to sell identical products in the market. In such an environment of stiff competition, success in selling depends on the up to date detailed technical as well as non-technical knowledge of the products. A competent salesman generally remains well equipped with information about the product he sells and the product of the competitors, like a warrior in the field of selling. As a result, the salesman is able to sell in a competitive market.

Multiple earnings

With complete product knowledge the salesman is able to sell more. Earnings of the salesman usually depend on the sales volume. Thus, with the increase in the sales volume and profit of the organisation, the salesman is also able to increase his own earnings. In short, a salesman with thorough product knowledge is able to sell more and thus, earn more.

KNOWLEDGE ABOUT THE PRODUCT

(A) Knowledge of the organisation

First of all, salesman must know in details about the company he is working for. He must know about its history, board of directors, nature of business, product profile, product mix etc. He is also supposed to know the promotional strategy, pricing strategy, distribution strategy of the company. He should have an idea about company's expansion or diversification plans.

(B) Knowledge of the product:

(a) Background:

The salesman is expected to know the background of a product. He should know about the origin and history, past modifications, present position, the future plan of development, etc.

(b) Composition and construction:

The composition and construction of a product have a direct influence on its utility and durability. Therefore, the prospective buyer may ask questions and make queries regarding the composition and construction of a product.

(c) Use and performance:

The major and minor uses of the product and its performance should be known to the salesman. Such product knowledge enables the salesman to present the product in an impressive manner. The salesman must possess technical as well as non-technical knowledge of a product. Details like direct and indirect benefits, cautions to be taken during operations, installation procedure, operation process, maintenance, service and repair procedure and so on have to thoroughly understood by the salesmen. In case of products like textiles, certain features like colour, shrinkage or stretchability, wear and tear, heat resistance, maintenance, ironing instructions are also needed.

(d) Service and guarantee:

A salesman is also expected to know the specific services and guarantees offered along with the product. Durable products like washing machines, refrigerators, cars, scooters are offered free as for certain periods. Salesman is supposed to know the detailed of those services, terms and conditions.

Exhibit.3.1. Why does someone buy these items?

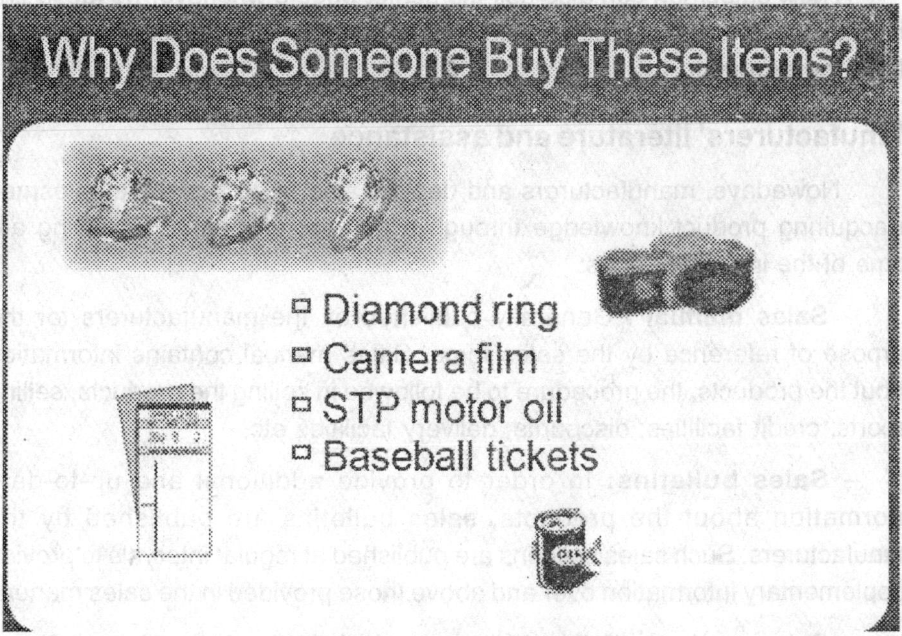

- **Diamond ring** – images of success, investment, to please a loved one
- **Camera film** – memories of places, friends, and family
- **STP motor oil** – engine protection, car investment or peace of mind
- **Baseball tickets** – entertainment, escape from reality or relaxation

METHODS OF ACQUIRING PRODUCT KNOWLEDGE

Personal Experience

More and more a salesman gets experience; he understands clearly the possible questions and thus, can prepare well and acquire sufficient knowledge about the products. Besides, salesman can gather a lot of information about a particular product by using it.

Libraries

Product information can also be gathered by going through related books in the library.

Senior and fellow salesmen

A new salesman can also ask the senior people whenever he faces any difficult situations and product related queries and thus, acquire lot of knowledge about the product.

Manufacturers' literature and assistance

Nowadays, manufacturers and dealers also try to assist the salesman in acquiring product knowledge through a number of means. Following are some of the important ones:

– **Sales manual :** Generally published by the manufacturers for the purpose of reference by the sales force. Sales manual contains information about the products, the procedure to be followed in selling the products, selling reports, credit facilities, discounts, delivery facilities etc.

– **Sales bulletins:** In order to provide additional and up-to-date information about the products, sales bulletins are published by the manufacturers. Such sales bulletins are published at regular intervals to provide supplementary information over and above those provided in the sales manual.

– **Salesman's portfolio:** While sales bulletins and sales manuals are meant exclusively for the company's sales force, salesman's portfolios are usually handed over to the dealers. Sales portfolio are usually prepared in a book form containing instructions and devices regarding the method of display, advertising materials, testimonial letters etc., for the benefit of the retailers.

– **Visit to factories:** Manufacturers often arrange visit of sales force to the factories to have first-hand knowledge about the products.

– **Meeting and conferences:** Manufacturers arrange meetings and conferences of the salesmen at regular intervals. These periodic meetings and conferences also help the sales force in enhancing their product knowledge through interactions, discussions, and deliberations. In such meetings and conferences, senior salesman also sales officers deliver lecturers and demonstrate important features of the products.

– **Education and Training:** In order to improve the selling skills of the existing sales force the manufacturer often arranges education and training programmes. Such orientation programmes are usually conducted by experienced professional people who equip the sales people with new techniques and methods to improve their sales performance. Salesmen are also offered correspondence courses to update their product and organisational knowledge as well as selling skills. Thus, education and training are important sources for the salesman to acquire detailed product knowledge.

KNOWLEDGE OF COMPETITIVE PRODUCTS:

In order to prove the superiority of his product, he must have full knowledge about the competitive products, their positive and negative features. Knowledge of competitors' sales policies, their brands and prices, etc., is also helpful. In all companies, marketing department has an additional sub-department known as MkIS (Marketing Intelligence System); its function is to collect competitor's information on marketing techniques, product modification, sales techniques, promotional strategy etc. Salesman can have enough information from the department as well.

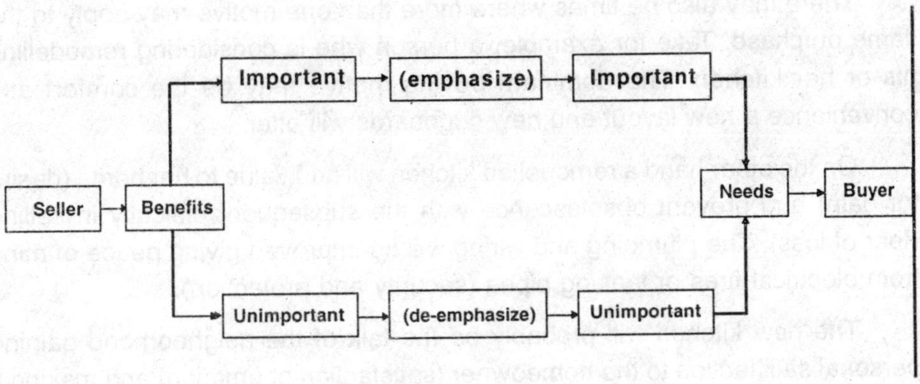

Fig.3.2. Match Buyer's Needs to Product's Benefits and Emphasize Them in the Sales Presentation

BUYING MOTIVES

As a salesperson you might think that people buy your product or service because of the reasons you give them. On the contrary, people buy not because of your reasons, not your company's reasons but for their very own reasons.

These reasons may not seem sensible, logical or even intelligent to us but they seem that way to the prospect. There are six different motives and they are not presented in any special order nor are they more important than the other. They are:

- ❖ Desire for gain (usually financial)
- ❖ Fear of loss (again, usually financial)
- ❖ Comfort and convenience
- ❖ Security and protection

- ❖ Pride of ownership
- ❖ Satisfaction of emotion

We refer to these as the six buying motives. You may notice that all these buying motives are emotional, not logical. People buy emotionally, not logically. In order to sell effectively you must keep this point foremost in your mind. They may buy in anticipation of financial gain or fear of financial loss. They want to feel secure and safe. They desire the comfort and convenience that a service or product may provide. They want to feel the pride and ownership of a product or they may purchase to satisfy the needs of love and ego.

There may also be times where more than one motive may apply to the same purchase. Take for example, a person who is considering remodelling his or her kitchen. The dominant buying motive may be the comfort and convenience a new layout and new cupboards will offer.

On the other hand a remodelled kitchen will add value to her home (desire for gain) and prevent obsolescence with the subsequent difficulty in selling (fear of loss). The plumbing and wiring will be improved giving peace of mind from electrical fires or leaking pipes (security and protection).

The new kitchen will probably be the talk of the neighborhood gaining personal satisfaction to the homeowner (satisfaction of emotion) and making it the center of attention for visiting friends (pride of ownership). Any one or any combination of all the six buying motives could apply to influencing this homeowner to remodel his or her kitchen.

If you were the salesperson who is trying to sell this person the remodelling job you need to know the dominant buying motives — the emotions that underline the decision — because you will want to appeal to those motives in your sales presentation.

It is extremely important that you uncover these underlying buying motives because the prospect in all likelihood will not come out and tell you. They are sometimes only vaguely aware of their motives themselves.

The primary reason people don't readily admit their buying motives is because it would make them feel too exposed. Psychologists tell us that people feel vulnerable admitting, even to themselves, what they care about, desire or fear on a deep, emotional level.

If you were to try to sell the prospect above a kitchen renovation based on the comfort and convenience of a new kitchen and the prospect is focused on the desire for gain on the resale value of the house, you won't be nearly as successful as you could be.

People do not readily admit their dominant buying motives. If you sat down and asked your prospect his or her dominant buying motives for a recent purchase, he or she would not or could not tell you. Psychologists report, even over a long period of time, most of their patients seem reluctant or unable to reveal their dominant motives for any of their actions.

Why? One reason is that our motives often overlap. Suppose you just purchased a new jacket. What was your dominant motive in making that purchase? Maybe you bought the jacket for comfort; you expect it to keep you warm. You might have bought it simply because it has a style or label that you are proud to wear or show your friends. Maybe you bought it because the color makes your eyes look bluer, or it makes you look taller and thinner, or in some way it makes you feel good about yourself — it gives you emotional satisfaction. Maybe you bought the jacket for all three reasons merged together: It's comfortable, you are proud to own it, and it makes you feel good about yourself.

Who wants to admit that we bought a jacket because it makes our eyes look blue? People would think we were conceited. Who wants to admit that we bought a jacket as a status symbol — that it has the "right" label, and we feel proud to own it? We do not like to admit these things. The six buying motives are real, but if we openly admit our real reasons for making a purchase, other people might laugh. We tend to hide our real reasons, because we just do not want to feel that vulnerable.

Well, your prospects are no different. They are not going to tell you or anyone else that the real reason they want to buy the copy machine you are selling is because it has a prestigious name. Who wants to admit to that kind of vanity?

They are not going to tell you or anyone that the real reason they want to contract your interior decorating service is because a well-decorated office will make them feel more important and appear more successful to others. Who wants to admit to that kind of vanity?

Your prospects are not going to tell you or anyone that the real reason they are interested in your computer system is because they are scared stiff that without it, their competitors will beat their socks off. Who wants to admit to that kind of fear?

Do not expect your prospects to be totally forthright and honest about the real reasons that motivate them to buy. In the next column, we will show you how to appeal to your prospect's dominant buying motive.

This lesson will make you understand various buying motives.

UNDERSTANDING CONSUMER BEHAVIOUR

Much of what we know about today's consumer is drawn from the behavioural sciences, including psychology, sociology and anthropology. Through application of this knowledge, salespeople can increase their ability to satisfy the needs and wants of consumers.

Developing a Customer Strategy

- The greatest challenge to salespeople is to improve responsiveness to customers.
- Salespeople must distinguish between similar products and services and help customers perceive important difference.
- The customer strategy is a carefully conceived plan that will result in maximum customer responsiveness.
- The customer strategy is built upon three prescriptions that help salespeople add value.
- Understand buyer behaviour
- Discover individual customer needs
- Build prospect base (discussed in Chapter 8)
- Consumer vs. business buyer behaviour
- Consumer buyer behaviour refers to the buying behaviour of individuals and households who buy products for personal consumption.
- Business buyer behaviour refers to the organizations that buy goods and services for use in the production of others.

Complex Nature of Customer Behaviour

- Customers perceive the product in their own terms.
- Buyers have different needs and motives.
- Current trends that influence buying decisions
- More consumers are moving upscale toward premium and luxury goods.
- Customer respect is central to success in every market.
- Customers come from more diverse racial, ethnic and cultural backgrounds than ever before.

BASIC NEEDS THAT INFLUENCE BUYING DECISIONS

Maslow's Hierarchy of Needs

- ❖ According to Abraham Maslow, basic human needs are arranged in a hierarchy according to their strength.

Physiological needs

- ❖ Physiological needs, sometimes called primary needs, are basic needs (hunger, thirst, shelter, and so forth), which tend to be very strong in the minds of most people.
- ❖ As basic needs are met, a person seeks to satisfy higher needs.
- ❖ Satisfaction of higher needs is postponed until basic physical needs are satisfied.
- ❖ Security needs

Security needs represent our desire to be free from danger.

- ❖ Desire to satisfy this need may motivate people to purchase security systems, smoke alarms, medical and life insurance, traveler's checks, and so forth.

Social needs

- ❖ Social needs reflect the desire for friendship, companionship, and long-term business relationships.
- ❖ Customers want to be treated as partners.

Esteem needs

- ❖ Esteem needs reflect the desire to feel worthy, competent, or adequate in the eyes of others.
- ❖ Customers want salespeople to involve them in the transaction.

Self-actualization needs

- ❖ Self-actualization needs refer to the need for self-fulfillment, a full tapping of one's potential. Highest-level needs on the hierarchy.
- ❖ Group influences that shape customer behaviour
- ❖ Group influences are role, reference group, social class, and cultural influences.

ROLE INFLUENCE

Definition: Role is a set of characteristics and expected social behaviors based on external expectations.

- ❖ Roles influence general behavior and buying behavior.
- ❖ Reference group influence

Definition: Reference group is a group of several people who have well-established interpersonal communications and tend to influence the values, attitudes and behaviours of one another.

May act as a point of comparison and a source of information for the individual member.

Norms of the group–become a guide for purchasing activity according to the strength of the individual's involvement with the group and the individual's degree of susceptibility to reference group influence.

SOCIAL CLASS INFLUENCE

Definition: Social class is a group of people who are similar in values, lifestyles, interests, behaviour, and occupational prestige.

- ❖ Entry into various social classes, differences among societies.
- ❖ To some degree, individuals within social classes have similar attitudes, values and possessions.
- ❖ Sociologists have determined that there are between three and six social classes.

Cultural influence

Definition: Culture is the accumulation of values, rules of behaviour, forms of expression, beliefs, and the like for a group of people who share a common language and environment.

- ❖ Culture has considerable influence on buying behaviour.
- ❖ Subculture is a group whose members share ideals and beliefs that differ from those held by the wider society of which they are a part.

Perception – How Customer Needs are Formed

- ❖ Perception is the process whereby we receive stimuli (information) through our five senses and then assign meaning to it.
- ❖ Perception is shaped by group influences and psychological and physiological conditions within us.

- Perception influences buying behavior because it determines what is seen and felt.
- Selective perception is screening out or modifying stimuli.
- Impossible to be conscious of all inputs at one time.
- Social and cultural background plus physical and psychological needs condition the use of selectivity.
- Buyers may screen out or modify information if it conflicts with previous attitudes or beliefs.
- Salespeople should review their own perceptions for accuracy.

Buying Motives

- Buying motive is an aroused need, drive or desire.
- It acts as a force that stimulates behaviour intended to satisfy that aroused need.
- Perceptions influence or shape this behaviour.
- Successful salespeople have adopted a product strategy that involves discovery of buying motives that influence purchase decisions.
- Emotional versus rational buying motives
- Emotional buying motives are those motives that prompt the prospect to act because of an appeal to some sentiment or passion.
- Rational buying motives are those motives that appeal to the prospect's reason or better judgement.

Emotional buying motives

A surprising number of purchases are guided by emotional buying motives. Salespeople should discover emotions that influence the buying decision.

Rational buying motives

A purchase based on rational buying motives is generally the result of an objective review of available information. The buyer closely examines the product or service in an unemotional manner and has a functional use in mind.

- A professional buyer or purchasing agent is likely to be motivated by rational buying motives.
- A professional buyer will welcome the advice and counsel of a well-trained salesperson.

- Rational buying motives include:
- Saving time
- On-time delivery
- Increased profits or financial gain
- Competent installation and servicing
- Durability
- Patronage versus product buying motives
- Patronage buying motives cause the prospect to buy products from one particular business.
- Prospect usually has had prior direct or indirect beneficial contact with the business.
- Highly important where there is little or no appreciable difference between two products.
- Patronage buying motives include
- Superior service
- Selection
- Competence of sales representative
- Product buying motives lead a prospect to purchase one product in preference to another.
- Sometimes made without direct comparison between competing products.
- Product buying motives include
- Brand preference
- Quality preference
- Price preference
- Design and/or engineering preference

PRODUCT BUYING MOTIVES: EMOTIONAL MOTIVES

Why do people buy? People always have their own reasons for buying. Their reasons are not necessarily rational, intelligent or sensible. However, whatever their buying motives, it is theirs. And you must be aware of which ones are motivating your prospect at all stages in the sales process. Then you can tailor your sales approach accordingly.

- ❖ No one buying motive is any more important than any other;
- ❖ They do not come in any particular order.
- ❖ These buying motives are emotional, not logical; people buy emotionally, not logically – even in B2B purchases.
- ❖ People do not readily admit to their buying motives:
- ❖ Who is going to admit to vanity or fear?
- ❖ Do not expect prospects to be open and honest about the real reasons that motivate them to buy.

Get better at observing or hearing your prospects. Know all six buying motives. Then you can appeal to them in turn, looking for which provokes the strongest responses in a prospect.

For example, suppose you see a reaction to a benefit of your product or service that appeal to comfort and convenience. Keep returning to that motive throughout the remainder of the meeting. Do not stop when you have uncovered just one motive that is important to your prospect. More than one buying motive may apply, and motives you leave undiscovered may turn out to be more important.

Uncover other buying motives with open, feeling-finding questions to discover additional reactions. Suppose you have already discovered that profit - desire for gain - is important to your prospect.

You might also ask: "How important is security to you?" and you would find out how the person feels about security and protection. As the meeting progresses, you can focus on areas that are important to your prospect.

Once the sale has been made, people stop responding emotionally and begin concentrating on the sound, practical, rational, business reasons why the purchase was made. Later on most people will not even remember their emotional motives. They sincerely believe that they bought the product or service for straightforward, logical reasons. If you ask, they can list these logical reasons for you.

People buy emotionally, then justify their decisions logically. Remember to provide your prospects with logical as well as emotional reasons why your product or service will benefit them.

Habits

Habits are easy to make but hard to break, habits once made become the basic need and repetitive act on the part of the individuals. Knowingly or unknowingly, most of the activities of people from dawn to dusk are based habits. Habits like smoking beedies, cigarettes, hard drinks of a particular brand, clothes at a particular place, cutting hair at a particular saloon, etc., very often *vide* the necessary stimulus for the consumer to buy articles or services.

Pride

Human beings by their sheer nature always wish to be admired and appreciated in the society. They invariably try to keep themselves above others in terms of social status, activities and achievements. They are very conscious about their dignity, status and class. In view of the same, people purchase certain expensive and luxury goods in order to maintain their dignity and prove their status in the society.

Fashion or imitation

People generally try to copy or imitate others, particularly, movie stars, sportsmen, business personalities, politicians, etc. Imitation takes place only when they are impressed by the dress, behaviour, hair style and other manners like walking, speaking, etc., of the person who is being imitated. Therefore, companies prefer to advertise their products or services with endorsements of celebrities to receive immediate response from the prospective buyers. It is the desire to live like the elite which motivates the present day consumers to purchase dress material, tooth paste, shampoo, watches, soft drinks, goggles, automobiles etc.

Sex and romance

One of the basic needs of all human beings and very strong, is basically based on emotions. Men want to be attractive to women and women want to attract them. The appeal of sex and romance is very important in case of articles like fancy dress, cosmetics, travel, clothing and automobiles. It is natural that buyers want to love and be loved by the opposite sex. Appeal to this motive is therefore made to sell a number of products like perfumes, deodorants, shaving lotions, hair grooming cream, shampoo, face powder and cream, clothing, sunglasses, shoes and chappals and services

Comfort

The desire to live in comfort is very strong with every individual. Goods include sofa sets, cushioned chairs, washing machines, pressure cookers, refrigerators, air coolers, air conditioners, dish washers, microwave ovens, automobiles, cell phones, etc. These articles save effort and time and provide pleasure at the same time. Factors like softness, noise, space, thirst, hunger, humidity, heat, cold, etc., affect the comfort.

Love and affection

Most human beings have an inborn tendency to care for their near and dear ones, and love for family, society, and country often drive consumers to buy certain (Affection for children is mostly responsible for buying things, like baby food, toys, dresses, life insurance policies, etc. Love for wife may lead to purchase articles like sarees, jewellery, cosmetics, etc., while love for husband may lead to buying gifts like ties, pens, purses, readymade, etc., Attachment to one's own country may make one buy goods made within the country. Care for loved ones may induce an individual to take up insurance policies.

RATIONAL BUYING MOTIVES

Rational Product Buying Motives

Generally people are rational in buying i.e., selective, with due consideration to factors like price, quality, durability, etc. Consumers usually purchase products by testing, comparing and observing the products keenly. The rational buying motives are based on wise thoughts, reasoning and judgement. However, there are certain rational buying motives which are product-related. They are:

a. Durability

b. Suitability

c. Multiple uses

d. Economy

e. Safety

f. Convenience

Rational Patronage Motives

A large number of buyers, by their rational choice, prefer to buy from a particular shop or store. They apply their judgement and intelligence before patronizing a particular shop. They always measure the benefits of extending their loyalty to a particular shop or store. The rational patronage motives include the following:

a. Credit facilities

b. Close location

c. Treatment

d. Wide choice

e. Additional services

PRODUCT BUYING MOTIVES: PATRONAGE BUYING MOTIVE

Appearance

Some customers are attracted to a particular shop or store by its appearance. The appearance mainly constitutes the decoration of the shop. A well decorated, attractively furnished shop with all modern amenities tends to attract the attention of customers automatically. It actually becomes a case of love at first sight.

Recommendations

Customers also visit a specific shop on the recommendations of their friends and relatives. Usually, these friends and relatives happen to be the satisfied customers of that particular shop. As a result, they recommend the store to others so that they can also avail the same type of facilities.

Imitation

Mostly, customers are motivated to follow others, particularly, the elites, the fashion leaders, the opinion leaders and so on. Most often, it seems easier and safer for many customers to go to a particular shop imitating others. This motive is stronger in case of fashion-oriented and style-based products and services.

Prestige

There are a number of customers who possess adequate wealth, and therefore, sufficient purchasing power. For them, the most important buying motive is the prestige and the feeling of superiority. The motive of prestige remains quite strong with them. As a result, they often purchase goods which they might not be needing at all at that time. Sometimes, they buy the latest and most exclusive products in the market as a display of prestige. They purchase articles and avail services even at higher price mostly driven by the motive of prestige.

IMPORTANCE OF BUYING MOTIVES

Many psychologists believe that the desire to feel important is one of the most powerful of all motivating forces. We all want to be appreciated as unique individuals. We love to feel important! and we like to have people around us who give us this feeling of importance.

There are hundreds of examples you can see every day of the importance of this motive. The child who "shows off" in front of company, the wife who spends the better part of a day preparing an outstanding dinner just so that she can enjoy the praise of her family, a man not used to public speaking who will go through the ordeal of preparing and delivering an after dinner talk so that he can he considered a person of influence, these are just a few of the many examples of the need for a feeling of importance.

A bellboy who makes a point of calling you by name as he shows you to your hotel room! the clothing salesman who compliments you on your good taste, the head waiter who makes a fuss over you when you enter the dining room, and the airline that actually rolls out a red carpet for the passengers on certain luxury flights, have learned that it is just good business to make the customer feel important.

Your prospect's need to feel important is a powerful force that can work either for or against you. To wound a person's ego or to take away the feeling of importance is a sure way to lose friends and alienate people. For example, people nearly always feel that their actions are logical. Therefore any criticism will usually be resented as a reflection of their motives.

By appealing to your prospects' ego, and feeling of importance, you are placing them on a pedestal. You are appealing to a wish to accomplish something worthwhile, to be recognized for achievements, to be useful to someone, and to be held in high esteem. These are all wrapped up in this powerful need for importance

In a child, this motive can be expressed as "hero worship." In adults, the motive of living up to what others expect is a desire to conform to group demands. There is a fear of being conspicuous and of being the object of ridicule. As a result there is an urge to be one of a group, to follow the crowd by doing what it does.

Although many outstanding sales representatives make good use of this motive, it is not as widely used as perhaps it should be. The use of testimonials is a practical way to put this motive to work for you. If other people are buying insurance from you, and "it is the thing to do," then there is that extra motive for your prospect also to buy from you.

This motive is also important in developing "nests" or related prospect groups. If you are the "insurance pro" for your prospects' co-workers or friends, then there is a certain amount of group acceptance in doing business with you. One of the benefits of a Referred Lead prospect is that you have the advantage of this extra power of motivation.

In most cases, you will find prospects who love their families and have a high measure of self-respect. On the other hand, you must condition your self to meeting many prospects with negative attitudes and an unwillingness to accept financial responsibility This is all just part of the job of being a sales representative.

As you go about your daily work of finding, meeting, studying, and interviewing prospects for your insurance subject, keep a few additional facts in mind:

1. Your prospect's own problems are of paramount importance. An emergency in the next county will not cause as much personal concern as a cut on the finger. Be sure you relate everything you say to your prospect.

2. Your sales talk must never be over the prospect's head; if it is, your ideas will not be understood. Conversely, nothing is more fatal in attempting to gain the prospects' confidence, goodwill, and signature than to "talk down" to them or below their mental capacity.

3. Finally, as you look at this intricate human being, your prospect. Consider that personal motivations are the positive drives that can stimulate individuals to action. They may also have a strong tendency! However, for inaction because of a natural resistance to change. They may prefer seeking an easy way out, escaping from the hard facts of life, or they may lack the will power to continue a savings program. This set of contradictions within the same individual is what makes the job of the sales representative such a fascinating one.

As you continue your study of your prospects, you will want to make a determined effort to constantly sharpen your powers of observation and communication. In this way you will be able to seek out the dominating motive or motives of your prospects.

Product Planning and Development:

The manufacture's product decision with regard to size, colour, weight, dimension, design, packaging, taste, etc., depends a lot on the consumer psychology which is chiefly based on the buying motives. Thus, once the buying motives are known, the product planning and development can be done in accordance with the consumer likings, tastes and preferences.

Pricing Policies:

Pricing of products and services is extremely significant because survival, growth and the profitability of an organisation depends on the same, to a great extent. In case a large section of the consumers are influenced by rational buying motives, the pricing policies of the firm have to be competitive. On the other hand, a comparatively high pricing strategy can be adopted if a majority of the consumers are guided by emotional buying motives. Therefore, it is essential that sellers should examine the nature of buying motives closely, and pricing decisions can be made accordingly.

Distribution Channel:

Once the buying motives of the consumers are known to the seller, the distribution channel of an organisation can be planned effectively. In other words, if the consumers are primarily guided by the service facilities offered by the dealers, the manufacturer can plan the distribution pattern accordingly so as to make services available at different distribution points. If door-to-door service is the motivational factor for a majority of buyers, then such provisions have to be built up by the seller. Similarly, if consumers prefer a particular type of store, the distribution channel has to be modified accordingly.

Promotional Policies:

Promotional efforts usually aim at winning the confidence of the potential buyers in favour of products or services. Once the influencing factors or the buying motives of the consumers are known, the advertisement and sales promotion programmes can be directed towards appealing to those specific buying motives. Accordingly, a large section of the buyers can easily be influenced and motivated for making a purchase. Therefore, in order to build an effective sales promotional policy, studying and understanding buying motives of consumers are essential.

In any sales transaction, the buyer plays a pivotal role. It is the customer who can make or break sale. Therefore, the knowledge of customer is very important. Moreover, it is required to know about the motives of the buyer which influence their buying process.

NOKIA PLANS TO DESIGN HANDSETS FOR DISABLED — CASE STUDY-VI

In an effort to take the mobile phone to the next billion worldwide, Nokia has started research to roll out handsets, specifically designed for the disabled. The world's largest handset vendor plans to undertake extensive research in India to understand the consumer behaviour of people with visual or hearing problems, towards the mobile phone.

Nokia is exploring ways to make the mobile phone friendly for such consumers. This could be done through using a different user interface, using icons and pictures in the menu and the phonebook instead of text, using large fonts, louder ring tones and voice commands.

These phones might have a different design aspect where India will also play a vital role. Talking to ET during his recent visit to India, Nokia global director, product group (entry business unit, mobile phones) Heikki Koivu said the challenge to sustain growth will be to reach out to consumers who do not use a mobile phones.

"We then have to address issues like physical disabilities, low vision, poor hearing and illiteracy. We also need to design phones that can support hearing aids," he said. Mr Koivu said India is a focus market for Nokia to understand consumer behaviour of mobile phones among the disabled.

"It is due to the sheer size of the population in this country. We have started adapting such features in some entry-level handsets like Nokia 1650 shipped to emerging countries like India. But, this will now attain bigger scale," said Mr Koivu.

India and China are two of Nokia's largest markets for entry level phones. The entry-level portfolio includes handsets, which are priced between Rs 1,500 and Rs 5,000. Nokia is also planning to bundle its internet services 'Ovi' in the entry level phones sold in India.

"We are planning to bundle most of the Ovi applications in handsets shipped to India, including the music services Nokia Music Store. All such integration will take place over the next three years for the entry-level handsets. We need to simplify these applications to suit the consumer preferences in emerging markets," said Mr Koivu.

Questions for discussion

(i) "Mobile for disables" – do you like this idea? Explain.

(ii) What could be the marketing strategy for Nokia to market mobile sets for disabled?

(iii) What could be the additional features can be associated with the mobile set? Explain.

CHECK YOUR PROGRESS

(A) True or False

(i) Without product knowledge also, a smart salesman can close a sale.

(ii) Salesman should be fully conversant with the history of the firm.

(iii) Sales Manual published by the manufacturer.

(B) Fill in the blanks

(i) Factors like price, quality, durability. etc,. comes under .... buying motive.

(ii) .... is one of the strong basic needs of all human beings.

(iii) .... are easy to make but hard to break.

LET US SUM UP

Most of the customers are ignorant about the features and utility of a product as so many varieties, types and design, are available in the market. Without the help of salesman, it is difficult for the customers to decide about their products. A salesman has to convince the customers about the utility of the product by removing their doubts. The salesman, therefore, must have complete knowledge about the product - its special features and uses. In order that the salesman could answer the questions of the customers, he should know the whole process of production – raw materials used, place of production, sources of supply, etc. He must also know the terms and conditions of sale – delivery, prices, packing, credit facilities available etc., and the distribution channels used.

In any sales transaction, the buyer plays a pivotal role. It is the customer who can make or break sale. Therefore, the knowledge of customer is very important. There are various buying motives which influence buyers to purchase a product/service. These motives are briefly:

Emotional buying motives like pride, sex and romance, habit, fashion etc.

Patronage buying motives: Appearance, recommendation, imitation, prestige etc.

Rational buying motives: Durability, suitability, multiple uses, economy, safety, convenience, credit facilities, treatment, wide choice, additional services etc.

LESSON END ACTIVITY

1. Interview a salesperson on how the internet has impacted her or his job responsibilities.
2. Visit the website www.monster.com and compile data on current salary levels for sales people in different industries and different parts of the country.

KEY WORDS

Salesmanship:

A concise effort on the part of the seller to induce a prospective buyer to buy even if he had not thought of it favourably.

Personal Selling:

It refers to oral presentation in conversation (by a sales rep) with one or more prospective customers for the purpose of making sales.

Marketing Mix:

Product, price, place and promotion collectively known as Marketing mix.

Product Mix:

It includes packaging, branding, labelling.

Promotion:

Efforts usually aim at winning the confidence of the potential buyers in favour of products or services

Distribution Channel:

Set of intermediaries to move the products from company to customer.

Sex and Romance:

The basic motives in human beings as expressed by Maslow's need hierarchy theory.

Rational buying:

It is selective with due consideration to factors like price, quality, durability etc.

Patronage:

Application of judgement and intelligence before selecting a particular shop.

REVIEW QUESTIONS

1. Write a short note on importance of product knowledge?
2. Explain the different product knowledge, what a salesman must have?
3. Is product knowledge is essential to make a sale? Explain.
4. Explain the different methods of acquiring product knowledge.
5. "Understanding government policy is critical for salesman's success" – explain.
6. Why salesman needs to know about competitor's product – explain.
7. "Salesman must know in details about his organisation"- explain in your own words.
8. Why customers buy product? Explain briefly.
9. Write short notes on (i) buying motives (ii) patronage motives (iii) emotional motives.
10. Explain in details the concept and component of patronage motives.
11. Explain different types of buying motives.
12. Explain importance of buying motives. What is a rational buying motive? Explain briefly
13. Explain the factors that influence in patronizing a particular shop.
14. Explain how pricing polices influence buying motives?
15. Explain the factors that influence patronage buying motives in detail.

CHECK YOUR PROGRESS: MODEL ANSWER

(A)

(i) False

(ii) True

(iii) True.

(B)

(i) Rational

(ii) Sex

(iii) Habits

SUGGESTED READINGS

P.K. Sahu & K.C. Raut: *Salesmanship and Sales Management,* Vikas Publishing House Pvt Ltd, New Delhi, 2003.

S. A. Chunawalla: *Sales Management,* Himalaya Publishing House, Mumbai, 2005.

Spiro, Stanton, Rich: *Management of a Sales Force,* Tata McGraw Hill, New Delhi, 2008.

☒☒☒

Chapter

4

Knowledge of Customers, Selling Process

There are worse things in life than death. Have you ever spent an evening with an insurance salesman?"
– Woody Allen

Knowledge of Customers - Introduction - Sizing up of Customers - Character Analysis - Classification of Customers.

Selling Process- Introduction – Prospecting – Pre-approach – approach - Need Assessment – Presentation - Meeting Objections - Gaining Commitment - Follow up - Theories of selling.

OBJECTIVES

At the conclusion of this lesson you should be able to understand :-

- ❖ The concept of sizing up of customers.
- ❖ Customers character analysis techniques.
- ❖ Different types of customers based on different factors.
- ❖ The selling process in details.
- ❖ Insight into each stage in details.

IIM-AHMEDABAD GRADUATE AIMS TO MAKE BIHAR — A VEGETABLE HUB - CASE STUDY- VII

It may come as a shock to many that after topping the elite Indian Institute of Management (IIM), he opted to sell vegetables on the rough streets of this city. But then Kaushalendra is a man on a mission.

He is not moving around with his loaded pushcart to earn a livelihood but to make his home state, Bihar, the vegetable hub of India. Kaushalendra, who is in his late 20s, is an IIM-Ahmedabad graduate of the 2007 batch. He could, like his peers, have chosen to sit in the plush air-conditioned premises of a top MNC like his peers. But he is roughing it out instead.

"I am here to do something. It was my childhood dream to contribute to the development of rural Bihar," he said."I have opted to make vegetables the new brand of Bihar," Kaushalendra, the native of a village in Nalanda, which happens to be the home district of Chief Minister Nitish Kumar.

Clad in a simple shirt and trousers, the bespectacled youth is popularly known as the "MBA sabziwalla" among his loyal customers, particularly women in the Kankarbagh colony, a middle class locality. Hailing from a farmer family himself, he started his venture about 10 days ago.

After passing out of IIM-A, he did extensive fieldwork, meeting farmers, studying cultivation techniques and finally taking a bank loan of Rs 40 lakh to start the project."Till date the response has been better than expected," Kaushalendra said, well aware of the attention he attracts.

Unlike other vegetable vendors, he is minutely studying consumer behaviour as he goes along. "It is important for me to study consumer behaviour when they purchase vegetables from my pushcart to help prepare a blueprint of expansion," he said.

Kaushalendra recalled that after doing his MBA, he along with some of his friends and teachers from IIM-A developed a pushcart to make it easy for vendors to carry a vegetable load of up to 200 kg. His pushcart is made of fibre with an attached weighing machine, is ice cooled to keep vegetables fresh for up to five days, and sold under the brand name of 'Samridhi'. "Initially, there was only one pushcart for trial but now I have already ordered 50 more. It will go up in the next phase," he said. He plans to take Samridhi, launched by his NGO Kaushalya Foundation, across the country and abroad within five years. His vegetables are priced slightly lower than those sold by other vendors.

"I am confident that all major players in the vegetable market, including Reliance Fresh, will purchase from us in the next five years," Kaushalendra said. In a bid to establish direct links with vegetable growers or farmers, Kaushalendra has tied up with over 250 vegetable growers in different villages in Nalanda and Patna districts. He has also tied up with the Agriculture Training and Management Agency (ATMA) to take his dream to vegetable producers in different parts of state.

Kaushalendra said Bihar has an enormous untapped potential for vegetables. The vegetables produced in fertile land near the Ganges river can mark a turnaround for the state if marketed properly. "It will assure better returns to growers," believes Kaushalendra. It was not easy for him to take to his pushcart selling vegetables as his family members initially opposed the idea and wanted him to go for a job with a fat salary.

INTRODUCTION

The success of salesmanship depends, to a large extent, on the approach of a salesman and his winning capability over customers. As a matter of fact, customer is the focal point of the modern marketing and all selling efforts centre around him. Seller is totally dependent on customers, for achieving success in selling. While dealing with the customers, training, knowledge and efficiency of the sales force are tested. Therefore, salesmen are expected to know and understand their prospective customers well because it is the customers who determine the fate and fortune of the business. The success of all selling efforts largely depends on the ability of the salesman to recognise the needs, problems, likes, dislikes of the customers and treat them accordingly. It has been rightly said that, 'know the customers, for, they are the paymasters'.

SIZING UP OF CUSTOMERS

Generally, different individuals buy products with different motives. Accordingly, they should be treated in such a manner that it matches their temperament and need, to achieve positive results. The process of recognizing or diagnosing the customer is known as sizing up the customers.

'Sizing up of customers' is nothing but understanding the taste and temperament of customers and tackling them in such a manner that their desire for products or services are converted into demand.

In other words, the salesman should be able to identify the quality and character of each customer. This is necessary because different types of customers need different types of persuasion and treatment. Therefore, it is essential that a salesman should, while sizing up the prospective buyers observe their carriage, clothes, expression, conversation and actions. This is known as character analysis of customers. Their buying policies need closer attention of the salesman.

CHARACTER ANALYSIS

Carriage:

Carriage means the way or the style in which a customer walks. By observing closely the way the customer walks, the salesman can know a lot about his nature and character. This observation also enables the salesman to decide whether the customer is a shopper or a looker.

The shopper generally walks straight, erect and to his full height with his head high and chest thrown out. They are confident and determined type of customers who walk straight to the salesman and ask for the goods they want. On the other hand, the looker type or indecisive customers usually walk casually into the shop. Generally they do not have anything definite to purchase and try to keep away from the salesman. There are also some nervous type of customers who walk up and down the shop because of their nervousness. Their unsteady looks indicate the wavering mind they possess.

Clothes:

The economic status and taste of a prospect can be known by his clothes. The clothes he wears are an indication of his taste and his ability to spend. The clothes may be expensive or cheap, latest or outdated, well cared and ironed or crumpled. However, at times it is not possible to judge the status of a prospect by his clothes. Extremely rich persons may wear cheap clothes whereas, snobs and cheats may wear expensive clothes.

Expression :

An expression usually indicates the overall impact that the salesman is able to create through the sales talk. Face is the mirror of a person and an index of his mind. The facial expression of the customer reveals the extent to which he is interested in the proposition of the salesman. Similarly, the salesman can easily know the mood and willingness of the customers by observing the eyes of the customers. Facial expression also shows whether a particular customer is frank or sullen, cheerful or gloomy, confident or diffident. Thus, a keen observation of the expression of customers can indicate their character.

Conversation:

Conversation is another useful source of information about the nature, attitude, likes and dislikes of a customer, for the salesman. The language and tone of the customer should be observed carefully and the salesman should adjust his manner, language and tone accordingly, to suit the customer.

Actions :

It has been rightly pointed out by someone that actions speak better than words. Therefore, the actions of the customers must be observed carefully. To be clearer, the salesman must watch the customers dealing with the product, his reactions, his eagerness, his craziness about the latest products, and so on. In case the customer is interested in the product, he will enquire about the same. If the customer argues by asking vague questions and starts bargaining, it shows he has not much interest in the product.

CLASSIFICATION OF CUSTOMERS

On the basis of sex

Men:

Male customers are generally experienced and learned. They are comparatively less interested to shop for longer periods as most of them consider it as a wastage of time. Usually they have a time saving attitude. They get bored if they are asked to wait while purchasing. They are quick decision makers and usually interested in qualitative and long lasting products. Usually, male customers do not consider price as a major and important factor for making their purchases. In many cases, it has been found out that they hardly go for the latest design and fashions. They also happen to be more adventurous and inventive. Usually, they like their work being done in a modern, improved, scientific and better, way. This attitude of the male customers should be given prime importance by the salesmen while dealing with them.

How to deal with them? It is comparatively easy to handle the male customers as they require little explanation about the products. The salesman should persuade, create and hold their interest by right approach, proper presentation of the article, appealing statements and appropriately handling objections. The salesman should possess adequate product knowledge to convince and handle such customers. In other words, an educated and experienced salesman can handle such customers efficiently. The salesman, while dealing with male customers should emphasize on the quality and durability of goods he intends to sell. He should attend to them quickly and avoid detailed sales talk. Such customers are also very particular about the behaviour of the salesman. The salesman, therefore, should be very cordial and courteous in his behaviour while dealing with such customers. Latest model and quality products only should be shown to them.

Women:

Generally, women constitute the most difficult type of customers to handle. They are very often termed as home ministers and most of the family purchases directly or indirectly, are made by them. Statistics indicate that nearly 65 per cent of the family purchases in the world are made by women. This, clearly points out the importance and status of women in the modern marketing environment.

There are certain unique characteristics of women customers. They are generally interested in the latest fashion, design, style, colour, etc. They take more time to make a selection and hardly trust the salesman. Generally, they are hard bargainers and late decision makers. To make women consumers agree to a particular point is really difficult for the salesman. They are usually economy oriented and even go to the extent of bargaining by moving to different shops. They are a suspicious type of customers and make minute enquiries about the products. They even irritate the salesman by asking vague and unnecessary questions. They are generally proud, egoistic and jealous. They want to showoff their superiority in society and most often seek variety. They prefer to have the best with the least.

How to deal with them? While dealing with women customers, the salesman must be very careful about his manners. He must greet, treat and pay due respect to them. It has been rightly pointed out by some experts that women customers want to be treated like queens and the salesman should provide them a red carpet treatment. The salesman should avoid discussion about the complex technical points of the product with the women consumers. As they are fond of examining the articles minutely, the salesman should allow them to feel, smell, look, lift, handle the product. Phrases like 'you get more for you money,' 'these articles save your money', 'this is more economical', should be cleverly used by the salesman while dealing with the women consumers. The salesman should point out discounts, free gifts, prizes, etc. Their craze for fashion and variety must be exploited fully by the salesman. Besides, the salesman should never insist on a quick decision while dealing with women customers. The selling points should be used cleverly and tactfully so that along with the products, customers are also praised and flattered.

On the basis of age

(i) Children

(ii) Youngsters

(iii) Middle aged

(iv) Elderly Children

How to deal with them?

Children:

Children are one of the easier type of customers as compared to others. The salesman should behave with love and affection to them. Sweet talk and cordial behaviour can easily win their hearts. Once they are satisfied with the shop and the salesman, they become regular customers automatically. Small children usually like to be treated well and expect importance like grown-up persons. The salesman should never cheat them either in transaction or in quality.

Youngsters:

How to deal with them? Youngsters are one of the easiest type of customers to be handled by the salesman. While dealing with young customers the salesman should offer friendly treatment to them since they are sensitive type of persons. These customers should be provided with the latest designs and colours to choose from. The salesman is expected to talk in a lighter vein and friendly manner to such customers. However, he should never try to offer advice to them. As a matter of fact, any intelligent salesman can deal and satisfy young consumers easily.

Middle aged :

How to deal with them? Middle aged customers are to be handled carefully and intelligently. The salesman should be very clever and tactful while dealing with such customers. The salesman should never try to bluff about the quality and the price of goods. The salesman should give them compliments for their achievements in life and their status in the society. The salesman must emphasize on "buying motives especially pride, possession, position, vanity and profit to win over such customers. The sales talk should also be effectively represented before such customers. Usually, middle aged customers are easily impressed by the courteous behaviour of the salesman.

Elderly:

How to deal with them? The salesman has to thoroughly study the psychology of such customers since they are basically difficult type of customers. The salesman should appreciate their wisdom and experience. He should give respect and regard to such customers and try to seek advice in order to please them. Elderly people are usually quite sensitive and therefore the salesman should be very cautious while dealing with them. The salesman has to talk about every detail of the product to such customers and therefore the sale is supposed to take a long time. Physically handicapped customers should be treated accordingly and should be looked after very well. It should be seen that they are comfortable in the shop. These type of customers feel gratified and satisfied when the salesman talks to them sympathetically, treats them well and sends them off in a courteous manner

On the basis of geographical area

Urban Customers :

Customers living in towns or cities are called urban customers. Generally, they are educated, well informed and cultured. They are usually polite in their behaviour. The buying motives of urban customers are generally linked with pride, possession, etc. They are always crazy about the latest fashion, style, colour, because of their awareness about the outside world. Usually, they are not the argumentative type and do not bargain much while purchasing. Usually, they expect good behaviour from the salesman. In short, they are the easy type of customers to deal with.

How to deal with them? The salesman is supposed to pay due respect and show adequate courtesy to the urban customers. They should be given the information about the latest arrivals and should be provided with a variety of goods to choose from. The salesman must explain technical details and avoid providing general information about the products. They hardly need any persuasion in purchasing. They are gentle and educated, and hence easy to handle.

Rural Customers:

Customers living in villages and muffosil areas are called rural customers. They are mostly illiterate or less educated and are simple and humble. They hardly care for good manners and polished behaviour. Most of them prefer bargaining and try to get the best goods at the least price. The main motive is to get maximum satisfaction out of the money spent. Unlike urban customers, they are not so crazy about the latest style and fashion. They are always suspicious and afraid of being cheated. Sometimes, they move in groups while buying as they think that chances of being cheated will be less in company. Lack of education often makes them argumentative and rude. They are usually guided by the motives of economy, durability, performance, and price.

How to deal with them? The salesman while dealing with the rural customers must try to convince them about the authenticity of the goods. These customers should not be neglected or cheated because they continue to patronise the shop once they are satisfied with the store and the product purchased thereof. While selling to rural customers the salesman must emphasize on the price, quality, durability, and performance of goods. Every detail of the goods must be provided to the rural customers. The salesman has to be tolerant with the bad habits of such customers who indulge in chewing paan, smoking, etc. Since they visit several shops for bargaining, the salesman has to be lenient to such behaviour. Their common sense and sense of choice need to be appreciated by the salesman.

On the basis of Purpose

Industrial Buyers:

Generally, industrial buyers purchase goods for use in the production process so as to manufacture a final product. Every manufacturer appoints a purchasing agent or a purchasing officer to purchase the required goods. These purchasing agents are usually experts in purchasing and have specialised knowledge in purchasing the goods which are needed by the organisation. They purchase in large quantities at regular intervals. Generally, industrial goods are sold more through salesman than by advertising and publicity. Industrial purchasers are very much rational in their buying decisions because they have thorough knowledge about the product and are considered as experts in purchasing. Industrial buyers are generally interested in the price and quality of the product and the services offered along with the product. They are also concerned about regular, dependable and adequate supply of such industrial goods.

How to deal with them? As pointed out earlier, industrial buyers are usually guided by the price and the quality of goods. They are also particular about door-delivery, prompt and regular supply and after sales technical and repair services. The salesman who deals with industrial purchasers must be honest and prompt and should have thorough knowledge of the product. It should be noted that expert industrial purchaser looks for the services offered along with the product. At times, industrial buyers do not bother much about the price even if it is a bit high. These customers also need assurance of continuous supply of goods and they should be assured accordingly. They should be dealt with utmost care because they always purchase in bulk quantities. Hence, the salesman should keep a very cordial sales relationship with them.

Resale Buyers:

The customers who buy for resale are wholesalers and retailers. They purchase goods in large quantities and are generally experts in the field because they purchase at regular intervals. They are well informed about the products, market conditions, changing fashion, tastes, etc. Usually, they prefer to purchase fast moving goods, i.e., the goods which are sold rapidly. Resale buyers are also keen in purchasing goods having high profit margins.

How to deal with them? In dealing with such resale purchasers, the salesman must have a thorough knowledge of the products. Because the purchasers are experts in buying and selling of goods, they expect the salesman to be honest and efficient in dealing. Moreover, the salesman must be prompt in answering their queries and assure them regular delivery, quality and price. The salesman should keep them in good humour and deal with utmost care because finally they are the persons who sell the goods to the ultimate buyers. As such, they can push up or bring down the ultimate demand of the goods in the market.

The Government Purchasers:

Every government department has some buying officers who purchase on behalf of their respective organisations. Generally, they purchase in bulk. For example, defence department purchases weapons, electronic equipment, vehicles, warships, tanks, airplanes, etc.

How to deal with them? The salesman should meet these buying authorities at their respective offices. He should meet them on the appointed day and time. These customers should be kept satisfied by friendly and courteous behaviour. The salesman should be very prompt in discharging orders received from such customers.

On the basis of Characteristics

Argumentative type:

Some customers are argumentative by nature. They enjoy and take pleasure in finding faults with the goods, the salesman, and the organisation. In fact, they find fault with every one and consider themselves as the most capable and intelligent person in doing so. Usually, they lack patience to listen to the salesman and his selling points. Rather, they argue with the salesman without any aim. They are basically quite emotional. For no reason, or for a silly reason, they become annoyed and get irritated. Some of them are clever and intelligent and keep detailed information about the product. They always compare prices of different stores and purchase their requirements at comparatively cheaper prices.

How to deal with them? While dealing with argumentative type of customers, the salesman must be very tactful. The salesman must remain cool and should have lots of patience to deal with such customers. At times, the salesman is bound to remain silent to handle the situation and sometimes he should present facts and truths tactfully. He must have a lot of patience to listen to the customers and answer their queries and provide necessary explanations, wherever required. Such type of customers must be given enough scope to argue because by arguing, they feel they are showing their knowledge and intelligence and ultimately get satisfied. At no point of time, should the salesman lose his temper because once he loses his temper he loses the sale too. If the customer is right they must be properly appreciated. Further, the salesman should never try to avoid the arguments of the customers. 'The customer is always right', should be his principle while handling argumentative type of customers. He should try his best to please such customers by his sweet words and flattery talks and avoid confrontation with such customers.

Shy type:

Generally they are of nervous type and lack experience in purchasing goods. Therefore, they remain shy and timid and lack own judgement in buying. Usually they take quick decisions in purchasing articles. They do not like to criticise others and also do not like to be criticised by others. Because of their shyness, they do not express their dissatisfaction. If they are dissatisfied with the product or the salesman or the store, they never express it. They simply discontinue purchasing their requirements from that shop. This indicates their sensitiveness. They are generally very polite and conscious about self-respect.

How to deal with them? Dealing with a shy type of customer is comparatively easier for the salesman. Such customers should never be neglected since they are very sensitive. Such customers should be dealt with utmost care and should be given best possible services without indulging in unnecessary details. Only specific questions should be asked and limited suggestions made to such customers. They should be given wise advice and best services so that they visit the shop regularly with a favourable impression. The salesman should be friendly and polite in his behaviour while dealing with such type of customers. However, the salesman should never try to dominate over such customers. Rather, he should suggest things tactfully and nicely.

Silent type:

This is one of the most difficult type of customer to deal with. These customers are always calm, inactive and introvert and hence do not speak much. In most cases, they are sober and mild. It becomes difficult on the part of the salesman to study and judge their

feelings, thought process and also their reactions. By their very nature these customers remain silent. However, in most cases their product knowledge remains much better as compared to others. Silent customers generally have self-confidence and therefore make their own judgments. They do not talk much but think deep. Usually they do not like to waste their valuable time talking to the salesman. They just listen to the salesman without much fuss but finally make their own decision.

How to deal with them? Dealing with such customers is a very difficult task for the salesman. To make them speak, the salesman has to strive hard. The salesman should try to make them speak by asking certain questions like, 'May I help you?, What can I do for you ?', etc. Here the salesman plays a secondary role by giving much importance to the feelings of the customers. These customers should be treated with dignity and respect. The salesman should not get irritated because of the customers' silence. He should not develop fear psychosis due to the customers' silence. These type of customers are generally impressed by facts and figures. They should be offered proofs of benefits and values associated with the product. A lot of imagination, tactfulness and foresight is essential for the salesman while dealing with silent type customers.

Talkative type:

Talkative types of customers are the opposite of silent type of customers and are comparatively easier to handle. By their sheer nature, they are talkative and good listeners. Generally they go on talking endlessly unless there is some obstruction. They go on talking on any subject. These customers think that they are well informed even though they are not. Generally they do not allow the salesman to talk about the product.

How to deal with them? While dealing with talkative customers, the salesman should give them ample opportunity to express their views and should allow them some time to talk. Then he should try to draw their attention towards the products tactfully. Patient hearing and tactful handling can help a salesman to deal with such buyers. The salesman need not talk in detail about the selling points of a product because such customers generally lack interest as well as patience for the same. Short and sweet sales talk most often motivates talkative customers. The salesman should mix words of flattery to please them.

Suspicious type:

These type of customers are in the habit of disbelieving each and everyone. These customers generally neither believe in the talks and statements of the salesman, nor the genuine of the products. They always carry an impression that the salesman is trying to exploit and trap them by his sweet talks. They always believe that salesmen are usually kept to cheat the customers. It is quite difficult to convince such customers since, by nature, they never believe in what others say. They often cross examine the salesman with many questions in order to subdue him. Usually they have a poor opinion about the salesman.

How to deal with them? It is usually difficult for the salesman to deal with such type of customers. They are not so easily convinced and at times behave erratically.

Sometimes additional purchases can also be pushed since these customers never say no as they are prestige conscious. Such customers rarely bargain and worry little about the price because they feel it is below their dignity to do so. These type of customers need to be praised and admired throughout the sales process in order to clinch a sale.

Rude type:

There are certain customers who are basically ill-mannered and rude. They lack the minimum manners. They get annoyed over silly matters and petty issues. Their ill manners are usually influenced by factors like education, family atmosphere, friend circle, financial conditions, cultural background, etc. Such type of customers never bother about the feelings of others while talking, look down at everything, ready to apply their physical strength, and possess high ego. They like utmost freedom within a shop and if objected, react harshly. Such customers are in the habit of making strong remarks and ironic statements.

How to deal with them? The salesman should avoid all possible arguments while dealing with ill-mannered or rude customers. Moreover, the salesman should never try to mend their behaviour since it is inborn. The salesman should have a firm control over his temper while dealing with such type of customers. He should maintain his cool and tolerate their rude remarks with patience. He should politely and patiently explain the selling points about the goods to them. The salesman should never feel insulted about their ill manners. Rather, he should give an impression that the manners shown by the customer are to his liking.

Handicapped type:

These type of customers suffer from some physical disabilities. Such type of customers may be deaf, dumb, blind, lame or may have defective speech, etc. Such customers are very sensitive and deserve some special care, attention and kind treatment from the salesman. These customers should never be discarded or ignored. They like to be treated at par with others, like the normal individuals in the society.

How to deal with them? The salesman must have respect towards handicapped customers. They should be given some special treatment, importance and extra care so that they feel gratified. These type of customers are usually very loyal and once they are satisfied with a particular shop they buy from that shop regularly. However, the salesman should never express his sympathy for their physical disabilities. Rather, he should treat them as normal persons. By giving special care and attention to such customers, the salesman earns goodwill for the firm as well as for himself. Other customers present in the shop generally carry a good impression about the salesman and the company. The salesman has to adjust himself accordingly to deal with the handicapped customers. For example, he can raise his voice for partially deaf customers; he can use symbolic language for dumb and deaf customers. He can carry goods to lame persons who cannot come to the counter, and so on.

Untruthful type:

Some customers try to deceive or cheat the salesman. They are also known as 'deceitful customers'. These customers believe that dishonesty is the best policy. They always try to take undue advantage of the salesman. They often persuade a salesman to allow discount or credit by telling him that other shops are offering the same. They also quote low price for the articles at other shops and claim the same price. Sometimes they continue to bargain about the price and often threaten that unless the salesman is prepared to sell at a lower cost, they would go to another shop for making their purchases.

How to deal with them? While dealing with such customers, the salesman must be thorough with the price list as well as well informed about the prices of the competitor's goods. He should also be sufficiently aware of the terms and conditions of discount and credit allowed by the competitors. Thorough market information makes the salesman more comfortable and confident to handle such type of customers.

Impulsive type:

Some customers, like business executives and administrators take quick decisions. They are usually impatient and always remain in high gear. Because of their preoccupations and heavy work pressure, they are not able to pay adequate attention to the products. They do not bother much about the features of the product and the sales talk of the salesman. Of course, they have a clear cut idea about various product characteristics and predetermined choice of the product which they intend to buy.

How to deal with them? While dealing with such type of customers, the salesman must be brief in providing the selling points. As time is always a constraint for such type of customers, the salesman should avoid talking in detail about the product. They should be attended to promptly. Otherwise they may get bored and leave the shop. The salesman has to deal with such customers in a friendly manner and with dignity. They are easy to deal with and they bother little about the price and avoid bargaining with the salesman.

Group shopper:

It is quite common to find customers moving in groups, coming to shops for making purchases. In fact, nowadays, it has become a fashion to purchase in a group. For example, wife accompanies her husband, young persons go with their girl friends, and family members go with their parents and so on. This type of group shopping is popular among the ladies. These people move from shop to shop to choose their requirements and do not get bored easily. Sometimes they bargain and ask for discount.

How to deal with them? In dealing with such shoppers, the salesman has to give more importance to the group leader. The group leader usually has greater voice in making purchase decisions. However, he should never ignore or neglect the persons accompanying the prospect. Rather, he should try to make all of them happy. The person who is paying should be given due weightage because of his decision making capacity. For example, in case of a couple, the husband may have an upper hand whereas in a family, the earning member has got an upper hand with regard to purchases.

SELLING PROCESS

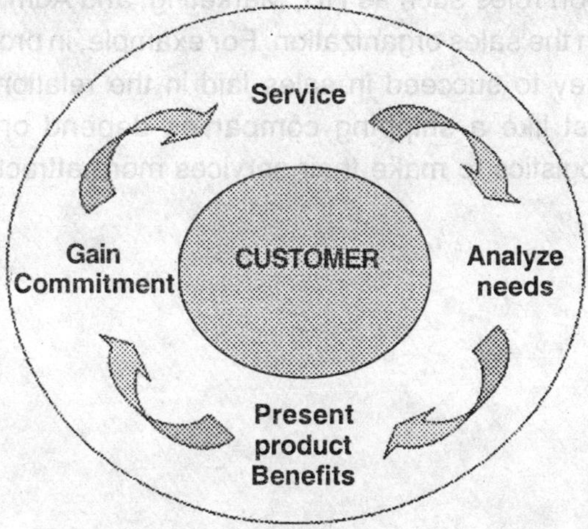

Fig.4.1. Selling Cycle

Academically, selling is thought of as a part of marketing however, the two disciplines are completely different. Sales often form a separate grouping in a corporate structure, employing separate specialist operatives known as salespeople (singular: salesperson). Selling is considered by many to be a sort of persuading "art". Contrary to popular belief, the methodological approach of selling refers to a systematic process of repetitive and measurable milestones, by which a salesperson relates his or her offering of a product or service in return enabling the buyer to achieve their goal in an economic way.

Selling is one of the oldest human activities and it has been recorded in every civilization. The Egyptians build one of the first empires based on trade. Later, during his conquest of much of the east, Alexander the Great was able to open route of trade. Caravans travel from east to west to sell good such as spices, textiles goods, and jewelry in exchange for gold, silver, and other commodities. Less developed societies such as the Tainos, used to trade food items such as fish or casaba for jewellery.

Buying and selling is one of the most pervasive of human activities at its done several times a day. To sell is to give up some of value in exchange for a financial instrument, such as money. Generally speaking, every member of society has something to sell. For example, a worker gives up skills, time, and effort in exchange for a salary. Some people make a living at the selling, often those people are called, salesman, salesperson, sales executives, account executives, etc.

Sales are at the core of every corporation. It is the blood the gives life to a company. Sales, Finance and Operations are the only functions that are indispensable to a corporation. Every other role is considered support. The top person of a company is usually the CEO, who is also the top salesperson who is responsible to sell the company to potential investors and customers. The CFO is responsible for finances and usually gets involved in negotiations with financial institutions and potential vendors. COO is responsible for operations. Support roles such as HR, Marketing, and Administration are now more integrated in the sales organization. For example, in professional services organization, a key to succeed in sales laid in the relationship with the HR organization. Just like a shipping companies depend on improvement in operations and logistics to make their services more attractive.

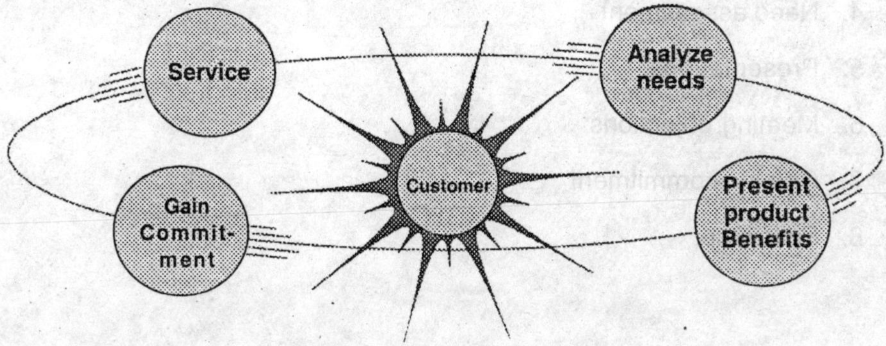

Fig.4.2. Selling revolves around Customer

Selling is the profession-wide term, much like marketing defines a profession. Recently, attempts have been made to clearly understand who is in the sales profession, and who is not. There are many articles looking at marketing, advertising, promotions, and even public relations as ways to create a unique transaction.

Two common terms used to describe a salesperson are Farmers and Hunters. The reality is that most professional sales people have a little of both. A hunter is often associated with aggressive personalities who used aggressive sales technique. In term of sales methodology a hunter refers to a person whose focus is in bringing deals and closing deals. This process is called "sales capturing". An example is a commodity sale such as a long distance sales person, shoe sales person and to a degree a car sales person. Their job is to find and convert buyers. Sales farmer is some who creates sales demand by activities that directly influence and alter the buying process.

Many believe that the focus of selling is on the human agents involved in the exchange between buyer and seller. Effective selling also requires a systems approach, at minimum involving roles that sell, enable selling, and develop sales capabilities. Selling also involves salespeople who possess specific set of sales skills and knowledge are required to facilitate the exchange of value between buyers and sellers that is unique from marketing, advertising, etc.

The actual selling process can be likened to a chain, each link of which must be closed successfully or the seller will fail to get the order. However, each step overlaps others, and their sequence may be altered to meet the situation at hand.

The eight steps of the sales process are:

1. Prospecting
2. Preapproach—planning the sale
3. Approaches

4. Need assessment
5. Presentations
6. Meeting objections
7. Gaining commitment
8. Follow-up

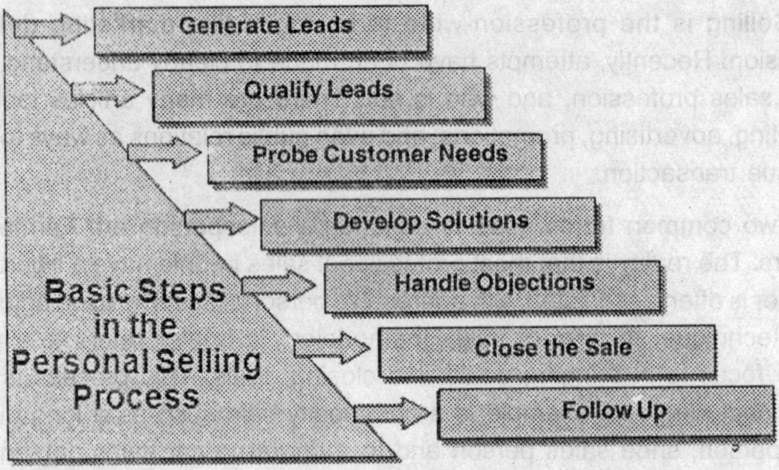

Fig.4.3. Selling Process

PROSPECTING

Succeeding in today's competitive environment means that a company must constantly find new customers. A salesperson's basic strategy should be to spend as much time as possible with excellent prospects—people who recognize their need and are ready to buy. As Phil Clark, an IBM regional sales manager in Dallas, succinctly told his sales force, "The idea is that through our advertising and promotional efforts we stand on a ladder shouting loudly all over Dallas, 'Everyone who is ready to buy a computer please raise their hands.' Then we go sell one to each person who responds."

Prospecting is the method or system by which salespeople learn the names of people who need the product and can afford it. There are two steps in successful prospecting. The first step is identifying leads—generating potential customers. The second step is qualifying leads according to who is most likely to buy.

Identifying Leads

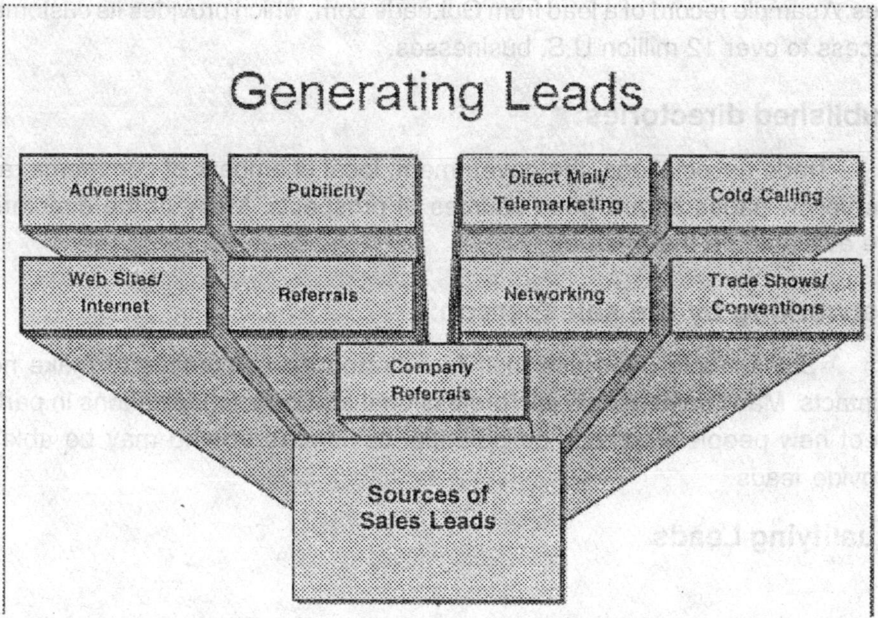

Fig.4.4. Generating Leads

Names and addresses of good prospects can be obtained in a number of ways:

Referrals from customers:

Salespeople indicate that their number one source of referrals is their existing customers, who provide nearly two-thirds of their leads. Referrals from customers are arguably the best, most credible source of leads. "If you provide valuable, worthwhile products and services to your clients, they will want to share you with others," says Maribeth Kuzmeski, founder and president of Red Zone Marketing. "It's just human nature! But sometimes they need a little nudge. So whatever your business is, you should have a system in place for promoting this positive 'word of mouth.'"!

Referrals from internal company sources such as the sales manager, themarketing department, or the telemarketing department:

Customer inquiries may be generated from company advertising, direct mail, company websites, trade shows, and teleprospecting efforts. Sales people report that these sources provide approximately 23 per cent of their leads.

Referrals from external referral agencies:

Some companies turn to outside agencies for the generation and qualification of leads. This trend is on the upswing due to an increasing number of dot-com businesses, which typically provide a list of leads for reasonable fees. A sample record of a lead from GoLeads.com, which provides its customers access to over 12 million U.S. businesses.

Published directories:

Trade associations, the government, local chambers of commerce, and the yellow pages all are good sources of prospects. Many of the directories are available on the Internet.

Networking by the salesperson:

Salespeople often use their friends and acquaintances to make new contacts. Many salespeople join professional and civic organizations in part to meet new people who may be potential customers or who may be able to provide leads.

Qualifying Leads

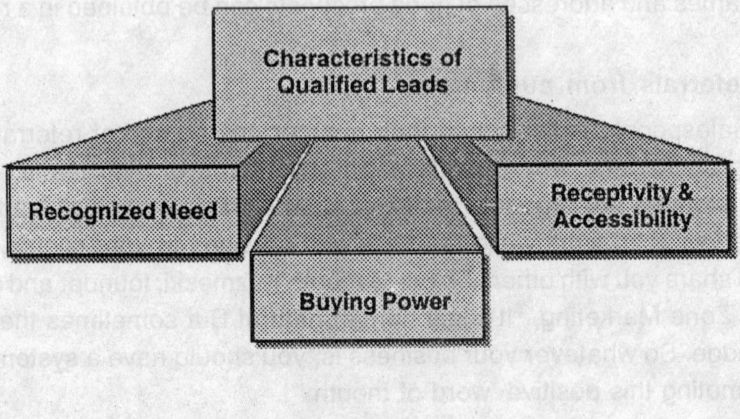

Fig.4.5. Qualifying Leads

Whatever the source of the lead, it is important that the lead be qualified. Philo sophically, professional salespeople do not want to bother people who have no need for their products. Moreover, it is very expensive for salespeople to make calls that have little chance of success because the customer does not need, does not want, or cannot afford the products. In order to qualify a prospect, the sales person or the person providing the referral should determine whether the prospect is a good one. To determine this, the prospect must satisfy three conditions:

1. The customer has a need for the products being sold.
2. The customer can afford to buy the products.
3. The customer is receptive to being called on by the salesperson.

PREAPPROACH: PLANNING THE SALE

The preapproach step includes all the information-gathering activities salespeople perform to learn relevant facts about the prospects, their needs, and their overall situation. Then, based on this information, salespeople plan their sales presentations, selecting the most appropriate objective for each call.

Customer Research

The sales rep should learn everything possible about the prospective customer's business—its size; its present purchasing practices; the location of its plants; the names of its executives; and, most important, the names of people who make the buying decision as well those who influence the purchase. It is also helpful to learn something about the buyers' backgrounds, such as their education, social affiliations, or personalities. If the prospective buyer has been having problems, the seller should, if possible, become familiar with those problems.

When researching a current customer or one that has been called on previously by a sales person from your company, start by reading the company files. They should provide a wealth of background information on the company and possibly on the buyers as well—sales records, correspondence, past sales call reports, and other relevant information. Many companies store information about their customers in a database to which their salespeople have easy access using laptop or notebook computers.

For new customers, you can easily obtain a great deal of information by using the Internet or online information services such as LexisNexis, Dialog, and Dow Jones News/Retrieval. Other sources include trade magazines, industrial directories, magazine and newspaper articles, chambers of commerce, and government publications, as well as the annual reports of companies. Sometimes the company's current suppliers, customers, and certain employees can provide information.

Planning the Sales Presentation

The most important part of planning the sales presentation is defining the objective or goal for the particular call. The goal is not necessarily to close or complete the sale on each call. In fact, salespeople report that, on average, it takes four calls to close a sale. However, on each call the salesperson does want to obtain from the buyer some type of commitment for action that moves the sale forward. For example, the salesperson may try to obtain a list of the customer's ven dor selection criteria or get the buyer to set up a meeting with some of the other people who will be involved in the decision. The objective may be any agreement on an action that moves the sale forward.

Salespeople may also plan how they are going to approach the buyer and what kind of questions they want to ask. It is important that salespeople recognize differences across selling situations and adapt their presentations accordingly. Based on their precall customer research, they will make a tentative judgment as to which of their products best meet their customers' needs and then formulate a tentative plan for presenting the features and benefits of those products. Of course, the information gained by salespeople during the actual call may often cause them to alter their initial objectives or plans. This is called adaptive selling.

THE APPROACH

Once the sales rep has the name of a prospect and adequate preapproach information, the next step is the actual approach. Making an appointment to see the buyer increases the chances that the salesperson will have the buyer's attention during their meeting.

A good approach makes a favorable impression and establishes some degree of rapport between the salesperson and the buyer. In order to make a favorable impression with customers in the United States, the salesperson should have a firm handshake, be professionally attired, and make good eye contact. Usually each call starts with an introduction (unless the salesperson has called on this customer before) and a limited amount of small talk. Sometimes salespeople will draw attention to their products by handing the buyer a sample or by highlighting some benefit in which the buyer will likely be interested.

The approach usually takes up only the first minute or so of a call, but it can make or break the entire presentation. If the approach fails, the salesperson often does not get a chance to give a presentation. At the end of the approach, the salesperson must gain the buyer's agreement to move into the need assessment stage of the call.

NEED ASSESSMENT

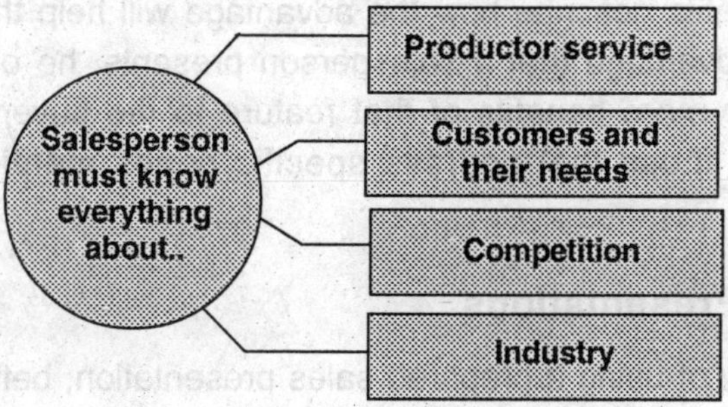

Fig.4.6. Probing Needs

Companies and consumers purchase products and services to satisfy needs or to solve problems. In a business situation, the company's purchases are always related to the need to improve performance—to become more efficient and effective at fulfilling customer needs. Need assessment is the stage in which the salesperson must discover, clarify, and understand the buyer's needs. The best way to uncover and understand needs is by asking questions. In fact, research has determined that the more questions salespeople ask, the more likely it is that they will be successful.

Salespeople ask these questions in the logical order just presented. The situational questions shuld be asked first, followed by the problem discovery questions, the problem impact questions, the solution value questions, and then the confirmatory questions. Each type naturally leads to the following type, and each one helps build the buyer's interest in hearing about the solutions the salesperson has to offer. It should be noted that studies by Neil Rackham of 35,000 sales calls demonstrate that the most successful salespeople are those who use fewer situational questions and more problem discovery, impact, and solution value questions.

THE PRESENTATION

After assessing the needs and desires of the customer, the salesperson moves into the main body of the sale, the presentation. The presentation is primarily a discussion of those product and/or service features, advantages, and benefits that the customer has indicated are important. While most presentations are oral, they often include written proposals and supporting material as well as visual aids. The goal of the presentation is to convince the customer that the product or service being sold will satisfy the customer's needs better than that of a competitor.

Features describe the characteristics of the product or service, advantages describe how the feature changes the performance of the product or service, and benefits describe how the advantage will help the buyer. For each feature and advantage that a salesperson presents, he or she should also present one or more benefits of that feature to the buyer. In fact, the benefits should be those that address specific needs mentioned by the customer

Prepared Sales Presentations

The advisability of using a prepared sales presentation, better known as a canned sales talk, is debatable. Without doubt, a prepared presentation done poorly and without feeling is a dismal experience. However, many firms do use canned talks successfully. The prepared presentation has several advantages:

- It gives new salespeople confidence.
- It can use tested sales techniques that have proven effective.
- It gives some assurance that the complete story will be told.
- It greatly simplifies sales training.

The use of a prepared presentation does not mean that sales reps must use some one else's words. Above all, the salesperson's own feelings and personality should be evident in the presentation.

Developing Effective Presentations

The task of developing a presentation is not an easy one. Some simple advice may be helpful here:

Keep the presentation simple .

The temptation to tell everything is overwhelming. Do not it. The prospect can absorb only a limited amount of information at any one time. Do not overload the system.

Talk the prospect's language.

Do not build the presentation around industry jargon or product model numbers. If customers do not understand what the rep is talking about, they seldom say so. That would be an admission of ignorance. They usually pretend to understand and then say, "I'll have to think it over for a while."

Stress the application of the product or service to the prospect's situation .

Tailor the presentation to the application or person at hand. Even within the same firm, different individuals place different priorities on what is important about the product. You must adapt your presentation to the situation and person.

Above all, seek credibility at every turn.

The entire presentation is nothing if it is not believed. Each statement must be credible. Prove points one by one. A critical point is not complete until the prospect believes it. The real key to successful selling lies in this credibility.

MEETING OBJECTIONS

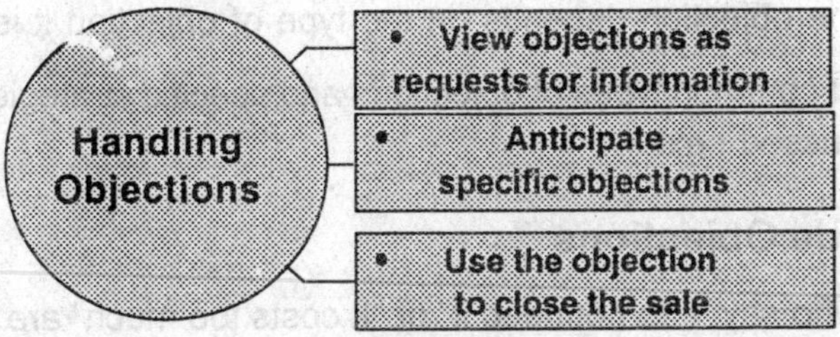

Fig.4.7. Handling Objections

Objections are encountered in practically every presentation. They should be welcomed because they indicate that the prospect has some interest in the proposition. A prospect who is not interested in buying seldom raises any objec-tions, silently going along with the presentation but saying at the end, "I'm not interested in your deal." There are several important techniques that should be used in responding to a buyer objection:

Listen to the buyer.

It is important that you listen actively. "Learn as much as you can about the objection," says certified professional sales trainer and speaker Rick Grosso. "Encourage your prospect to expand and tell you more."Do not assume that you know what the buyer is going to say, and never interrupt—nothing annoys a buyer more!

Clarify the objection.

Repeat and clarify the objection by asking for more information, using questions such as "Let me see if I understand you correctly, [repeating the objection as you understand it]. Is that correct?" The buyer may confirm that you are correct in your understanding or provide additional information. Sometimes this step can uncover a misunderstanding that the buyer has about your product and/or service.

Respect the buyer's concern.

Acknowledge that you understand and appreciate the concerns. Remember that the buyer is not attacking you personally, so you should not become defensive.

Respond to the objection.

It is important that you respond to the buyer's concern. The specific response to the objection depends on the type of objection it is.

The most common types of objections and specific strategies for handling them are discussed next.

Price or Value Objections

Buyers who say "I do not need it" or "It costs too much" are indicating that they do not think the value of solving the problem or meeting the need is worth the cost. In this case, the salesperson must convince the buyer of the importance of the problem and of the value of the solution. It may be necessary to go back to the need assessment part of the call to ask some additional problem impact and solution value types of questions to increase the buyer's perception of the seriousness of the problem and the importance of a solution. If the buyer acknowledges the importance of the problem but still feels that the company can not afford the product/service or that it is not a price-competitive solution, then the salesperson can offer some price value comparisons of alternative solutions.

Product/Service Objections

Sometimes the buyer acknowledges the importance of a problem but doubts whether the product or service can solve his problem or improve his operations. The buyer may disagree with the salesperson's assessment or, in some cases, even doubt the genuineness of the salesperson. In this case the salesperson needs to convince the buyer that her product will do what she says. She must demonstrate or prove that the product has the capability to fulfill the need.

Hidden Objections

Prospects may state their objections to a proposition openly and give the salesperson a chance to answer them. This is an ideal circumstance, because everything is out in the open and the salesperson does not need to read the prospect's mind. Unfortunately, prospects often hide their real reasons for not buying. Further, stated objections may be phony. A prospect may say she does not like the looks of a product, when she really thinks the price is too high. The rep must determine the real barrier to the sale to be able to overcome it.

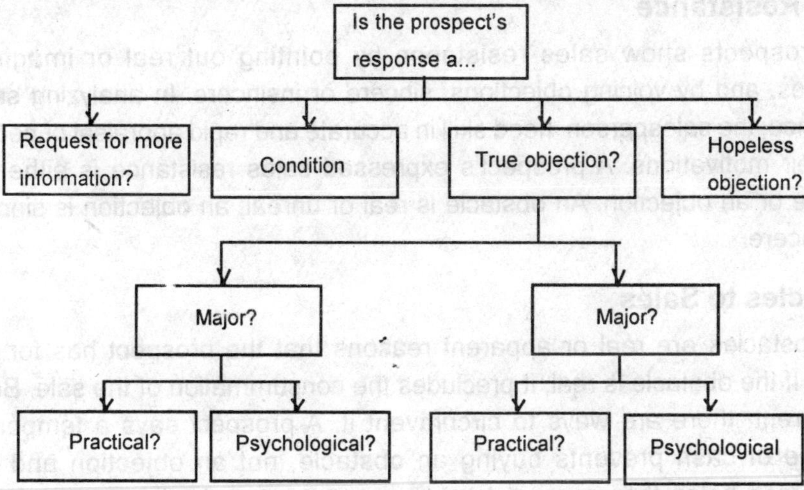

Fig.4.8. What Does a Prospect Mean by Objection

GAINING COMMITMENT

At some point after the salesperson has convinced the buyer that his or her products at least warrant further attention, the salesperson must ask the buyer to commit to some action that moves the sale forward. This is called gaining com-mitment. In a relatively simple sale, it is important for the salesperson to get a commitment from the buyer to purchase the product on the first call (usually the only call) or she will have lost the sale. Some of the techniques frequently used to close these transaction sales are highlighted in the box titled "Common Sales Closes."

However, sales of complex business products usually require more than one call. In fact, some large sales may take several years to complete. To get the buyer to agree to some action that moves the buyer closer to the sale, the salesperson may suggest a demonstration, review the specifications, or offer a sample. The keys to obtaining commitment are, first, to plan realistic objectives for each sales call and, second, to ask for a commitment. If the salesperson does not ask, then he or she will not move the sale forward. To ask for an action that in effect finalizes the sale, the salesperson may simply say, "Can I place an order for you today?"

Sometimes the buyer may volunteer to take an action that moves the sale forward or even finalizes the sale. For example, the buyer may say, "We have decided that we need to make a change and we think your company is in the best position to serve our needs." But often it does not happen this way, and the salesperson must ask for the commitment.

CLOSING THE SALES AND FOLLOW UP

Sales Resistance

Prospects show sales resistance by pointing out real or imagined obstacles, and by voicing objections, sincere or insincere. In analyzing sales resistance, the salesperson need skill in accurate and rapid appraisal of people and their motivations. A prospect's expressed sales resistance is either an obstacle or an objection. An obstacle is real or unreal; an objection is sincere or insincere.

Obstacles to Sales

Obstacles are real or apparent reasons that the prospect has for not buying. If the obstacle is real, it precludes the consummation of the sale. But it is apparent; there are ways to circumvent it. A prospect says a temporary shortage of cash prevents buying an obstacle, not an objection and the salesperson helps the prospect to circumvent it by explaining a method for financing the purchase. Some obstacles can be circumvented, theirs cannot, when an obstacle arises, the salesperson determines whether or not there is a way to get around it. If the salesperson recognizes the specific obstacle and knows a way to circumvent it, the next move is to present the solution to the prospect.

Sales Objection

Objections are never good reason for failing to complete the sale, but they nearly always divert the salesperson's presentation from its main course. At best, an objection requires a satisfactory answer; at worst, it blocks the sale. Adroitness in handling objection is a difference between effective and ineffective salespeople. Sincere objections trace to incompleteness, inaccuracy, or vagueness in the sales presentation. Prospects may not recognize the nature of their needs, or they may have doubt about the appropriateness of the product to fulfill those needs.

Prospects may be confused in some respect, or may react unfavorably to the salesperson's personality. Except when personality conflict cannot be resolved (a real obstacle, not an objection), sincere objections are overcome by patient and thorough explanations. Prospects raise insincere objections to discourage salespersons, to get rid of them, to test their competence, and as false excuses for not buying. When sales persons sense that an objection is insincere, they seek to regain the offensive as soon as possible.

They do not permit an insincere objection to provoke an argument one of the surest ways to lose a sale. Some sales executives say that every objection, no matter how insincere, should be treated with the utmost courtesy. Others say that insincere objections should be ignored. The best defensive strategy often is the strong counterattack, and the salesperson should seek to regain the initiative as soon as he or she can gracefully do so.

CLOSING SALES

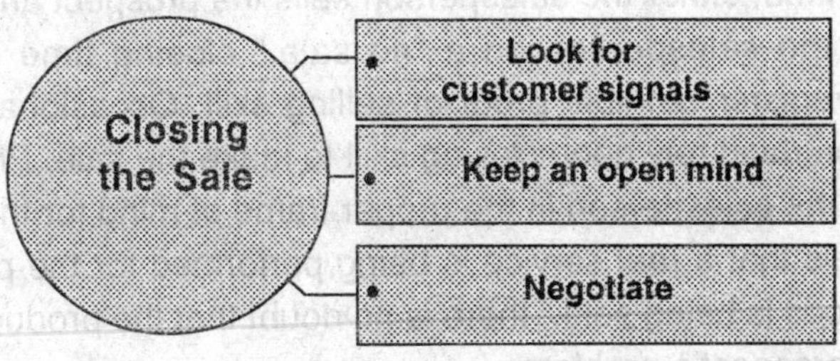

Fig.4.9. Closing the Sale

The selling tactics followed affect the ease of closing the sale. Low pressure sales are closed more easily than are high pressure ones. On low pressure sales, prospects feel that they are reaching the buying decisions themselves, and primarily through rational processes of thought, so there is no need for extra push just before the sales are consummated. In high pressure sales, the main thrust is to the prospects' emotions, so salespersons attempt to propel prospects into buying decisions. Often, the prospect, regains normal perspective as the sale nears its climax, and, if this happens, the salesperson needs unusually effective persuasion to close the sale.

Every salesperson approaches certain closings with apprehension.

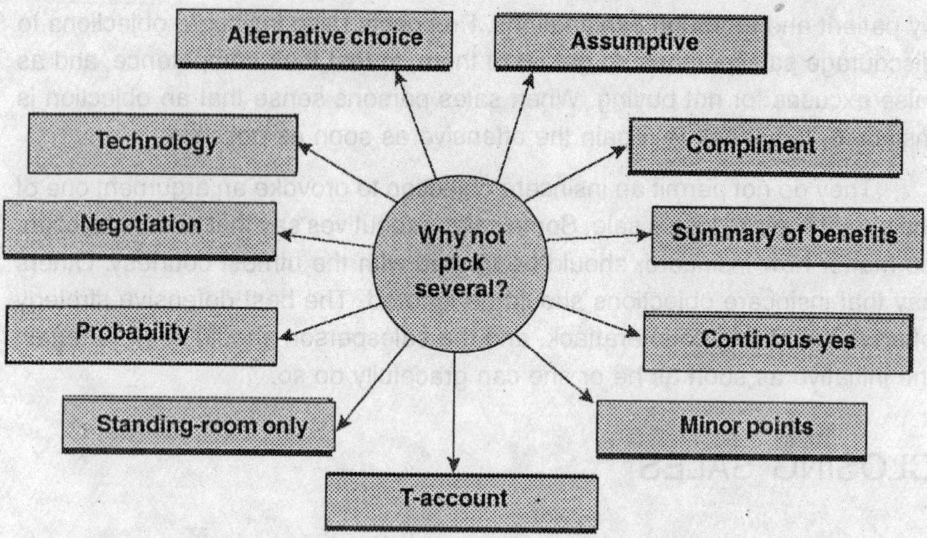

Fig.4.10. Techniques for Closing the Sale: Which Close Should be Used?

At closing time, either the salesperson sells the prospect an order or the prospect sells the salesperson on a "no sale." closing time provides an opportunity to register tangible proof of selling skill. Occasionally even the best salesperson must rely upon closing skill to make the sale. Prospecting, if well done, puts the salesperson in the proper frame of mind for the close. The salesperson feels that a real service is being performed for the prospect, not that "a bill of goods is being sold." there is no doubt that the product is the best solution to the prospect's problems.

But even after an excellent presentation, and in spite of thorough prospecting, some prospects refrain from positive commitments. The natural tendency of many people is to let inertia guide their reactions many are happy to leave things as they are, and salespersons leave empty handed unless they jolt these prospects into buying. The skilled closer gives the extra push that triggers a buying response. But failures to get an order result as much from poor prospecting and inept presentations as from ineffective closing.

When an attempted close fails, the salesperson should normally try another. The refusal does not necessarily imply an unwillingness to buy; it may indicate the prospect's need for additional information or for clarification of some point. Some executives recommend that sales personnel attempt as many as five closes before giving up. Early closing attempt should be so expressed that a refusal will not cut off the presentation. A salesperson judges the sincerity of a prospect's refusal, surrendering gracefully when it is clear that no sale will be made.

The salesperson first uses an indirect close, that is, attempts to get the order without actually asking for it. The salesperson may ask the prospect to state a preference from among a limited number of choice (as to models, delivery dates, order size, or the like), so phrasing the question that all possible responses are in the salesperson's favor except for one: "none at all." Or the salesperson may summarize, emphasizing features that visibly impress the prospect, showing how the reasons for the purchase outweigh those opposed to it. Then the salesperson pauses for the prospect's response, which is expected to be, "Go ahead and write the order." Sometimes, the extra push may be a concession that makes the sale. Or the salesperson may assume that the sale is made, write out the order, and hand it to the prospect for approval if the prospect balks, the issue is clearer. Perhaps one last objection is voiced, but after it is answered, the sale is made. Many indirect closes are in common use, and books on selling contain numerous examples.

When open or more attempts at a indirect close fail, the salesperson uses the direct approach. Few prospects respond negatively to a frank request for the order in fact, many people, especially those who are themselves engaged in selling, do not buy unless the order is asked for outright.

Reps must learn that the sale is not over when they get the order. Good sales reps follow up in various ways. They make certain that they have answered all the buyer's questions and that the buyer understands the details of the contract. If the merchandise is delivered at a later date, the reps are present at the time of delivery or call soon afterward to ensure that everything is in order.

The follow-up step of the sales process has become critical to the success of contemporary sales organizations. This is especially true given recent sales management trends toward the concepts of relationship marketing and consultative selling. That is, instead of focusing on one-time, transactional sales, today's sales-people work to build and maintain long-term, mutually beneficial partnerships with their customers. Of course, customers would never form partnerships with organizations whose salespeople forget about them after the sale!

Indeed, the concepts of relationship marketing have made sales organizations rethink the steps of the sales process. Organizations realize that it is much more expensive to acquire new customers than it is to retain existing customers. So, although generating new accounts is still important, salespeople must be careful not to sacrifice effective follow-up for prospecting. Further, effective follow-up essentially consists of asking questions to customers in an ongoing attempt to monitor their needs. Thus, when dealing with loyal customers, salespeople must continually revisit the need assessment step of the sales process.

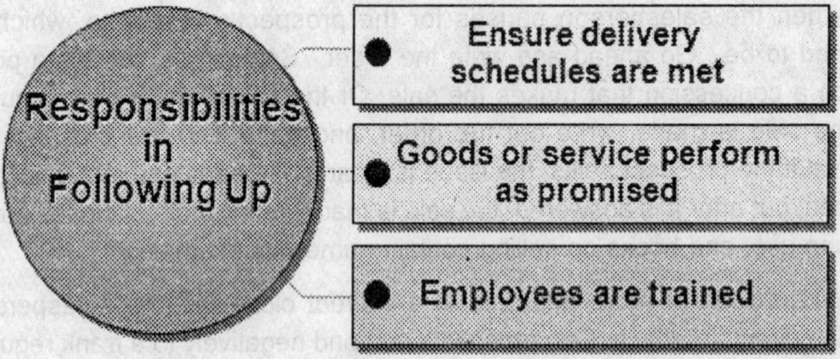

Fig.4.11. Following Up

Source: Adapted from William C. Moncrief III, "Selling Activity and Sales Position Taxonomies for Industrial Sales forces, " Journal of Marketing Research23 (August 1986), pp. 266-71.

Fig.4.12. Selling Job Factors

THEORIES OF SELLING

Selling is both an art and a science. Many consider it as an art evolving into a science. Selling is viewed differently by those who consider it as an art and those who treat it as a science. This gives rise to two contrasting theories of selling.

Selling is studied as the cumulative experience of sales persons and advertising professionals. It distils knowledge from practice, and psychology learnt through experience. It teaches how all this can be put into practice. The emphasis is on 'how to' rather than 'why'. Empirical evidence is considered more valuable than a systematic body of knowledge. But such knowledge can never be full-proof.

In the second approach, theories of behavioural sciences are applied to selling.

The seller-oriented theories are AIDAS theory and right set of circumstance theory. The buyer-oriented theory is 'buying-formula' theory. The behavioural equation considers the mutual influences of the buyers and sellers.

(i) AIDAS Theory of Selling

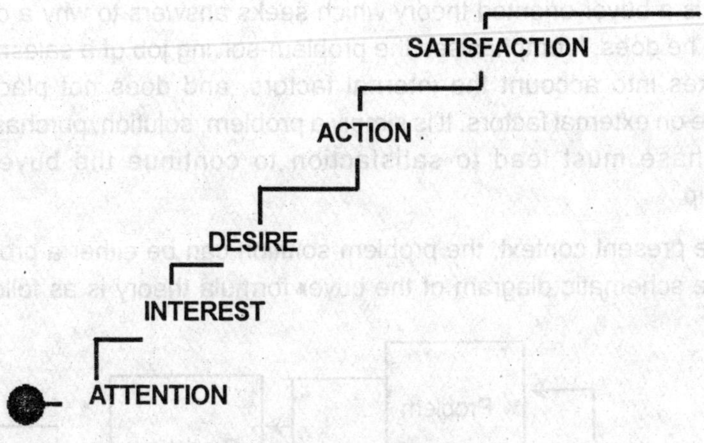

Fig.4.13. AIDAS Model

The salesman, in order to affect a sale, must persuade the customer to buy his products. This act of persuasion needs proper planning of strategy and tactics. The customer must be taken through certain stages of the mind. These stages are very effectively summarized by what is known as the AIDAS model:

'A' Attention: It is the starting point in the sales process. The attention of the customer must be attracted to the product, and the want that the product is able to satisfy.

'I' Interest: The salesman must create an interest in the mind of the customers. The customer must be made to realize how the product will benefit them, and must feel curious to know more about the product, its features and its merits.

'D' Desire: The salesman must ignite the desire of the prospect after securing his attention and after arousing his interest in the product. The salesman must use all his powers for persuasion and conviction to create an urge to buy.

'A' Action: It means gaining an order. The culmination of the first three stages should be in to the actual purchase of the product. The customer must be induced to buy the product or place an order for the product. The want must be converted into demand.

'S' Satisfaction: Follow-up or post-sale contact is necessary to ensure customer satisfaction and to remove any post-sale problems. It is also a source of feedback from the customer. Satisfaction leads to repeat orders.

(ii) Buying Formula Theory

This is a buyer-oriented theory which seeks answers to why a consumer buys what he does. It emphasises the problem-solving job of a salesman. This theory takes into account the internal factors, and does not place all the importance on external factors. It is simply a problem, solution, purchase theory. The purchase must lead to satisfaction to continue the buyer-selling relationship.

In the present context, the problem solution can be either a product or a brand. The schematic diagram of the buyer formula theory is as follows:

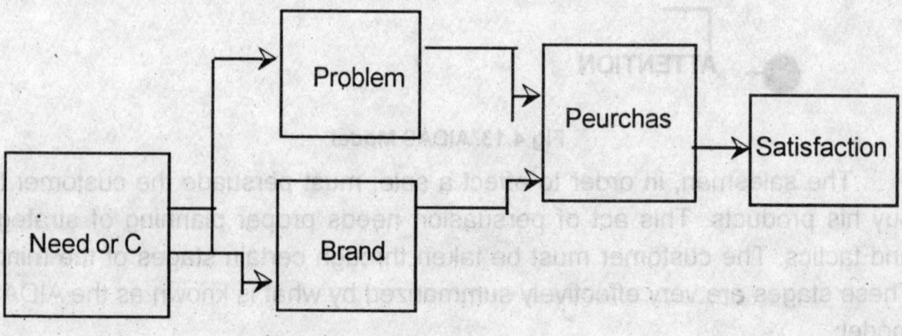

Fig.4.14. Buying Formula Theory

Product or brands must be considered as adequate in solution and must induce pleasant feelings. Both adequacy and pleasant feelings can be simultaneously present. Sometimes it is either-or situation. The buying formula in its modified form looks as follows:

A buyer should be aware why the product/brand is an adequate solution and should have pleasant feeling towards it. This establishes his buying habit. There is an assault on this habit by rival ads, competing sales person's presentation and a friend's remark. He defends his decision on the strength of adequacy and pleasant feelings. These act as good defence mechanism. In most purchases, this defence mechanism is not at work. Just there is a direct association of a problem and solution.

Each selling problem has its answers in the above formula, and the variations in the answers are in effect the variations of emphasis on the elements constitution this formula.

(iii) Behavioural Equation Theory:

Howard explains buying behaviour as phases of the learning process resulting into purchasing. Basically, this is modified stimulus-response (SR) model. Drives, cues, response and re-enforcement are the four elements of the learning process. Drives are strong internal stimuli which can be innate like hunger, thirst, pain, sex etc. or can be learned like recognition, prestige, approval, etc., cues are weak stimuli which decide when the buyer will respond. They can trigger the decision making or may not trigger it. Product cues are directly received from the product. Information cues provide information of a symbolic nature about the product. Response is what a buyer does. Any event that strengthens this response is called reinforcement. Howard puts forward theis as an equation.

$$B = P \times D \times K \times V$$

B= Response or purchasing

P= Force or habit

D= Drive level or motivation

K = Value of the product to provide satisfaction

V= Intensity of all cues.

It is a multiplicative relationship. B is dependent variable and the rest are independent variables. If these independent variables have a zero value, B will also be zero. P increases if K increases. A salesperson influences P directly. The use of the product affects P much more. Sales affect D to exercise influence.

(iv) Selling process

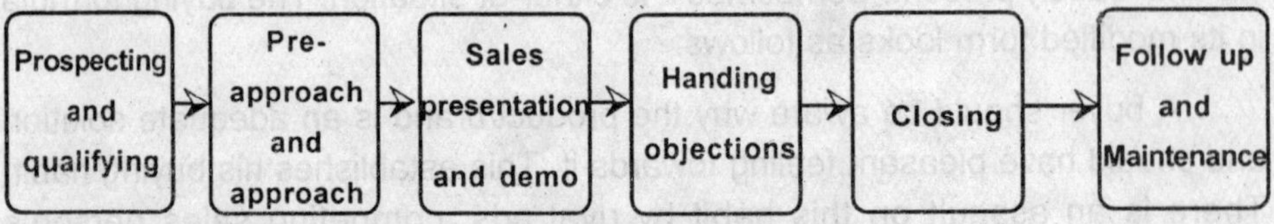

Fig.4.15. Steps in Selling Process

PROSPECTING AND QUALIFYING

The first step in selling is to identify and qualify prospects. More companies are taking responsibility for finding and qualifying leads so that the salespeople can use their expensive time doing what they can do best: selling. Companies can qualify the leads by contacting them by mail or phone to assess their level of interest and financial capacity. The leads can be categorized, with "hot" prospects turned over to the field sales force and "warm" prospects turned over to the telemarketing unit for follow-up. Even then, it usually takes about four calls on a prospect to consummate a business transaction.

PRE APPROACH

The salesperson needs to learn as much as possible about the prospect company (what it needs, who is involved in the purchase decision) and its buyers (personal characteristics and buying styles). The salesperson should set call objectives: to qualify the prospect, gather information, make an immediate sale. Another task is to decide on the best contact approach, which might be a personal visit, a phone call, or a letter. Finally, the salesperson should plan an overall sales strategy for the account.

PRESENTATION AND DEMONSTRATION

The salesperson now tells the product "story" to the buyer, following the AIDA formula of gaining attention, holding interest, arousing desire, and obtaining action. The salesperson uses a features, advantages, benefits, and value approach (FABV). Features describe physical characteristics of a market offering, such as chip processing speeds or memory capacity. Advantages describe why the features provide an advantage to the customer. Benefits describe the economic, technical, service, and social benefits delivered by the offering. Value describes the worth (often in monetary terms) of the offering. Too often, salespeople spend too much time dwelling on product features (a product orientation) and not enough stressing the offering's benefits and value (a customer orientation).

OVERCOMING OBJECTIONS

Customers typically pose objections during the presentation or when asked for the order. Psychological resistance includes resistance to interference, preference for established supply sources or brands, apathy, reluctance to giving up something, unpleasant associations created by the sales rep, predetermined ideas, dislike of making decisions, and neurotic attitude toward money. Logical resistance might consist of objections to the price, delivery schedule, or certain product or company characteristics.

To handle these objections, the salesperson maintains a positive approach, asks the buyer to clarify the objection, questions the buyer in a way that the buyer has to answer his or her own objection, denies the validity of the objection, or turns the objection into a reason for buying. Handling and overcoming objections is a part of the broader skills of negotiation.

One potential problem is for salespeople to give in too often when customers demand a discount. One company recognized this as a problem when its sales revenues went up by 25 per cent but its profit had remained flat. The company decided to retrain its salespeople to "sell the price," rather than "sell through price." Salespeople were given richer information about each customer's sales history and behavior. They received training to recognize value-adding opportunities rather than price-cutting opportunities. As a result, the company's sales revenues climbed and so did its margins.

CLOSING

Now the salesperson attempts to close the sale. Salespeople need to know how to recognize closing signs from the buyer, including physical actions, statements or comments, and questions. There are several closing techniques. They can ask for the order, recapitulate the points of agreement, offer to help the secretary write up the order, ask Whether the buyer wants A or B, get the buyer to make minor choices such as the color or size, or indicate what the buyer will lose if the order is not placed now. The salesperson might offer the buyer specific inducements to close, such as a special price, an extra quantity, or a token gift.

FOLLOW-UP AND MAINTENANCE

Follow-up and maintenance are necessary if the salesperson wants to ensure customer satisfaction and repeat business. Immediately after closing, the salesperson should cement any necessary details on delivery time, purchase terms, and other matters that are important to the customer. The salesperson should schedule a follow-up call when the initial order is received to make sure there is proper installation, instruction, and servicing. This visit or call will detect any problems, assure the buyer of the salesperson's interest, and reduce any cognitive dissonance that might have arisen. The salesperson should also develop a maintenance and growth plan for the account.

DYNAMICS OF THE INDIAN CONSUMER — CASE STUDY-VIII

Fast-changing consumerism in India over less than two decades has made life more than a little difficult for marketers and analysts who have been trying to understand the changing dynamics of the Indian marketplace.

Gone are the days when consumers could be neatly slotted into a definite category based on a single indicator since consumers and consumerism have turned into more complex proposition, looking for more value and satisfaction for their money.

For instance, two decades ago, ownership of consumer durables by the SEC-A profile consumer and the SEC-C consumer would have been distinctly different. Not anymore. Today, you can expect both groups of consumers to have access to mobile phones, television sets, and computers and other gizmos.

Similarly, absolute income data no longer provides validity over a long period of time. To illustrate, going by the income data of 1985-86 those that were classified as the 'low income group' has almost ceased to exist as of 2007-08.

As a result, the conceptual framework and approach of consumer research, resulting in meaningful insights have come into play. Psychographics today play a significant role in determining spending patterns of consumers. As linkages between rural and urban India have grown, the rural-urban divide in consumer behaviour too has begun to be less stark than it used to be.

Increasingly, the challenge for analysts is to come up with an integrated model that factors in income data, product ownership data, demographics related information and expenditure and savings data to create holistic, reliable and a multi-dimensional profile of today's Indian consumer.

Let's take income data, for instance. Typically, income refers to new earnings of individuals and households during a year. It is an indicator of the earning capability of the household and in combination with consumption data should be able to provide useful information for marketers who are seeking to understand key consumer segments, their purchasing power consumption behaviour.

However, the problem with income data is that there is rampant understatement of income which often raises doubts about the interpretation of this data. It also raises concerns about the validity of the data.

However, where income data does come in handy is when it is analysed in terms of income distribution by "quintiles". That is, to measure income distribution, the households are first ranked from highest to lowest income and then the households are divided into five groups, or quintiles, to determine the share of total income of each quintile, ranging from the Bottom (or first quintile) up to the Top (or fifth quintile). It provides a clear picture about the different consumer segments and how they compare with each other. In a diverse country such as India where there is significant diversity in socio-economic conditions and the gap between the top-earning households and the lowest-income earning families is huge, it becomes necessary to look at the data through the filter of quintiles and deciles.

Questions for Discussion

(i) Explain the complexities of the problems faced by Indian consumers because of fast changing consumerism.

(ii) What kind of role psychographics plays in determining spending pattern of Indian consumers?

(iii) Is there any difference between Urban and Rural consumer behaviour today?

CHECK YOUR PROGRESS

(A) True or False

(i) For all customers buying motives are same.

(ii) Men and women differ in their buying motives.

(iii) Industrial buyers purchase products for their own consumption.

(B) Fill in the Blanks

(i) The majority of the sales person's time is spent on .... Activities.

(ii) The first step of selling process is ....

(iii) Follow up takes place after the ....

LET US SUM UP

The success of salesmanship depends, to a large extent, on the approach of a salesman and his winning capability over customers. As a matter of fact, customer is the focal point of the modern marketing and all selling efforts centre around him. Seller is totally dependent on customers, for achieving success in selling. While dealing with the customers, training, knowledge and efficiency of the sales force are tested. Therefore, salesmen are expected to know and understand their prospective customers well because it is the customers who determine the fate and fortune of the business. The success of all selling efforts largely depends on the ability of the salesman to recognise the needs, problems, likes, dislikes of the customers and treat them accordingly.

Prospecting: A salesman has to prepare himself first. He has to be up-to-date on product knowledge. He is aware of the market conditions. He knows about the competition. He has mastered the technique of selling. Once prepared, he has to locate the customers. For this, he has to decide the profile of his ideal prospect. He has been assisted in identifying the prospects by the organisation, which provides him the leads. Moreover, the salesman himself develops his own leads.

He can get references from the existing customers, suppliers, distributors and dealers, other sales people and trade associations.

Poor leads must be eliminated skillfully. What is needed is qualification. Prospects are qualified on the basis of some important factors – their employment, marital status, number of dependents, the products they use now.

Pre-approach: Before actually visiting the prospects, sales people must know as much as possible about the prospects. It is possible to know their present consumption and usage. If it is a corporate organisation, we can use stock-exchange records about the company. There also should be some attempt to choose between several methods of approach–a written communication, a telephone call or a personal visit. The sales strategy is decided as a part of re-approach.

Approach: When we are face to face with the buyer, we must know how to greet him. The interview must have a cordial start. Much depends upon the personal appearance of the salesman, his opening remarks, and his follow-up conversation. All this should be on a positive note, e.g., we should do everything possible to help you and your company.

Presentation and Demonstration: The crucial task of selling is communicating the product story to the buyer. A typical sales presentation follows the AIDA.

Handling Objections: During the course of a sales presentation or at the time of closing the sale, a salesman many encounter objections from the prospect. Just because the prospect voices his objection, the salesman should not become unduly disturbed.

Closing the sale: This is the most important step in the selling process. Closing the sale results into an order for the product or service. It is a climax of the whole game of selling. Several salesmen falter in closing

A salesman must have his closing material ready at all times and at all places. We might close the sale at many unimaginable laces like a race course , a restaurant, swimming pool or a golf course.

LESSON END ACTIVITY

Speak with a sales representative and find out the difficulties he/she faced while dealing with customers.

Identify prospects for a new brand of special occasion and novelty cards.

KEY WORDS

Sizing up of customers :

It is nothing but understanding the taste and temperament of customers and tackling them in such a manner that their desires for products or services are converted into demand.

Carriage:

It means the way or the style in which a customer walks. By observing closely the way the customer walks, the salesman can know a lot about his nature and character. This observation also enables the salesman to decide whether the customer is a shopper or a looker.

Urban Customers :

Customers living in towns or cities are called urban customers.

Argumentative type:

Some customers are argumentative by nature. They enjoy and take pleasure in finding faults with the goods, the salesman, and the organisation.

RURAL CUSTOMERS:

Customers living in villages and muffosil areas are called rural customers.

Industrial Buyers:

Generally, industrial buyers purchase goods for use in the production process so as to manufacture a final product.

Prospecting:

It is the method or system by which salespeople learn the names of people who need the product and can afford it.

Pre-approach:

The pre-approach step includes all the information-gathering activities salespeople perform to learn relevant facts about the prospects, their needs, and their overall situation.

Approach:

A good approach makes a favorable impression and establishes some degree of rapport between the salesperson and the buyer.

REIVEW QUESTIONS

1. Explain the concept of sizing of customers?
2. What is customer character analysis? Explain briefly.
3. What are the types of customers and how to deal with each of them explain briefly.
4. Write short notes on (i) Talkative customer (ii) Argumentative customer (iii) Shy customer (iv) Rude customer.
5. On the basis of age, how customers can be classified? Explain.
6. On the basis of geographical area how customers can be classified? Explain.
7. On the basis of purpose, how customers can be classified? Explain.
8. What do you understand by prospecting explain?

9. Explain the concept of customer hierarchy?
10. Explain the sources of leads? How to find out the qualification of leads.
11. Explain the selling process in details.
12. Write briefly the importance of follow up and maintenance in the selling process.
13. What are the different kinds of objections can rise during handling customer queries? Briefly explain.
14. Write short notes on (i) hidden objection (ii) customer research.
15. Explain the different theories of selling briefly.
16. What is AIDAS model? Explain briefly.

CHECK YOUR PROGRESS: MODEL ANSWER

(A).

(i) False

(ii) True

(iii) False

(B).

(i) Selling

(ii) Prospecting

(iii) Purchase

SUGGESTED READINGS

P.K. Sahu & KC Raut: *Salesmanship and Sales Management*, Vikas Publishing House Pvt Ltd, New Delhi, 2003.

S. A. Chunawalla: *Sales Management*, Himalaya Publishing House, Mumbai, 2005.

Spiro, Stanton, Rich: *Management of a Sales Force*, Tata McGraw Hill, New Delhi, 2008.

☒☒☒

Chapter

5

Selling Jobs and Types of Salesman

"A salesman minus enthusiasm is just a clerk." - **Harry F. Banks**

Introduction - Types of selling jobs - Classification of salesmen - Salesman compensation – Motivation

OBJECTIVES

At the conclusion of this lesson you should be able to understand :-

- The different selling jobs
- Different categories of salesmen.
- Classification of salesmen.

AMERICAN EXPRESS OPEN FORUM - A SMALL BIZ COMMUNITY CASE STUDY - CASE STUDY-IX

American Express OPEN's social media approach at the OPEN Forum – the following presentation by VizEdu does a nice job capturing it:

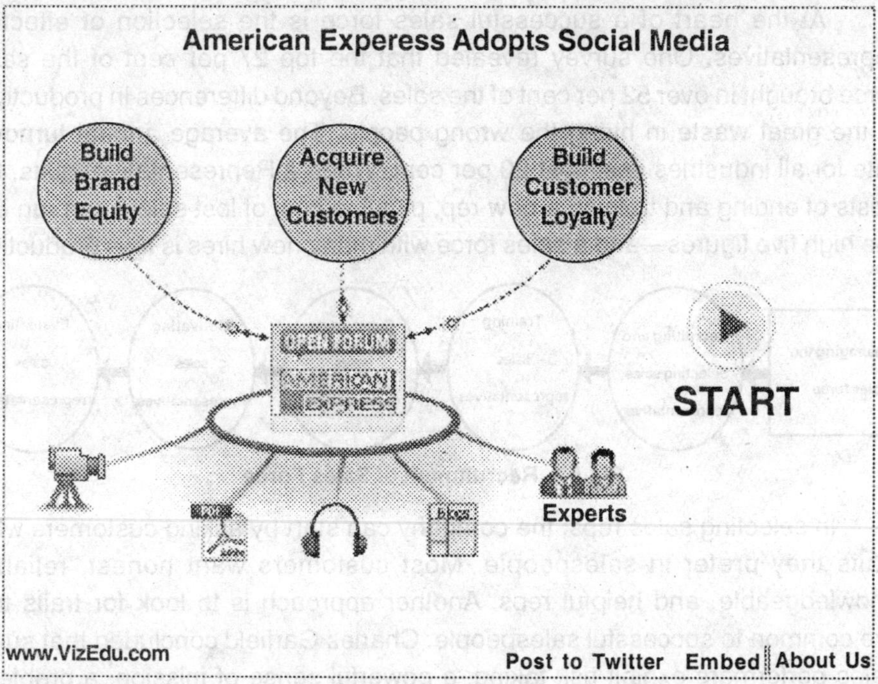

The idea is to provide information and strike up a conversation with small business owners, on a special conversational site that American Express OPEN has set up (separate and apart from its corporate website). Among the benefits to American Express OPEN from the OPEN Forum initiative are: building brand equity, acquiring new customers, and building loyalty of existing customers.

INTRODUCTION

A widely held **view about a** salesman is that he simply remains present at the counter and sells goods to the customers. But in reality, the job of the salesman is not that narrow and limited. In the modern business world, there are numerous types of selling jobs in any organisation. The duties and responsibilities are numerous and vary from salesman to salesman. This lesson will help you to understand the various types of selling jobs and different types of salesman.

MANAGING THE SALES FORCE

Effective management of the sales force is needed to implement the company's chosen sales force design and achieve its sales objectives. Sales force management covers the steps in recruiting and selecting, training, supervising, motivating and evaluating representatives.

RECRUITING AND SELECTING SALES REPRESENTATIVES

At the heart of a successful sales force is the selection of effective representatives. One survey revealed that the top 27 per cent of the sales force brought in over 52 per cent of the sales. Beyond differences in productivity is the great waste in hiring the wrong people. The average annual turnover rate for all industries is almost 20 per cent. When a Representative quits, the costs of ending and training a new rep, plus the cost of lost sales, can run into the high five figures—and a sales force with many new hires is less productive.

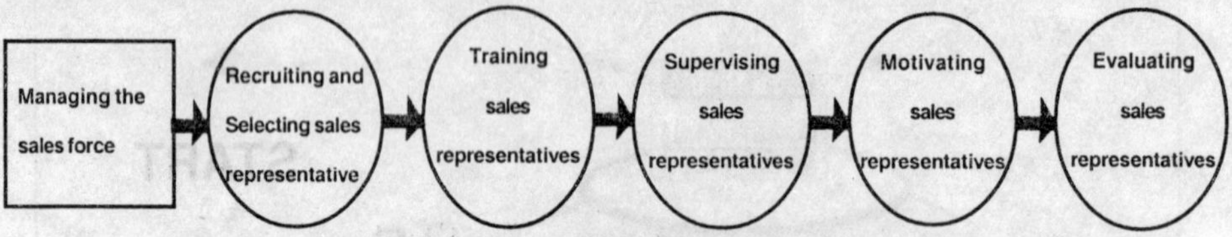

Fig.5.1. Recrultment of Sales Force

In selecting sales reps, the company can start by asking customers what traits they prefer in salespeople. Most customers want honest, reliable, knowledgeable, and helpful reps. Another approach is to look for traits that are common to successful salespeople. Charles Garfield concluded that super sales performers exhibit risk taking, a powerful sense of mission, a problem-solving bent, care for the customer, and careful planning.

Mayer and Greenberg noted that the effective salesperson has empathy, the ability to feel as the customer does, and ego drive, a strong personal need to make the sale. After management develops suitable selection criteria, the next step is to recruit applicants by various means, including soliciting names from current sales reps, using employment agencies, placing print and online job ads, and contacting graduating college students. Selection procedures can vary from an informal interview to prolonged testing and interviewing. Although test scores are only one information element in a set that includes personal characteristics, references, past employment history, and interviewer reactions, they are weighted quite heavily by such companies as IBM, Prudential, Procter & Gamble, and Gillette. Gillette claims that tests have reduced turnover by 42 per cent and have correlated well with the subsequent progress of new reps in the sales organization.

TRAINING SALES REPRESENTATIVES

Today's customers expect salespeople to have deep product knowledge, offer ideas to improve customer operations, and be efficient and reliable. These demands have required companies to make a much higher investment in training their sales reps. Companies use training to help sales reps: (1) Know and identify with the company; (2) Learn about the company's products; (3) Know customers' and competitors' characteristics; (4) Make effective sales presentations; and (5) Understand sales procedures and responsibilities. Training time varies with the complexity of the selling task and the type of person recruited into the sales organization. The median training period is 28 weeks in industrial-products companies, 12 in service companies, and 4 in consumer-products companies. At IBM, new reps receive extensive initial training and may spend 15 per cent of their time each year in additional training.

Training often involves a variety of methods, including role playing, audio and videotapes, CD-ROMs, and Web-based distance learning. For instance, reps at the tandem division of Compaq used to complain that they could not keep up with the printed information and training materials the company sent them. Now field reps carry their own miniature training rooms with them—they simply slip a CD-ROM disk into their laptop computers.

SUPERVISING SALES REPRESENTATIVES

New sales representatives need more than a territory, a compensation package, and training—they also need proper supervision. Reps paid mostly on commission generally receive less supervision, while those who are salaried and must cover definite accounts are likely to receive substantial supervision. In the course of supervising sales reps, successful companies set norms for calls on customers and prospects, and they help reps make the most efficient use of sales time.

Norms for Customer Calls

In the early 1980s, the average salesperson made five calls a day; by 1989, that number had dropped to just 4.2 sales calls a day. Today salespeople make even fewer in-person sales calls because they are using phone, fax, and e-mail to sell. In addition, more firms are using automated ordering systems to reduce reliance on sales calls.

How many calls should a company make on a particular account each year?

Research shows that additional calls generally produce more sales, but companies still need to determine whether the increase in sales justifies the increase in sales costs. Some studies and experiences suggest that sales reps may be spending too much time selling to smaller, less profitable accounts when they should be focusing more of their efforts on selling to larger, more profitable accounts.

Therefore, in setting norms, management needs to weigh the cost of a customer sales call against the sales and profit payback for that account.

Norms for Prospect Calls

Knowing the high cost of sales calls, companies often specify how much time reps should spend prospecting for new accounts. Spector Freight, for instance, wants its sales representatives to spend 25 per cent of their time prospecting and to stop calling on a prospect after three unsuccessful calls. Other companies set prospect and customer norms based on product sales, specifying, for example, that reps spend 80 per cent of their time selling established products and 20 per cent selling new products.

Companies set up prospecting standards because many reps, left to their own devices, will spend most of their time with current customers, who are known quantities, rather than with prospects, who might never buy. In general, selling to prospects tends to be more difficult and more time-consuming than selling to established accounts, yet it is the road to customer base expansion and closing more sales. This is why some firms deploy a special missionary sales force to open new accounts.

Using Sales Time Efficiently

Not surprisingly, studies confirm that the best sales reps are those who manage their time effectively. One popular efficiency tool is configurator software to automate the order preparation process. This type of program is offered by Massachusetts-based Concentra Corporation, among others. On a sales call, reps can use configurator software to present product specifications and pricing information, show customization options, and handle scheduling. Integrating all of this information, the configurator software can virtually write up the order in minutes. This software not only saves time; it also builds goodwill by reducing errors and letting both customer and supplier see the same information from the same source. Concentra's customers say this software has helped them increase sales and reduce cancellations.

Another tool is time-and-duty analysis, which helps reps understand how they spend their time and how they might increase their productivity. In general, sales reps spend time in (1) preparation (getting information and planning call strategy); (2) travel (which can be more than 50 per cent of total time); (3) food and breaks (some portion of every workday); (4) waiting (to see buyers);

(5) selling (time spent with the buyer); and (6) administration (writing reports, billing, attending sales meetings, and so on). With so many duties, it is no wonder that actual face-to-face selling time can amount to as little as 25 per cent of total working time!

To improve sales force productivity, many companies train their reps in the use of "phone power," simplify record-keeping, and use computerized methods to develop call and routing plans and to supply reps with customer and competitive information.

Seeking to reduce the time demands on their outside sales force, many firms have increased the size and responsibilities of their inside sales force. Inside salespeople are of three types. Technical support people provide technical information and answers to customers' questions. Sales assistants provide clerical backup for the outside reps by confirming appointments, carrying out credit checks, following up on deliveries, and answering customers' questions. Telemarketers use the phone to find new leads, qualify and sell to them, reactivate former accounts, and give more attention to neglected accounts.

The best sales reps spend time getting to know their customers' preferences, needs, and buying patterns so they can plan their calls accordingly. Technology speeds up this process. For example, before telecommunications reps at TimePlex go on a sales call, they use their laptops to dial into the firm's data network and retrieve status reports on that account's previous orders and other background information. When deals are struck, the reps use their laptops to record each order, double-check for errors, and then transmit everything electronically to the firm's New Jersey headquarters.

In addition, Internet technology is helping to make prospecting more efficient. Company Web sites provide an introduction to self-identified potential customers and, for some businesses, may lead to on-line orders. For more complex transactions, the site provides a way for the buyer to contact the seller—for example, through a link to an e-mail address. The Pall Corporation, which makes fiuid filtration and purification technologies, has all e-mail directed to company headquarters, with leads going directly to the appropriate sales rep. The quality and quantity of leads generated by its Web site (www.pall.com) has prompted the firm to promote its home page more aggressively.

As another example, Lucent Technologies (www.lucent.com) combines e-mail with Web marketing to generate more qualified sales leads. A typical campaign starts with an e-mail inviting prospects to learn more about a particular offer (and qualify for a free gift) by visiting a customized Web page. Once there, prospects answer a few qualifying questions and can then request information to be sent by mail. Lucent's automated system separates these leads based on product needs; and contacts the best prospects 2 weeks later, offering free, downloadable software for analyzing total product costs. Prospects who choose the download are considered hot leads, so the system sends Lucent's sales force complete contact data on these prospects for immediate follow-up. "We never had to pick up the phone, and we have already established a relationship with them," notes Lucent's senior manager of marketing services.

TYPES OF SELLING JOBS

Special characteristics of the sales job:

A salesman is an ambassador of his company to the external world. He leaves a lasting impression on those with whom he interacts and forms an opinion about the company from his behaviour. By no stretch of imagination, we can consider the production staff or, for that matter any other staff of the organisation wielding the same influence as the salesman does.

A salesman is out in the field; with no direct or little direct supervision, whereas other employees have to work under close super vision. Field involve hard physical work and are never a bed of roses. Besides, selling demands creativity, doggedness and initiative. Thus, a successful salesman should have a combination of brain and brawn. As he is to be self-directed, he needs strong motivation.

A salesman needs human relation skills much more than others. As he interacts with a variety of people in diverse situations he must show diplomatic skills and composure. He should show tact and intelligence while dealing with his customers.

A salesman is authorised to spend company's money for his lodging, boarding, travelling and entertainment. Very few in the company are so authorised to use the company's funds.

A salesman cannot enjoy family life like people in other walks of life do. He has to travel his territory while servicing it. Besides, selling is a high pressure job. All this makes him prone to stress. Thus a salesman has to brave all kinds of adverse situations, while being away from home. It is, thus, a very tough job.

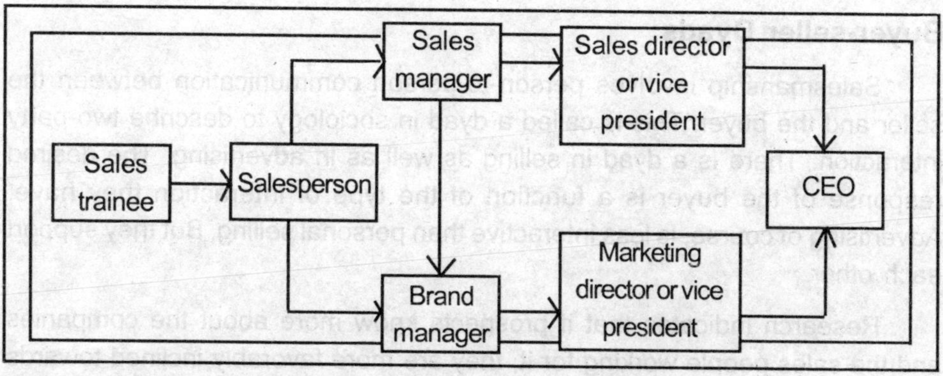

Fig.5.1. Possible career track in sales job

Exhibit.5.1. Salesperson to CEO

• With companies increasingly focusing on customer satisfaction and building long-term relationship with customers, they are tapping the sales and marketing ranks to fill CEO positions. Here are five steps you can take to place yourself in that corner office.	• *Show you want it.* Knowledge and experience are important for attaining the spot, but proving your desire is vital. Let the people above you know your aspirations and constantly prove to them why you're qualified.
• *Understand the whole business.* Sales and marketing people can become quite focused on just sales and marketing. Customer relationships are vital, but make sure to gain knowledge of how the rest of company works. No executive can be CEO without being able to talk the talk about every aspect of a company.	• *Gain self-awareness.* No CEO can be good at leading without fully understanding his or her strengths and weaknesses. Ask for honest assessments from your employees, your bosses,and your customers. Process that knowledge and improve on it.
• *Take on extra responsibilities.* In an effort to understand other parts of your business, spend time with other departments. Learn what it's like to be a factory worker or a researcher. Not only will this give you overall insight, but it will undoubtedly get you respect throughout the organisation	• *Network, network, network.* You have to know the top people to become one of them. It may feel like a game at some point, but no executive can get the head job unless he or she continuously has meaningful conversations with top brass.

Source: Eilene Zimmerman, "So you Wanna be a CEO", Sales and Marketing Management, January 2000, p. 33.

Buyer-seller Dyads:

Salesmanship involves person-to-person communication between the seller and the buyer. This is called a dyad in sociology to describe two-party interaction. There is a dyad in selling as well as in advertising. The desired response of the buyer is a function of the type of interaction they have. Advertising of course, is less interactive than personal selling. But they support each other.

Research indicates that if prospects know more about the companies and the sales people working for it, they are more favorably inclined towards the products. Research also indicates that the matching of prospects and sales person in terms of physical and demographic characteristics also increases the chances of a sale. This leads to a successful dyadic relationship. In industrial marketing, this type of matching is fairly common. The dyadic relationship is further enhanced by the perception of the buyer about a sales person's performance and its conformance to his concept of ideal performance.

Types of selling jobs:

We can see a very wide spectrum of selling jobs – ranging from mere order taking as in the case of a soft-drink salesman to a technological presentation as in the case of a sales engineer selling complex products like industrial machinery, aircraft and computer. Selling jobs can be classified on the basis of the creative input needed to perform them.

Order Getters

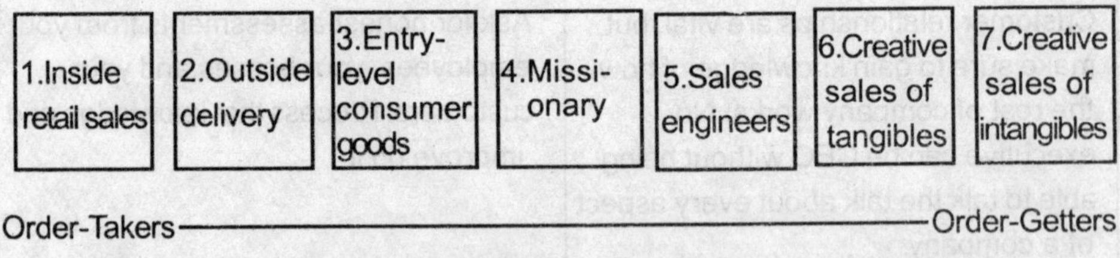

Fig. 5.2. The complexity and difficulty of these seven sales job categories increase as they move left to right

The role most synonymous with selling is a position in which the salesperson is actively engaged in using their skills to obtain orders from customers. Such roles can be further divided into:

New Business Development –

A highly challenging yet potentially lucrative sales position is one where the main objective is to find new customers. Sales jobs in this category are often in fields that are very competitive, but offer high rewards for those that are successful. The key distinguishing factor of these positions is that once a sale is made new business salespeople pass customers on to others in their organization who handle account maintenance. These positions include:

Business Equipment Sales –

These salespeople are often found in industries where a company's main profits come from the sale of supplies and services that come after an initial equipment purchase. The key objective of business equipment salespeople is to get buyers to purchase the main piece of equipment for which supplies and service are needed in order for the equipment to function. For instance, in the photocopier industry certain salespeople only seek out new accounts and once a photocopier sale is made they pass along the account to other sales personnel who handle the sales of maintenance and supply products.

Telemarketing –

This category includes product sales over the phone, whether aimed at business or consumer. While in the US laws restrict unsolicited phone selling, the practice is still widely used in the business market.

Consumer Selling –

Certain companies are very aggressive in their use of salespeople to build new consumer business. These include: retailers selling certain high priced consumer products including furniture, electronics and clothing; housing products including real estate, security services, building replacement products (e.g., windows); and in-home product sellers including those selling door-to-door and products sold at "home party" events such as cosmetics, kitchenware and decorative products.

Account Management –

Most people engaged in sales are not only involved in gaining the initial order, but work to build and maintain relationships with clients that are intended to last a long time. Salespeople involved in account management are found across a broad range of industries. Their responsibilities involve all aspects of building customer relationships from initial sale to follow-up account servicing. These include:

Business-to-Business Selling –

These salespeople sell products for business use with an emphasis on follow-up sales. In many cases, business-to-business salespeople have many different items available for sale (i.e., broad and/or deep product line) rather than a single product. So while the initial sale may only result in the buyer purchasing a few products, the potential exists for the buyer to purchase many other products as the buyer-seller relationship grows.

Trade Selling –

Sales professionals working for consumer products companies normally do not sell to the final user (i.e., consumer). Instead their role is focused on first getting distributors, such wholesalers and retailers, to handle their products and once this is accomplished, helping distributors sell their product by offering ideas for product advertising, in-store display and sales promotions.

Order Takers

Selling does not always require a salesperson use methods designed to encourage customers to make a purchase. In fact, the greatest number of people engaged in selling are not order getters, rather they are considered order takers. In this role, salespeople primarily assist customers with a purchase in ways that are much less assertive than order getters. As might be expected, compensation for order takers is generally lower than that of order getters. Among those serving an order taker role are:

Retail Clerks –

While some retail salespeople are involved in new business selling, the vast majority of retail employees handle order taking tasks, which range from directing customers to products to handling customer checkout.

Industrial Distributor Clerks –

Industrial purchase situations, such as distributors of building products, will also have clerks to handle customer purchases.

Customer Service –

Order taking is also handled in non face-to-face ways through customer service personnel. Usually this occurs via phone conversations, though newer technologies are allowing for these tasks to be handled through electronic means such as online chat.

Order Influencers

Some salespeople are not engaged in direct selling activities at all. That is, they do not sell directly to the person who is the ultimate purchaser for their product. Instead these salespeople concentrate on selling activity that targets those who influence purchases made by the final customer. The primary example of an order influencer is the missionary salesperson:

Missionary -

These salespeople are used in industries where customers make purchases based on the advice or requirements of others. Two industries in which missionary selling is commonly found are pharmaceuticals, where salespeople, known as product detailers, discuss products with doctors (influencers) who then write prescriptions for their patients (final customer) and higher education, where salespeople call on college professors (influencers) who make requirements to students (final customer) for specific textbooks

Sales Support

A final group involved in selling mostly assist with the selling activities of other sales professionals. These include:

Technical Specialists -

When dealing with the sale of technical products, particularly in business markets, salespeople may need to draw on the expertise of others to assist with the process. This is particularly the case when the buying party consists of a buying center. In business selling many people from different functional areas may be involved in the purchase decision. If this buying center includes technical people, such as scientists and engineers, a salesperson may seek assistance from members of their own technical staff, who can help address specific questions.

Office Support –

Salespeople also may receive assistance from their company's office staff in the form of creating promotional materials, setting up sales appointments, finding sales leads, arranging meeting space or organizing trade shows exhibits.

There are other types of selling jobs as well as mentioned below:

(i) There are manufacturer's salesmen, wholesaler's salesmen and retailer's salesmen.

(ii) Some are counter salesmen while some others are travelling salesmen.

(iii) Some salesmen sell consumer goods like soaps, shoes, toothpastes etc. some sell industrial goods like hand tools, nuts and bolts, motors, machineries, etc. and some others sell agricultural products like fruit, vegetables, grains, seeds etc.

(iv) Some salesmen sell tangible products like textiles, soaps, cycles, watches, etc. while some others sell intangible goods like insurance policy, securities, advertisement space, etc.

(v) New and competitive goods need expensive selling efforts. Therefore, energetic, hardworking and aggressive salesmen are required for selling new and competitive goods.

(vi) For selling products like medicines, books, magazines, etc. extensively travelling by salesmen is required.

(vii) Some selling jobs require detailed and technical knowledge about the product like machines, electronic equipment, medicine, etc. Some other selling jobs are quite single and therefore do not require thorough and detailed knowledge about the product as in case of consumer goods and grocery articles.

(viii) Some salesmen are required to sell directly to the ultimate consumers. Another set of salesmen sell to the middlemen like wholesalers and retailers instead of the final consumers.

(ix) Some selling jobs like insurance policies, motor cars, land, etc. require continuous effort on the part of the salesman. Therefore, it takes time to finalise sales in such cases. Some sales may even take months and years to finalise. On the other hand, some sales are finalized immediately and on the spot like pen, food articles, grocery items, etc. since little effort is required to sell these articles.

(x) Costly items like automobiles, video cassette recorders, refrigerators, vacuum cleaners, televisions, air conditioners, etc. require technical advice and service both before and after the actual sales. Therefore, for selling these articles technically qualified salesmen who possess adequate knowledge about the various aspects of the products are needed.

(xi) There are certain selling jobs which can be best performed by women. Products most ideally suited for saleswomen are ladies garments, cooking utensils, cosmetics, etc. Hence, sales women are preferred to sell such articles.

CLASSIFICATION OF SALESMAN

Exhibit.5.2. Traditional and Other Salespeople

Traditional Salespeople	Professional Salespeople	Golden Rule Salespeople
• Do what they think they can get away with.	Do what they are legally required to do	Do the right thing.
• Guided by self-interests.	Take care of customers.	Finds others' interests most important.
• Atribute results to personal efforts.	Atribute results to personal efforts, employer, customers, economy.	Atribute results to others.
• Seek recognition for efforts; sharing not important. Pride and ego driven	Enjoy recognition; may share if it suits their purpose. Pride ego driven.	Feel that an individual's performance is due to others; not motived by pride and ego.
• Money is life's main motivator.	Money is important, but not to the customer's detriment	Service is most important; money is to be shared.

There are several methods of classifying salesmen's job. They may be classified on the basis of: (a) organisation, (b) goods they sell, and, (c) services offered.

Salesmen can be divided into the following three categories on the basis of organisation.

Manufacturer's Salesmen

There are some salesmen who do the selling on behalf of the manufacturing organisation. They usually possess specialised knowledge about the products or the services. They can be divided into three categories: namel pioneer or promotional salesmen, dealer or middlemen servicing salesm and merchandise salesmen.

(i) Pioneer Salesmen or Promotional Salesmen:

Such salesmen usually undertake the responsibility of introducing new products or services in the market. Therefore, pioneer or promotional salesmen have to be highly skilled and experienced. They should possess, considerable amount of imagination, aggression and self-confidence. With the possession of these qualities only, such salesmen are able to present the utility and usefulness of the product or service in an interesting and innovative manner before the dealers or the customers. Consequently, the interest of the dealers and the customers is automatically aroused about the product or service which motivates them to purchase. As such, the job of a pioneer salesman is comparatively difficult as well as time consuming and requires efficient and high level of salesmanship. Since high level of skill and efficiency is required from such salesmen, they are usually handsomely paid with attractive perks.

(ii) Dealer Servicing Salesmen or Middlemen Servicing Salesmen:

Usually, manufacturers employ these middlemen servicing salesmen to book orders, visit dealers at regular intervals and convince them about goods and services. These salesmen provide information to the dealers about the selling points, salient features, product improvements, etc,. besides meeting queries about the goods and services. Sometimes they also train the dealer's salesmen about various aspects of selling and selling methods. Such types of salesmen need to be enthusiastic, energetic and friendly in nature so as to push sales and help the dealers. The job of those dealer servicing salesmen are comparatively easy since they deal with goods and services which are usually established in the market and well supported by promotional measures. Another important duty of these salesmen is to provide detailed information about the dealer's attitude, market conditions and competitive position to the manufacturer. They usually enjoy a steady income and job security. However, they are paid less than the pioneer salesmen.

(iii) Merchandise Salesmen :

These kinds of salesmen are generally appointed to assist dealers to expand their sales volume. Merchandise salesmen visit dealers at regular intervals and point out ways and means to increase sales. They provide sound advice to the dealers with regard to the arrangement of showrooms, choosing appropriate advertising media, display provisions, interior decorations, credit policies, etc., which have a direct influence on the volume of sales. Such types of salesmen are usually employed in trades involving sale of medicines, cigarettes, detergents, soft drinks, etc.

These types of salesmen have to possess detailed information about the various features of the product and their utilities. Besides, they should also have adequate samples and sufficient literature about the product or service. Since their main job is only to promote sales through the dealers, merchandise salesmen usually do not receive or book direct orders. The importance of these kind of salesmen is gradually increasing since they have wide scope. They generally enjoy steady income and attractive commissions.

Wholesaler's Salesmen

Usually the job of the wholesaler is to purchase goods from the manufacturer and sell the same to the retailers or industrial users. Therefore, a wholesaler is the main link between the manufacturer and the retailer. Wholesaler therefore, appoints salesmen whose main job is to inform the retailers about the various products or services. As the wholesalers usually deal with a number of products of various manufacturers, the wholesaler salesmen have to handle with a number of items. They help the retailers in selecting the products and show them ways and means to increase their sales volume. The wholesaler salesmen usually visit retailers at regular intervals. During visits, it is the duty of the wholesaler salesmen to see that goods are supplied to the retailer regularly and in adequate quantities. They usually persuade retailers to stock a particular brand or brands of product in which the wholesaler is interested. Another duty of these salesmen is to collect all possible information on behalf of the wholesaler regarding dealer's attitude, market condition and competitive position of the product. They also inform the wholesaler about the credit worthiness of the retailers. Accordingly, the wholesaler is able to know the financial strength of the dealers and thereby can avoid future bad debts to a great extent. Sometimes, these wholesaler's salesmen act as collection agent of the manufacturers also.

Wholesaler's salesmen have to depend much on persuasive technique while dealing with the retailers since the success of their job lies in convincing the retailers. In other words, once the retailers are convinced, a major part of the selling job of the wholesaler salesmen is over. Therefore, such salesmen need to build up reliability and confidence in the minds of the retailers.

Retailer's Salesmen

Retailers constitute the end part in the chain of distribution of goods and services. Usually, retailers purchase goods from the wholesalers and sell them to the ultimate consumers. In the distribution process, retailers are those middlemen who directly come in contact with the final consumers. As such they deal with numerous consumers. Retailers play an all important role in the sale of products or services. To carry out their selling activities, retailers employ salesmen. The salesmen appointed by the retailers can be broadly of two types namely, (i) counter or indoor salesmen and (ii) travelling or outdoor salesmen.

1. Counter or Indoor Salesmen:

Counter salesmen are basically meant to pass on the goods across the counter in exchange for money. Such type of salesmen usually sell commodities by remaining present at the counter and are most commonly found in every shop whether big or small. Unlike other type of salesmen, counter salesmen usually do not search for the customers. Instead, customers always approach such type of salesmen. In such a sales exchange, the money and the goods pass across the counter, one after another. In other words, the salesman receives the price in exchange for the goods he sells, whereas, the buyer receives the goods in exchange for the price he pays. As it can be observed, there is comparatively less effort on the part of the counter salesmen to sell products and services. In fact, there is very little use of the art of salesmanship by the counter salesmen. Customers usually approach the counter salesmen for goods and get the same in exchange for money. Sometimes cash memo is also issued to the customers. The job of the counter salesman is comparatively easy than other type of salesmen. The essential qualities of such salesmen are that they need to have insight and proper imagination. Such qualities help the indoor salesmen to find out the additional needs of the customers and make additional sales. For example, if a person buys a pair of shoes, the salesman should find out whether he needs a pair of socks, shoe polish, etc. This is known as 'suggestion' in sales. Thus, the salesmen can create additional sales by offering related articles. However, additional selling needs to be done skillfully. He should never attempt to force a sale. It is the duty of the salesman to assist the customers in purchas-ing the right products of their choice in right quantities to meet their requirements. The experience of a counter salesman is always an asset and helps him in his dealings. In comparison to other type of salesmen, these salesmen do not get an attractive salary as their job is more or less routine in nature.

2. Outdoor or Travelling Salesmen:

Travelling salesmen are usually employed to contact prospective customers scattered in different areas of a country. Generally, these salesmen are required to sell high unit value and speciality goods. They are creative salesmen and sell commodities by approaching prospective buyers personally. They travel extensively in search of prospective customers, to introduce new products and popularise existing products in the market. Unlike the indoor salesmen, these salesmen visit existing as well as prospective customers in order to make sales. These kind of salesmen have to be experts in the art of selling. Success in travelling salesmanship requires high degree of initiative, persistence and motivation. The sales talk of the travelling salesmen need to be lively so that they can hold the attention, convince, and finally sell goods to the customers. Travelling salesmen are required to possess sound health and appealing personality. They need to have enough patience in order to sell well. Further, these kind of salesmen need to possess a detailed knowledge of the product, its utility, price and stock. This helps them tackle the customer queries intelligently and convincingly.

On the basis of goods they sell, travelling salesmen can be classified into two categories: (i) staple salesmen (ii) speciality goods salesmen.

Staple Salesmen :

These kinds of salesmen specialize in selling necessities like food, clothes, stationery, grocery, etc. These goods are usually sold in many, shops and similar types of goods are produced by many manufacturers. Consumers of these articles are free to compare the quality, price and utility of various products available, and choose the best one which suits their needs. Demand for these goods remains more or less stable and very little effort is needed to create demand for such goods.

These kinds of salesmen are of average type. They need to possess the ability to meet the customers' demand promptly. They should have patience and should be friendly in nature so as to create a favourable impression and win the heart of the customers. They should give fair and equitable treatment to all consumers. They should also have thorough knowledge of the stock position, the prices and the various attributes of the goods offered for sale. These salesmen are usually paid moderately.

Speciality Goods Salesmen:

There are certain goods which are fairly durable, non-consumable and have high unit value. Some of the examples of specialty goods are: vacuum cleaners, electronic water purifier, sophisticated sewing machines, industrial products, materials supplies, etc. The speciality goods salesman specializes in introducing new products as well as the novel features of existing products, in the market.

Salesmen of these goods need to have a lot of imagination and self-confidence like creative salesmen. Specialty goods require special efforts to sell. Therefore, the salesmen must have patience and detailed knowledge about the durability, service, unique features and prices of competing products. Such knowledge helps them to sell the products successfully and meeting the queries of the consumers. As the speciality goods are high priced and long lasting, customers usually collect sufficient information and make several queries before the final purchase. It is only after being satisfied about the utility of the product in meeting their needs that the consumers usually take the purchase decision. Therefore, the salesmen should be alert, fluent in speaking, tactful and well trained. As this kind of salesmanship requires high level of skill in selling, these salesmen are usually paid handsomely.

Salesmen can also be classified on the basis of service they render. They can be categorized as (i) house-to-house salesmen, (ii) missionary salesmen, (iii) service salesmen, (iv) exporter's salesmen and (v) industrial salesmen.

House-to-house Salesmen

House-to-house selling is usually done by travelling salesmen. This type of salesmen can be classified into several categories. The 'independent consumer salesmen' sell goods independently by moving from door-to-door, approaching each and every prospective buyer personally. Some of the notable varieties of such salesmen are peddlers and hawkers. The stocks and varieties of goods these salesmen sell usually remain very limited.

Peddlers generally carry goods on their head, shoulder, back or hands and sell them by moving from door-to-door. They usually deal with cheap cosmetic goods like bangles, vermillion, powder, comb, hair oil; eatables like biscuits, bread; and items like toys, vegetables, etc. Peddlers purchase their merchandise either from the manufacturers, the wholesalers or the retailers and sell them in small packs to suit the individual requirement of the buyers. Generally, they make cash sales. The market for goods sold by the peddler is limited to a particular area or locality in which he makes selling rounds. The Peddler should possess a sound health because physical strength is essential both for carrying goods and making selling rounds in a geographic area. As a local salesman, the peddler is expected to be polite in his behaviour and conversant with the local language, taste, and traditions. He must have persuasive nature in order to be successful in his trade. A thorough knowledge about the goods he is selling and the substitutes helps the peddler a lot to increase his sales.

A hawker is also a house-to-house independent salesman like the peddler. The only difference between these two is that while the peddler carries goods all by himself, the hawker carries goods on cycle, rickshaw, and cart or wheel barrow. As a result, the hawker is able to deal with more goods as compared to the peddler. The coverage of the market for the hawker is also larger than the peddler. The hawker moves from door-to-door to sell his product and just like the peddler, the hawker should also be strong and healthy. He should also be polite in his behaviour, honest in his dealings and conversant with the local language.

Both, peddlers and hawkers, draw the attention of the prospective buyers by shouting, singing songs or playing music. These type of salesmen are the owners of their business. The volume of the business depends much on the physical fitness of the salesmen. If they are able to move around a lot, they can sell more.

Another type of house-to-house salesman is the 'route salesman'. As the name implies these salesmen follow a specific route for selling their articles. Some of the notable examples of route salesmen are newspaper-boy, bakerman, milkman, etc. Similarly, house-to-house salesmen are employed by retailers, wholesalers or manufacturers. These salesmen also move from door-to-door to sell their products directly to the final consumers.

Missionary Salesmen

There are certain kinds of salesmen who are appointed by the manufacturers to the merits of their goods. These salesmen are responsible for promoting sales creating additional demand, thereby developing new sales territories. As their job is maintaining the goodwill of the manufacturer, they are called missionary salesmen, they give publicity to goods purchased by the wholesalers and retailers. This the wholesalers and retailers to sell the goods easily and quickly. As a result, they frequent orders with the manufacturers. They help the dealers in arranging store play, train the salesmen of the retailers and the wholesalers, and prepare advertisements for retailers and so on. Missionary salesmen help 'the dealers in all types of sales notion activities. Sometimes, they act as demonstrators at the retailer's store level. Salesmen must be properly trained, well experienced and able to convince the customers. They should have detailed knowledge about the product.

Service Salesmen

There are some kind of salesmen who do not sell tangible goods but sell only services. The insurance agents, bank deposit collectors, stock exchange brokers, persons engaged to push up sale of tickets for a movie or theatrical performance, space for advertisements, courier services, door-delivery services, are some of the notable example of service salesmen. The jobs of these salesmen are difficult and delicate. Usually, they have to deal with educated and highly placed persons. Therefore, they should be well educated and well trained. Otherwise, they can not be successful in their job. They have to be very polite and honest in their dealings. They should be alert, tactful and fluent in speech. They should also possess a detailed knowledge of the services they are selling. The remuneration of these salesmen usually depends on the volume of sales they make. The secret of success for service salesmen depends on the art of creativity and spirit of persuasion.

Exporter Salesmen

These salesmen are the representatives of their organisation in the overseas markets. Firms engaged in the export business employ these salesmen. The responsibilities of these salesmen are very complex. They generally supply goods to the foreign dealers and provide necessary information about the goods to the dealers. These salesmen must ensure prompt supply of goods to the dealers from the domestic organisation. These salesmen need to be well versed with the legal aspects in relation to import duties, custom duties and other taxes and above all, the law of the country to which the export is being made. The exporter's salesmen should take all necessary steps to ensure that the goods reach the distributors in time. These salesmen should be well conversant with the language of the country to which the goods are being exported. They must be honest, reliable and possess a good personality. They are generally paid high remuneration along with other facilities like housing, travelling, medical, expenses, etc.

Industrial Salesmen

There are some salesmen who sell industrial goods only. Machines, plants, components, computers, spare parts, lubricating oil, grease etc. are examples of industrial goods. These goods are generally sold to manufacturers and business houses. Salesmen of these goods need high technical knowledge and training. They must be capable of demonstrating and training the employees about the use of those products. For purchasing industrial goods, in most of the cases, purchasing agents are appointed who are professionals and experts in their own line. Therefore, they do not need much persuasion and selling effort. Rather, the customer or the agent of the customer approaches the seller to purchase the industrial products. In such transactions, customer or his agent have expert knowledge of the products. Thus, the job of the industrial salesmen is more of problem solving in nature. After sales, service plays an important role in industrial selling. Therefore, more emphasis is placed on this aspect of the industrial salesmen. As the job of these salesmen is more challenging, the reward is also better. They are generally paid a handsome salary as well as commission.

SALESMAN MOTIVATION

Motivation is the process through which hidden needs are aroused. Some sales people will put forth their best effort without any coaching from the management. For them selling is the most fascinating in the world. They are ambitious and self status, but majority of sales representative require encouragement and special incentives from the management to work at the best level. This is specially true of field selling for the following reasons:

The nature of the job

The selling job is frustrating, sales representatives usually work alone, their laws are irregular and they are other away from home, they confront aggressive, competing sales representative, they do not have the authority to do what is necessary to the account hence, they lose large orders that they have worked hard to obtain.

Human nature

Most people operate below capacity in the absence of special incentives such as financial gain or social recognition.

Personal problems

Sales representatives usually preoccupied with personal problems such as sickness in the family, marital discord or debt etc.

MOTIVATION MODEL

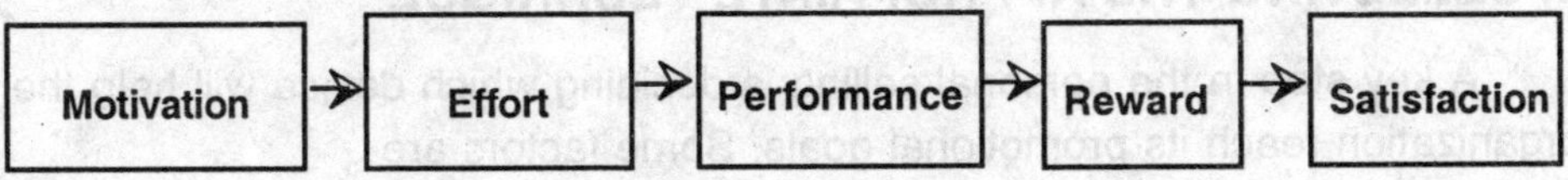

Fig.5.3. Motivation Model

The above model suggest that higher the sales person motivation the greater is his or her effort, greater effort will lead to greater performance which will lead to greater rewards and greater rewards will lead to greater satisfaction which will again lead to reinforce motivation.

The model implies following

- Sales manager must be able to convince sales people that they can sell more by working harder or being trained to work smarter. But if sales are largely determined by economic conditions or competitive action this linkage is undermined.
- Sales manager must be able to convince sales people that the rewards for better performance are worth the extra effort, but if the rewards are too small or of the wrong kind the linkage is undermined

DISCIPLINED WORK

Whatever the incentive package if the sales person are not organized and focused, and if they do not work hard they are not be able to meet the ever increasing demand of the customers these days, so following points are very important.

1. SET GOALS

First of all sales representatives has to set goals for their selves, what they want achieve in the future according to that than they make plans.

2. MAKE PLANS

Planning is very important in the sales person job, they make schedule for the future great sales person are very conscious about laying down detailed, organized plans than they follow through in a timely disciplined way (e.g.) if they say that they are going to make a follow up call on a customer in six months, you can sure that they will be on the doorstep in six month.

3. WORK HARD

They have to work hard because this job is very demanding and they have to work in Irregular hours travel a lot and most of the times have to work alone and away from home.

4. SELECTING THE APPROPRIATE TECHNIQUE

A key step in the personal selling is deciding which device will help the organization reach its promotional goals. Some factors are

- **Nature of the target audience:** weather target audience loyal to the company brand if not higher level of personal selling and convincing techniques are required
- **Nature of the product:** does the product level its self to sampling, demonstration or multiple item purchase.
- **Current economic conditions:** sales representatives must also see what the economic conditions of the country are. Premium and rebates are good in periods of recessions and inflation.

Motivation is goal-directed behaviour, underlying which are certain needs or desires. The term “needs” suggests a lack of something that reaching the goal could satisfy, while the term “desires” suggests positive ardor and strength of feeling. The complex of needs and desires stemming from within individuals leads them to act so as to satisfy these needs and desires.

Specifically, as applied to sales personnel, motivation is the amount of effort the salesperson desires to expend on the activities associated with the sales job, such as calling on potential accounts, planning sales presentations, and filling out reports. Expending effort on each activity making up the sales job leads to some level of achievement on one or more dimensions of job performance-total sales volume, profitability, and sales to new accounts, quota attainment, and the like.

Fig.5.4. Sales Manager's Motivation Mix

Motivational "Help" from Management

Most sales personnel require motivational "help" from management to reach and maintain acceptable performance levels. They require motivation as individuals and as group members. As individuals, they are targets for personalized motivational efforts by their superiors. As member of the sales force, they are targets for sales management efforts aimed toward welding them into an effective selling team. Four aspect of the salesperson's job affect the quality of its performance. The following discussion focuses on these aspects; each is an important reason why sales personnel require additional motivation.

Inherent Nature of the Sales Job

Although sales jobs vary from one company to the next, sales jobs are alike in certain respects. Every sales job is a succession of ups and downs a series of experiences resulting in alternating feelings of exhilaration and depression. In the course of day's work, salespersons interact with many pleasant and courteous people, but some are unpleasant and rude and are difficult to deal with. They are frustrated, particularly when aggressive competing sales personnel vie for the same business, and they meet numerous turndowns. Furthermore, sales personnel spend not only working time but considerable afterhours time away from home, causing them to miss many attractive parts of family life. These conditions cause salespersons to become discouraged, to achieve low performance levels, or even to seek non selling positions. The inherent nature of the sales job, then, is the first reason that additional motivation.

Salesperson's Boundary Position and Role Conflicts The salesperson occupies a "boundary position" in the company and must try to satisfy the expectations of people both within the company (in the sales department and elsewhere) and in customer organizations. There is linkage with four groups : (1) sales management, (2) the company organization that handles order fulfillment, (3) the customers, and (4) other company sales personnel. Each group imposes certain behavioral expectations on the salesperson, and, in playing these different role, the salesperson faces role conflicts, such as

1. Conflict of identification arises out of multi group membership. As the salesperson works with the customer, identification is with the customer rather than the company. On returning to the company, the salesperson drops identification with the customer and identified with the company.

2. Advocacy conflict arises when the salesperson identifies with the customer and advocates the customer's position to other groups in the company organization. This may be important and may be encouraged by the sale management group, but the advocator is in a difficult position.

3. Conflict is inherent in the salesperson's dual role as an advocate for both the customer and the company and the salesperson's pecuniary interest as an entrepreneur paid directly or indirectly on the basis of sales volume, the salesperson has an interest in selling as much as possible in the shortest time. However, the salesperson may uncover facts the customer's organization limit the product's usefulness. If the salesperson tells the customer about these conditions and that, in all probability, the product will not meet the customer's needs, the salesperson risks losing the sale and the income that goes with it.

Not much can be done to reduce the role conflicts of sale personnel. Some evidence exists that experienced sales personnel perceive significantly less role conflict than do those with less experience. This suggests that a salesperson's perceptions of, and ability to cope with, role conflict are influenced not only by experience but by the effectiveness of sales training. It also suggests that those who become experienced sales personnel may cope better with role conflicts (that is, psychologically) than those leaving the sales organisation earlier. So improving sales training effectiveness and revising selection criteria are two roads to reducing the impact of role conflict on sales force morale.

Role conflicts traceable to the salespersons linkage with groups that have divergent interests, then, is another reason why additional motivation is required.

Tendency toward Apathy

Some sales personnel naturally become apathetic, get into a rut. Those who, year after year, cover the same territory and virtually the same customers, lose interest and enthusiasm. Gradually their sales calls degenerate into routine order taking. Because they know the customers so well, they believe that good salesmanship is no longer necessary. Their customer approach typically becomes: "Do you need anything today, Joe? They fail to recognize that friendship in no way obviates the necessity for creative selling and that most customers do not sell themselves on new products and applications. the customer's response, as often as not, is: nothing today, Bill". Later a competing salesperson calls on the same account, uses effective sales techniques, and gets an order. Many salespeople require additional motivation to maintain continuing enthusiasm to generate renewed interest in their work.

Maintaining a Feeling of Group Identity

The salesperson, working alone, finds it difficult to develop and maintain a feeling of group identity with other company salespeople. Team spirit, if present at all, is weak. Thus, the contagious enthusiasm-conducive to improving the entire group's performance-does not develop.

If sales management, through providing added motivation, succeeds in developing and maintaining team spirit, individual sales personnel strive to meet group performance standards. Few people who consider themselves members of the sales team want to appear as poor performers in the eyes of their colleagues, providing the kind of working atmosphere in which all members of the sales force feel they are participating in a cooperative endeavor is not easy-nevertheless, effective sales management works continuously to achieve and maintain it.

Need Gratification and Motivation

Behavioural research studies show that all human activity including the salesperson's job behavior is directed toward satisfying certain needs (that is, reaching certain goals). Patterns of individual behavior differ because individuals seek to fulfill different sets of needs in different ways. Some salespersons, in other words, are more successful than others because of the differing motivational patterns and amounts and types of efforts they exert in performing their jobs.

How particular individuals behave depends upon the nature of their fulfilled and unfulfilled needs modified by their environmental and social backgrounds. The motives lying behind any specific action drive from tensions build up to satisfy particular needs, some beneath the threshold of consciousness. Any action taken is for the purpose of reducing these tensions (fulfilling a need or needs to reach a goal or goals). Needs are either primary or secondary. Primary need are the inborn or physiological needs for food, water, rest, sleep, air to breathe, sex, and so on, the fulfillment of which are basic to life itself. Until primary needs are satisfied, other needs have little motivational influence. Secondary needs arise from an in individual's interaction with the environment, and are not inborn but develop with maturity. Secondary needs include those for safety and security, belongingness and social relations, and self-esteem and self-respect

Motivation Theory

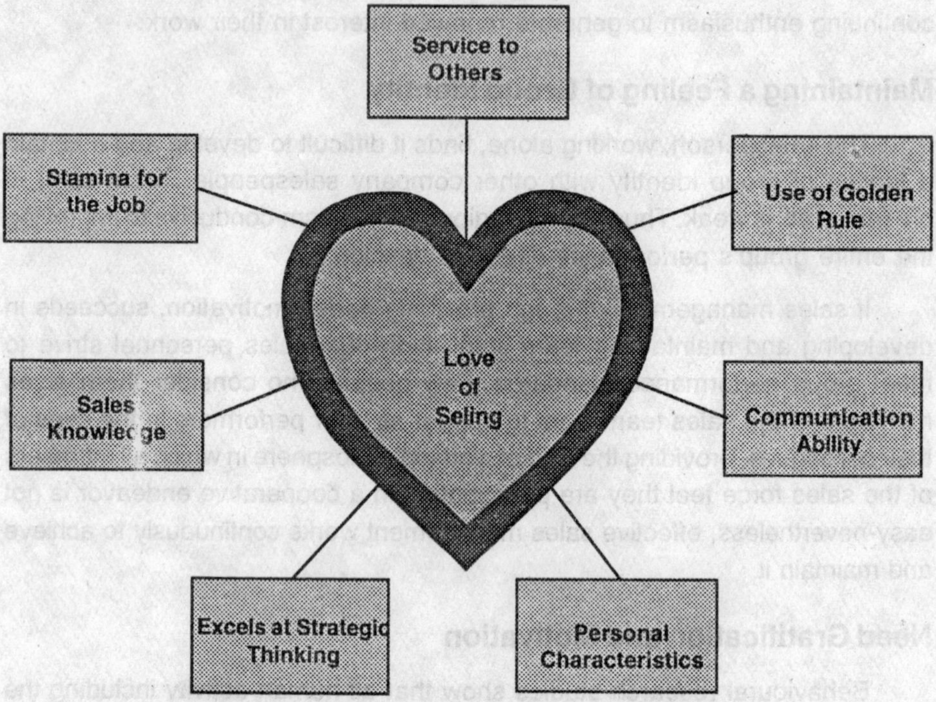

Fig.5.5. Love of Selling Is At the Heart of Helping Others

MASLOW'S HIERARCHY OF NEEDS:

The concept of a hierarchy of needs was advanced by Abraham Maslow, a psychologist. Maslow assumed that humans are "wanting" beings who seek to fulfill a variety of needs. He assumed that these needs can be arranged according to their importance in a sequence known as Maslow's hierarchy of needs.

At the most basic levels are physiological needs, the things we require to survive. These needs include food and water, clothing, shelter, and sleep. At the next level are needs, the things we require for physical and emotional security. They may be satisfied through job security, health insurance, pension plans, and safe working conditions.

Next are the *social needs*, the human requirements for love, affection, and a sense of belonging. To an extent, these needs can be satisfied through the work environment and the informal organization. But they also include relationships beyond the workplace. *Esteem needs* include the need for respect and recognition (the esteem of others) as well as a sense of accomplishment and worth (self-esteem). These needs may be satisfied through personal accomplishment, promotion to more responsible jobs, various honors and awards, and other forms of recognition.

At the uppermost level are *self-actualization* needs, the needs to grow and develop as people and to become all that we are capable of being. These are the most difficult needs to satisfy, and the means of satisfying them tend to vary with the individual.

Maslow suggested that people work to satisfy their physiological needs first, their safety needs next, and so on up the "needs ladder." In general, people are motivated by the needs at the lowest (most important) level that remain unsatisfied. However, needs at one level do not have to be completely satisfied before needs at the next-higher level come into play.

Maslow's hierarchy of needs provides a useful way of viewing employee motivation as well as a guide for management. By and large, American business has been able to satisfy workers' basic needs, but the higher-order needs present more of a problem.

HERZBERG'S MOTIVATION-HYGIENE THEORY:

In the later 1950s, Frederick Herzberg interviewed approximately 200 accountants and engineers in Pittsburgh. During the interviews, he asked them to think of a time when they had felt especially good about their jobs and their work. Then he asked them to describe the factor or factors that had caused them to feel that way. Next, he did the same regarding a time when they had felt especially bad about their work.

He found that feeling good and feeling bad resulted from entirely different sets of factors.

Herzberg's interviews convinced him that satisfaction and dissatisfaction may be different dimensions altogether. The idea that satisfaction and dissatisfaction are separate and distinct dimensions is referred to as the motivation-hygiene theory.

The job factors that Herzberg found most frequently associated with satisfaction are achievement, recognition, responsibility, advancement, growth, and the work itself. These factors are generally referred to as motivation factors because their presence increases motivation. However, their absence does not necessarily result in feelings of dissatisfaction.

Job factors cited as causing dissatisfaction are supervision, working conditions, interpersonal relationships, pay, job security, and company policies and administration. These hygiene factors reduce dissatisfaction when they are present to an acceptable degree. However, they do not necessarily result in high levels of motivation.

Using Herzberg's Motivation-Hygiene Theory :

Herzberg provides explicit guidelines for using the motivation-hygiene theory of employee motivation. He suggests that the hygiene factors must be present to ensure that a worker can function comfortably. But he warns that a state of no dissatisfaction never exists. Managers should make hygiene as good as possible but should then expect only short-term improvement in motivation.

Managers must work to provide the motivation factors, which will presumably enhance motivation and long-term effort. Employee pay has more effect than is explained by Herzberg's theory.

THEORY X AND THEORY Y

The concepts of Theory X and Theory Y were advanced by Douglas McGregor in his 1960 book, The **Human Side of Enterprise**. They are, in reality, sets of assumptions that underlie management's attitudes and beliefs regarding worker behaviour.

Theory X is a concept of employee motivation generally consistent with Taylor's scientific management. The basic assumptions of Theory X include the following:

People dislike work and try to avoid it. Because people dislike work, managers must coerce, control, and frequently threaten employees to achieve organizational goals.

People generally must be led because they have little ambition and will not seek responsibility. They are concerned mainly with security.

Theory Y is a concept of employee motivation generally consistent with the ideas of the human relation's movement. The basic assumptions of Theory Y include the following:

- People do not naturally dislike work. In fact, work is an important part of their lives.

- People will work toward goals to which they are committed. People become committed to goals when it is clear that accomplishing the goal will bring personal rewards.

- People often seek out and willingly accept responsibility. Employees have the potential to help accomplish organizational goals. Organizations generally do not make full use of their human resources. McGregor argued that most managers behave in accordance with Theory X. But he maintained that Theory Y is more appropriate and effective as a guide for managerial action.

Theory Z : In the 1970s, William Ouchi, a management professor at UCLA, began to study business practices in United States and Japanese firms. In Japan, Ouchi found what he calls **Type J** firms. They are characterized by lifetime employment for employees collective (or group) decision making collective responsibility for the outcomes of decisions slow evaluation and promotion implied control mechanisms non-specialized career paths a holistic concern for employees as people American industry is dominated by what Ouchi calls A firms. These firms are characterized by

- short-term employment
- individual decision making
- individual responsibility for the outcomes of decisions
- rapid evaluation and promotion
- explicit control mechanisms
- specialized career paths
- a segmented concern for employees only as employees

A few very successful American firms represent a blend of the **Type J** and **Type A** patterns.

These **Type Z** organizations emphasize

- long-term employment
- collective decision making
- individual responsibility for the outcomes of decisions
- slow evaluation and promotion
- informal control along with some formalized measures
- moderately specialized career paths
- a holistic concern for employees

Theory Z is the belief that some middle ground between Ouchi's Type A and Type J practices is best for American business.

REINFORCEMENT THEORY :

Reinforcement theory is based on the premise that behavior that is rewarded is likely to be repeated, whereas behavior that has been punished is less likely to recur.

Kinds of Reinforcement :

Reinforcement is an action that follows directly from a particular behaviour. Reinforcements can take a variety of forms and can be used in a number of different ways.

- ❖ A positive reinforcement strengthens desired behavior by providing a reward.
- ❖ A negative reinforcement strengthens desired behaviour by eliminating an undesirable task or situation.
- ❖ Punishment is an undesired consequence that follows from undesirable behaviour.
- ❖ Managers who rely on extinction hope to eliminate undesirable behaviour by ignoring it.

Using Reinforcement :

The effectiveness of reinforcement depends on which type is used and how it is timed. Generally, positive reinforcement is considered the most effective action, and it is recommended when the manager has a choice. Continual, repetitious reinforcement can become tedious for both managers and employees, especially when the same behavior is being reinforced over and over in the same way.

CONTEMPORARY VIEWS ON MOTIVATION

In recent years, managers have begun to explore four other models that take a more dynamic view of motivation: equity theory, expectancy theory, reinforcement theory, and Theory Z.

EQUITY THEORY :

The equity theory of motivation is based on the premise that people are motivated first to achieve and then to maintain a sense of equity. As used here, refers to the distribution of rewards in direct proportion to the contribution of each employee to the organization. Everyone need not receive the same rewards, but the rewards should be in accordance with individual contributions.

According to the theory, we tend to implement the idea of equity as follows:

First, we develop an input-to-outcome ratio. Inputs are the things we contribute to the organization. Outcomes are the things we get from the organization. Next, we compare this ratio with what we perceive as the input-to-outcome ratio for some other person, called the "comparison other." If the two ratios are roughly the same, we feel that the organization is treating us equitably and are motivated to leave things as they are. If our ratio is the lower of the two, we feel under-rewarded and are motivated to change things. We may decrease our own inputs by not working so hard.

- Try to increase our total outcomes by asking for a raise in pay.
- Try to get the comparison other to increase some inputs or receive decreased outcomes.
- Leave the work situation.
- Do a new comparison with a different comparison other.

Equity theory is most relevant to pay as an outcome.

EXPECTANCY THEORY:

Expectancy theory , developed by Victor Vroom, is a very complex model of motivation that is based on a simple assumption. According to expectancy theory, motivation depends on how much we want something and on how likely we are to get it.

Consider three sales representatives who are candidates for promotion to one sales manager's job. Bill has had a very good sales year and always gets good performance evaluations. But he is not sure he wants the job because it requires a great deal of travel, long working hours, and much stress and pressure. Paul wants the job but he doesn't think he has much chance of getting it. He has had a terrible sales year and gets only mediocre performance evaluations from his present boss.

Susan wants the job as much as Paul, and she thinks she has a good chance of getting it. Her sales have improved significantly this past year, and her evaluations are the best in the company. Expectancy theory would predict that Bill and Paul are not very motivated to seek the promotion. But Susan is very motivated to seek the promotion, because she wants it and thinks she can get it.

Expectancy theory is complex because each action we take is likely to lead to several different outcomes, some that we may want and others that we may not want. For example, if people work hard and put in a lot of extra hours, several things may happen.

- ❖ They may get a pay raise.
- ❖ They may be promoted.
- ❖ They may gain valuable new job skills.
- ❖ They may have less time to spend with their families.
- ❖ They may have to cut back on their social life.
- ❖ Expectancy theory is difficult to apply, but it does provide several useful guidelines for managers. It suggests that managers must recognize the following:
- ❖ Employees work for a variety of reasons.
- ❖ These reasons, or expected outcomes, may change over time.
- ❖ It is necessary to clearly show employees how they can attain the outcomes they desire.

GOAL-SETTING THEORY :

Goal-setting theory suggests that employees are motivated to achieve goals they establish together with managers.

- ❖ There are three requirements for the goals that are set.
- ❖ They should be specific.
- ❖ They should be moderately difficult.
- ❖ They should be goals that the employee will commit to achieve.
- ❖ Employee rewards should be tied to goal achievement.
- ❖ There are several benefits of using goal-setting theory.
- ❖ It allows managers to design rewards that fit employee needs.
- ❖ It clarifies expectations.
- ❖ It maintains equity.
- ❖ It provides reinforcement.

Unionization of Sales Personnel

There are several reasons why unions have made little progression organizing sales personnel. First, it is difficult to develop strong group identification in most sales departments because each person works alone and sees other members of the sales force infrequently. Little opportunity exists for mutual exchange of grievances. Second, in contrast to most employee groups, salespersons think of themselves as independent operators rather than as cogs in an industrial machine. Third, sales personnel have some control over their workday and workweek.

If they work excessive hours, it is often to add to their complementation, and there are no time clocks. Fourth, the prospect of higher wages has never served as a strong organizing incentive for sales personnel, as sales personnel have been made to feel that low earnings are the result of personal ineffectiveness, not of the employer's niggardliness.

Only about one in ten salespersons belong to a union. When unionization has occurred, it usually traces to a failure of sales management. Grievances stem from such failures as too many reports, competition of house accounts, inadequate expense allowances, poor territories, too many people on the sales force (which results in inadequate territories), and too many non-selling duties.

Unionization has made headway in industries where sales personnel are paid straight salaries, where they work together on the same premises (retail selling), and where the selling job is combined with that of delivery, as in the distribution of beer and soft drinks. Unions have made little progress in organizing sales personnel who sell directly to industrial users or those who make calls on middlemen. Sales personnel in these classifications, paid in whole or part according to productivity, frown upon union affiliation. Many sales executives oppose unionization. Their opposition is based chiefly upon the effect that unionization has on the motivation and control of sales personnel and upon the limitations that union contracts place on management. Managerial action is circumscribed by the collective-bargaining agreement, and uses of incentive compensation are restricted.

Commonly, unions object to sales contests and other devices for motivating the sales force; sometimes they insist that all additions to the sales force be recruited through the union, they discourage the use of quotas and other standards of performance, and a strict system of seniority is demanded. Sales executives maintain that the organizational structure of unions does not harmonize with the demands of the selling job. Selling and sales management require more flexibility than does running a plant or an office. They argue that all salespeople are called upon at times for extra effort, this being the price paid for freedom from day-to-day supervision.

SALESMAN COMPENSATION

Requirements of a Good Compensation Plan

A good sales compensation plan meets seven requirements. First, it provides a living wage, preferably in the form of a secure income. Individuals worried about money matters do not concentrate on doing their jobs well. Second, the plan fits with the rest of the motivational program-it does not conflict with other motivational factors, such as the intangible feeling of belonging to the sales team. Third, the plan is fair-it does not penalize sales personnel because of factors beyond their control within the limits of seniority and other special circumstances, sales personnel receive equal pay for equal performance. Fourth, it is easy for sales personnel to understand-they are able to calculate their own earning. Fifth, the plan adjusts pay to changes in performance. Sixth, the plan is economical to administer. Seventh, the plan helps in attaining the objectives of the sales organization.

Devising a Sales Compensation Plan

Whether contemplating major or minor changes or drafting a completely new sales compensation plan, the sales executive approaches the project systematically. Good compensation plans are built on solid foundations. A systematic approach assures that no essential step is overlooked.

Define the Sale Job

The first step is to reexamine the nature of the sales job. Up-to-date written job descriptions are the logical place to start. If job descriptions are outdated, it they are not accurate, or if complete descriptions of the sales job objectives and work are not given, then a revision is in order. The effective sales executive asks:

Does this description convey a realistic picture of what the salesperson is supposed to accomplish and to do? If there no written sales job descriptions, they are prepared. Other aspects of company operations are considered in relation to their impact upon the sales job. Sales department objectives are analyzed for their effect on the salesperson's job.

Sales volume objectives, for instance, whether in dollars, units of product, or numbers of dealers and distributors, are translated into what is expected of the sales personnel, as group and individually. The impact of sales-related marketing policies is determined. Distribution policies, credit policies, price policies, and other policies affect the salesperson's job. Current and proposed advertising and sales promotional programs assist in clarifying the nature of the salesperson's goal, duties, and activities.

Consider the Company's General Compensation Structure

Most large companies, and many smaller ones, use job evaluation systems to determine the relative value of individual jobs. Job evaluation procedure is not scientific; it is an orderly approach based on judgment. It focus on the jobs, without considering the ability or personality of individuals who do the work. Its purpose is to arrive at fair compensation relationships among jobs. There are four job evaluation methods. Two are non-quantitative: simple ranking and classification or grading. The other two are quantitative : the point system and the factor comparison method.

Simple Ranking

In this inexpensive job evaluation method, widely used by small businesses, an executive committee sorts job descriptions in the order of worth. This is done without considering the individuals currently in the jobs or their compensation levels. No attempt is made to determine critical factors inherent in the jobs; only overall appraisals of the relative worth of different jobs are made.

Classification or Grading

This approach utilizes a system of grades and grade descriptions, against which individual jobs are compared. The grades, sometimes called classes, are described in terms of job responsibility, skills required, supervision given and received, exposure to unfavourable and hazardous working conditions, and similar characteristics. Job descriptions are then classified into appropriate grades-this is done by an executive committee or by personnel specialists. The basic process is to compare job descriptions with grade descriptions. All jobs within a grade are treated alike with respect to base compensation.

Point System

The point system is the most widely used job evaluation method. It involves establishing and defining the factors common to most jobs that represent the chief elements of value inherent in all jobs. The specific factors chosen differ from one company to another, but generally include mental and physical skills, responsibility, supervision given and received, personality requirements, and minimum education required.

Each factor is assigned a minimum and maximum number of points, different ranges being associated in line with the relative importance of the factors, Net, appraised factor scores are combined into a total point value.

Finally, bands of points are decided upon and become the different compensation classes. Less arbitrary judgment is required than under the classification method; the use of point values makes it possible to determine the gap, or distance, between job classes.

Factor-comparison Method

This method resembles the point system but is more complex. It utilizes a scheme of ranking and cross-comparisons to minimize error from faulty judgment. In a process similar to that used in the point system, the factor-comparison method employs selected factors and evaluation scales. However, the scale values are in dollars and cents, and no upper limit exists to the valuation that can be assigned to any one factor. A selected

Number of key jobs, typical of similar jobs throughout the company, is then evaluated, factor by factor. This is done by arranging them in rank order, from highest to lowest for each factor. As a check against this judgmental evaluation, the compensation dollars actually paid for each job are allocated to the factors; the allocation automatically establishes the relationship among jobs for each factor. The judgment ranking and the ranking by allocation compensation are compared and differences are reconciled, or else the jobs are removed from the jobs are removed from the key list. On the basis of the dollar amounts assigned to the several factors making up key jobs, additional jobs are evaluated and their monetary values for each factor interpolated into the scale. This procedure is repeated until all jobs are evaluated.

Job Evaluation and Sales Positions

Job evaluation occurs whenever decisions are made about the relative worth of jobs, and it is inescapable in organizational life. If, for example the owner of an automobile dealership decides that the new car sales manager should be paid more than the service manager, the jobs have been evaluated. So informal job evaluation exists in firms not using formal job evaluation.

Traditionally, sales executives have opposed using formal job evaluations to determine the compensation levels of sales personnel. They contend that compensation levels for sales personnel are more closely related to external supply-and demand factors than to conditions inside the company. Sales personnel enjoy greater job mobility than most other employees, and are in everyday contact with potential employers.

If a company has a formal job evaluation program that includes the jobs of sales personnel, there should be sales department representation on the committee that arrives at quantitative evaluations. If the job evaluation program does not cover sales personnel program or the company does not use formal job evaluation, it is important for the sales executive to establish the value of sales jobs relative to other company jobs. This helps assure that the monetary attractiveness of sales positions is no less than for comparable jobs elsewhere in the company. If the sales executive keeps informed on the relative differences between sales jobs and other company jobs, he or she is preparing for the day, which is probably inevitable, when sales positions are regarded as appropriate for inclusion in formal job evaluation programs.

Consider Compensation Patterns in Community and Industry

Because compensation levels for sales personnel are related to external supply-and-demand factor, it is important to consider prevailing compensation patterns in the community and industry. Management needs answers to four questions:-

(1) What compensation systems are being used?

(2) What is the average compensation for similar positions?

(3) How are other companies doing with their plans? And

(4) What are the pros and cons of departing from industry or community patterns.

If there is a companywide formal job evaluation program, it should take into account the current rates for sales positions in the community and industry. A program for setting compensation of sales personnel is sound only if it considers the relation of external compensation practices to those of the company. Effective sales executives maintain constant vigilance against the possibility that the pay of sales personnel will get out of line with that paid for similar jobs in the community or industry.

Determine Compensation Level

Management must determine the amount of compensation a salesperson should receive on the average. Although the compensation level might be set through individual bargaining, or on an arbitrary judgment basis, neither expedient is recommended. Management should ascertain whether the caliber of the present sales force measures up to what the company would like to have. If it is too low or if the company should have lower-grade people than those currently employed, management should determine the market value of sales personnel of the desired grade. Management weigh the worth of individual persons through estimating the sales and profit dollars that would be lost if particular salespeople resigned.

Another consideration is the compensation amount the company can afford to pay. The result of examining these and other factors pertinent to the situation is a series of estimates for the total cost of salespeople's compensation. It is excellent practice to plot each cost estimate on a break-even style chart. When the several plots are compared with the company's cost goals, the sales volume needed to break even at each compensation level is revealed. The compensation levels for individual salespeople under the proposed plan also should be plotted in break-even style.

In some firms, companywide formal job evaluation programmes are used to set compensation levels for sales positions. The procedure recommended earlier serves as a check on the compensation levels prescribed through job evaluations. Any discrepancies should be reconciled. When the job evaluation program is sound, there should be few, if any, discrepancies. It is not unusual to find that two companies operate under similar selling conditions but with different sales compensation levels. Sales personnel in one company earn more than those who do essentially the same work in another company.

Relatively speaking, the first group of salespeople is overcompensated. What explains such situations? Sometimes, management does not know the true worth of individual sales personnel, or managerial inertia prevents adjustment of the compensation level to changed selling conditions. In still other cases, sales managers are biased in favor of high compensation for selling jobs.

Provide for the Various Compensation Elements

A sales compensation plan has as many as four basic elements:

(1) a fixed element, either a salary or a drawing account, to provide some stability of income; (2) a variable element (for example, a commission, bonus, or profit-sharing arrangement), to serve as an incentive; (3) an element covering the fringe or "plus factor," such as paid vacations, sickness and accident benefits, life insurance, pensions, and the like; and (4) an element providing for reimbursement of expenses or payment of expense allowances. Not every company includes all four elements. Management selects the combination of elements that best fits the selling situation. The proportions that different elements bear to each other vary. However, most companies split the fixed and variable elements on a 60:40 to an 80:20 basis.

Special Company Needs and Problems

A sales compensation plan is no panacea for marketing ills, but it is often possible to construct a plan that increases marketing effectiveness. If a company's earnings are depressed because sales personnel overemphasize low-margin items and neglect more profitable products, it may be possible, despite the existence of the managerial alternatives, to adjust the compensation plan to stimulate the selling of better balanced orders, Specifically, variable commission rates might be set on different products, with the higher rates applying to neglected products.

Or, as another example, a firm might have a "smaller-order" problem. It is possible to design compensation plans that encourage sales personnel to write larger orders. Comissionrates can be graduated so that higher rates apply to larger orders. However, it is desirable to supplement such a revised compensation plan with a customer classification and call scheduling system, enabling management to vary call frequency with account size.

As still another example, a company may want to obtain more displays or local advertising by retailers. The presence or absence of point-of-purchases displays can spell the difference between marketing success or failure. Securing retail displays is a task that sales personnel may neglect, especially if they are paid commissions based on sales volume. To overcome this tendency, an incentive payment for obtaining retail displays Is often incorporated in the compensation plan.

Numerous other possibilities exist for using the compensation plan to help solve special company problems. Plans may assist in securing new customers and new business, improving the quality of salespeople's reports, controlling expenses of handling complaints and adjustments, eliminating price shading by the sales staff, reducing traveling and other expenses, and making collections and gathering credit information.

Management, however, should recognize that other means exist for dealing with these problems, which are generally transitory in nature. Repeated tampering with the sales compensation plan frequently results in complex and difficult-to-administer plans.

Consult the Present Sales Force

Management should consult the present sales personnel, inasmuch as many grievances have roots in the compensation plan. Management should encourage sales personnel to articulate their likes and dislikes about the current plan and to suggest changes in it. Criticisms and suggestions are appraised relative to the plan or plans under consideration. But at this point, management compares the caliber of the present sales force with that of the people whom it would like to have. If the present salespeople are not of the grade that the company wishes to attract, their criticisms and suggestions are of limited usefulness. Since, however nearly every sales force has some people of the desired caliber, more weight can be attached to their opinions than to those of others.

Reduce Tentative Plan to Writing and Pretest it

For classification and to eliminate inconsistencies the tentative plan is put in writing. Then it is pretested. The amount of testing required depends upon how much the new plan differs from the one in use. The greater the difference, the more thorough is the testing. Pretests of compensation plans are almost always mathematical and usually computerized. Past payrolls, perhaps for a year or two, are reworked to check operation of the proposed plan against experience under the old system. Analysts compare what happened with what would have happened had the new plan been in effect. If the sales pattern has shown considerable fluctuation, calculations are made for period's representative of average, good, and poor business. Then a look is taken into the future. Utilizing sales forecast data, new and old plans are applied to future periods. The plan is tested for the sales force as a group and for individuals faced with unique selling conditions. Analysis reveals whether the plan permits earning in line with the desired compensation level. If deficiencies show up, the plan may not be at fault; weaknesses can trace to the way territorial assignments have been made or to inaccuracies in sales forecasts budgets.

To conduct a pilot test, several territories representative of different sets of selling conditions are selected. The proposed plan is applied in each one long enough to detect how it works under current conditions. Pilot tests are invaluable for spotting possible source of trouble and other deficiencies.

Revise the Plan

The plan is then revised to eliminate trouble spots or deficiencies. If alterations are extensive, the revised plan goes through further pretests and perhaps another pilot test. But if changes have been only minor, further testing is not necessary.

Implement the Plan and Provide for Follow-up

At the time the new plan is implemented, it is explained to sales personnel. Management should convince them of its basic fairness and logic. The sales personnel are made to understand what management hopes to accomplish through the new plan and how this is to be done. Details of changes from the old plan, and their significance require explanation. All sales personnel should receive copies of the new plan, together with written examples of the method used for calculating earnings. If the plan is at all complex, special training sessions are held and aimed at teaching sales personnel how to compute their own earnings. If sales personnel do not understand the plan or certain of its features, such as quotas and variable commission bases, they may think that the company is taking unfair advantage of them. Inadequate understanding of the sales compensation plan is common and often a cause of low morale. No effort is spared to make certain that everyone on the sales force fully comprehends the compensation plan and its workings. Provisions for follow-up are made. From periodic checkups, need for further adjustments are detected. Periodic checks provide evidence of the plan's accomplishments, and they uncover weaknesses needing correction.

Compensation Technique:

Straight-Salary Plan

The straight salary is the simplest compensation plan. Under it, salesperson receive fixed sums are regular intervals (usually each week or month but sometimes every two weeks), representing total payments for their services. The straight salary was once the most popular sales compensation plan, but it has been declining in importance. A recent study by Executive Compensation service, Incl. shows that under 17.5 per cent of all selling organizations use straight-salary plans. Such plans are more common among industrial goods companies than among consumer-goods companies. Firms that formerly used the straight salary have tended to combine a basic salary with a variable element—that is, they have switched to combination plans.

In spite of the trend away from its use, sometimes the straight salary plan is appropriate. It is the logical compensation plan when the selling job requires extensive missionary or educational work, when salespeople service the product or give technical and engineering advice to prospects or users, or when salespeople do considerable sales promotion work. If non-selling tasks bulk large in the sales-person's total time expenditure, the straight-salary is worthy of serious consideration.

Straight-salary plans are commonly used for compensating salespeople heavily engaged in trade selling: These jobs, in which selling amounts to mere order taking, abound in the wholesale and manufacturing fields, where consumer necessities are distributed directly to retailers. Frequently, too, the straight-salary method is used for paying driver-salesperson selling liquor and beverages, milk and bread, and similarly distributed products. From management's standpoint, the straight-salary plan has important advantages. It provides strong financial control over sales personnel, and management can direct their activities along the most productive lines. Component tasks making up salespersons' jobs can be recast with minimum opposition from those affected, so there is flexibility in adjusting field sales work to changed selling situations. If sales personnel prepare detailed reports, follow up leads, or perform other time-consuming tasks, they cooperate more fully if paid straight salaries cause of their basic simplicity, and compared with straight-commission plans, accounting costs are lower the main attraction of the straight-salary plan for sales personnel is that stability of income provides freedom from financial uncertainties inherent in other plans. In addition, sales personnel are relieved of much of the burden of planning their own activities (the practice of providing detailed instruction, for example, on routing and scheduling, generally goes along with the straight salary plan). And, because of its basic simplicity, sales personnel have no difficulty in understanding straight-salary plans.

The straight-salary plan, however, has weaknesses. Since there are no direct monetary incentives, many salespeople do only an average rather than an outstanding job. They pass up opportunities for increased business, until management becomes aware of them and orders the required actions. Unless the plan is skillfully administered, there is a tendency to under compensate productive salespeople and to overcompensate poor performers. If pay inequities exist for long, the turnover rate rises; and it is often the most productive people who leave first, resulting in increased costs for recruiting, selecting and training. Other problems are encountered in maintaining morale, as arguments occur on pay adjustments for ability, rising living costs, and length of service.

Because all the selling expense is fixed, it is difficult to adjust to changing conditions—a knotty problem during business downswings, when selling expenses can be reduced only by cutting salaries or releasing personnel. Moreover, during business upturns, there is difficulty in securing the company's share of rising industry volume, because salaried salespeople commonly are not disposed to exceed previous sales records by any large amount. However, many of the straight-salary plan's weaknesses are minimized through good administration.

In administering a straight-salary plan, individual sales personnel are paid, insofar as possible, according to their relative performance. The difficulty is in measuring performance. Management needs to define "performance" and the meanings of good, average, and poor performances. When management has these definitions and develops methods for performance measurements, it can set individual salaries fairly and intelligently. Users of the salary plan define performance as total job performance, not merely success in securing sales volume or in performing some other aspect of the job—and this is theoretically correct, because the payers of salaries assume they can exercise maximum control over to measure performance by relating the salesperson's total selling expense in using the expense-to-sales ratio as the sole criterion of performance overemphasizes the importance of cost control. In the absence of well-defined quantitative performance standards and few companies have them, the sales job description, if up to date and complete, is the place to start in appraising job performances of sales personnel.

All sales personnel need rating not only on their achievement of sales and cost goals but on their performance of each assigned duty. The total evaluation of an individual is a composite of the several ratings, weighted according to relative performance. Persons rated as average are paid average salaries. Salaries of to which their performances vary from the average. Each individual's performance is regularly reviewed and upward adjustments made for those showing improvements, and downward adjustments made for those with deteriorating performances.

Straight-commission Plan

The theory supporting the straight-commission plan is that individual sales personnel should be paid according to productivity. The assumption underlying straight-commission plans is that sales volume is the best productivity measure and can, therefore, be used as the sole measure. This is a questionable assumption. The straight-commission plan, in its purest form is almost as simple as the straight-salary plan, but many commission systems develop into complex arrangements. Some provide for progressive or regressive changes in commission rates as sales volume rises to different levels. Others provide for differential commission rates for sales of different products, to different categories of customers, or during given selling seasons. These refinements make straight commission plans more complex than straight-salary plans. Straight-commission plans fall into one of two broad classifications:

1. Straight commission with sales personnel paying their own expenses. Advances may or may not be made against earned commission.
2. Straight commission with the company paying expenses, with or without advances against earned commissions.

There is a general trend away from the straight-commission plan and today no more than 6 or 7 per cent of all companies use such plans. The straight-commission plan is used in situations where non-selling duties are relatively unimportant and management emphasizes order getting. Straight-commission plans are common in the clothing, textile, and shoe industries and in drug and hardware wholesalers. Firms selling intangibles, such as insurance and investment securities, and manufactures of furniture, office equipment, and business machines also are frequent users of straight-commission plans.

The straight commission plan has several advantages. The greatest is that it provides maximum direct monetary incentive for the salesperson to strive for high-level volume. The star salesperson is paid more than he or she would be under most salary plans, and low producers are not likely to be overcompensated. When a commission system is first installed, the sales personnel turnover rate accelerates, but usually the exodus is among the low producers.

Those remaining work longer and harder, with more income to show for their efforts. Straight-commission plans, in addition, provide a means for cost control—all direct selling expenses, except for travelling and miscellaneous expenses (which are reimbursable in some plans), fluctuate directly with sales volume changes and sales compensation becomes virtually an all variable expense. The straight-commission plan also is characterized by great flexibility— by revising commission rates applying to different products, for instance, it is possible to stimulate sales personnel to emphasize those with the highest gross margins. However, the straight-commission method has weaknesses. It provides little financial control over salespeople's activities, a weakness further compounded when they pay their own expenses. Salespersons on straight commission often feel that they are discharging their full responsibilities by continuing to send in customers' orders. They are careless about transmitting reports, neglect to follow up leads, resist reduction in the size of sales territories, consider individual accounts private property, shade prices to make sales, and may use higher-pressure tactics with consequent loss of customer goodwill. Moreover, unless differential commission rates are used, sales personnel push the easiest-to-sell low-margin items and neglect harder-to-sell high margin items; management seeks to correct this through using differential commission rates; it incurs increased record-keeping expenses. Under any straight-commission plan, in fact, the costs of checking and auditing salespeople's reports and of calculating payrolls are higher than under the straight-salary method. Finally, some sales-persons' efficiency may decline because of income uncertainties. If a sales force has many financially worried salespeople, management may have to invest considerable time, effort, and money to buoy up their spirits.

Determining Commission Base

One important aspect of designing a straight-commission system is to select the base on which to pay commission. Company selling policies and problems strongly influence selection of the base. If obtaining volume is the main concern, then total sales is the base. If sales personnel make collections on sales, commissions are based upon shipments, billings, or payments. To control price cutting by sales personnel, some companies base commission on gross margins. Other companies use net profits as the base, seeking simultaneously to control price cutting, selling expense, and net profit.

Drawing Accounts

A modification of the straight-commission plan is the drawing account method, under which the company establishes separate account for each salesperson, to which commissions are credited and against which periodic withdrawals are made. Drawing accounts resemble salaries, since customarily individual sales personnel are allowed to overdraw against future earning. If sales personnel become greatly overdrawn, they may lose in incentive to produce, because earned commissions are used to reduce the indebtedness. More important, some sales personnel become discouraged with the prospects of paying back overdrawn accounts and quit the company.

To forestall quitting by overdrawn salespeople, some firms use "guaranteed" drawing account plans. These do not require the paying back of overdraw. Sales executives in these firms are conservative in setting the size of guaranteed drawing accounts, for they are in effect combination salary and commission plans. Commonly, drawing account plans include a provision that covers the possibility of overdrafts. Legally, an overdraft cannot be collected unless the salesperson specially agrees to repay it, or it is really a personal loan, or the salesperson has given a note acknowledging its receipt. Without a formal understanding, most courts hold that the relationship between the salesperson and the company is a partnership in which the company agreed to finance the salesperson and that the resulting loss is a normal risk incurred in doing business. Even if the company has an ironclad agreement with its sales personnel, there is a problem in collecting money that overdrawn sales personnel do not have.

COMBINATION SALARY AND INCENTIVE PLAN

Salary plus Commission

Most sales compensation plans are combinations of salary and commission plans. Most developed as attempts to capture the advantages and offset the disadvantages of both the salary and commissíon systems. Where the straight-salary method is used, the sales executive lacks a financial means for stimulating the sales force to greater effort. Where the straight-commission system is used, the executive has weak financial control over non-selling activities. By a judicious blending of the two basic plans, management seeks both control and motivation. Actual results depend upon management's skills in designing and administering the plan. Unless there is skillful adjustment of salary and commission, weaknesses of both basic systems reappear.

Strengths and Weaknesses of Combination Plans

A well-designed and administered combination plan proves significant benefits. Sales personnel have both the security of stable incomes and the stimulus of direct financial incentive. Management has both financial control over sales activities and the apparatus to motivate sales efforts. Selling costs are composed of fixed and variable elements; thus, greater flexibility for adjustment to changing conditions exists than under the commission method. Nevertheless, selling costs fluctuate some with the volume of business. There are beneficial effects upon sales force morale. Disagreements on pay increases and territorial changes are less violent than under a straight-commission plan. Further, if salespeople realize that the company shares their financial risks, a cooperative spirit develops between them and the company.

The combination plan, however, has disadvantages. Clerical costs are higher than for either a salary or a commission system. More records are maintained and in greater detail. There are risks that the plan will become complicated and that sales personnel will not understand it. Sometimes a company seeking both to provide adequate salaries and to keep selling costs down uses commission rates so low that the incentive feature is insufficient to elicit needed sales effort. But, if the incentive portion is increased, salespeople may neglect activities for which they are not directly paid. Therefore, the ratio that the base salary and the incentive portion bear to the total compensation is critical. As mentioned earlier, most companies split the fixed and variable elements on a 60:40 to an 80:20 basis.

Use of Bonuses

Bonuses are different from commissions –a bonus is an amount paid for accomplishing a specific sales task; a commission varies in amount with sales volume or other commission base. Bonuses are paid for reaching a sales quota, performing promotional activities, obtaining new accounts, following up leads, setting up displays, or carrying out other assigned tasks. The bonus, in other words, is an additional financial reward to the salesperson for achieving results beyond a predetermined minimum.

Bonuses are never used alone—they always appear with one of the three main sales compensation methods. If used with the straight salary, the plan resembles the combination plan. If used with the straight commission, the result is a commission plan to which an element of managerial control and direction has been added. If used with the combination salary and commission plan, the bonus becomes a portion of the incentive income that is calculated differently from the commission. Certain administrative actions are crucial when a bonus is included in the compensation plan. At the outset, the bonus conditions require thorough explanation, as all sales personnel must understand them. The necessary records must be set up and maintained. Procedures for keeping sales personnel abreast of their current standings relative to the goals are needed. In addition, any bonus misunderstandings or grievances arising should be dealt with fairly and tactfully.

Fringe Benefits

Fringe benefits, which do not bear direct relationships to job performance, range from 25 to 40 per cent of the total sales compensation package. Some are required by federal and state law—for example, payments for social security premiums, unemployment compensation, and worker's compensation. Most, however, the company provides for other reasons; to be competitive with other companies in the industry or community, to furnish reasons for employees to remain in the company's service, and to comply with what employees expect as fringe benefits.

Fringe benefits, like monetary compensation, are not motivating factors. In the Maslow hierarchy, fringe benefits contribute to fulfillment of safety and security needs, although some (such as payment of country club dues) contribute to fulfillment of esteem and other higher-order needs. Since fringe benefits are given to all in the company's employ and do not vary with job performance, they help to prevent job dissatisfaction but do not add to job satisfaction (in line with Herzberg's motivation-hygiene theory).

Exhibit 5.3. Average Salary for Salespeople in 2004

Compensation trends in selling			
Average Salary for salespeople in 2004			
	Total compensation	Base salary	Bonusplus commissio
Executive	$144,653	$95,170	$49,483
Top performer	153,417	87,342	66,075
Mid-level rep	92,337	58,546	33,791
Law-level lep	63,775	44,289	19,486
Average of all reps	111,135	70,588	40,547

Source: Christine Galea, "2004 Compensation *Survey Sales & Marketing Management*, May 2004, pp. 28-34

FACTORS AFFECTING REMUNERATION PLAN

There is hardly any remuneration plan which can be called best and can be adopted to all types of organisation. An ideal compensation scheme necessarily maximizes the goals of the firm as well as of the sales force. No doubt, the method of remuneration differs from firm to firm but there are several factors which influence the remuneration plan of any organisation directly. These factors determine the nature and amount of remuneration of the sales force. The important factors which need to be considered while developing any method of remuneration for the salesmen are as follows:

(i)Nature of sales job:

First, a thorough study of the sales job should be made while determining a remuneration plan. A sales job analysis includes all aspects relating to the duties and responsibilities of salesmen. If the job is complex, time-consuming and need lots of hard work, the remuneration package should be high and handsome. On the other hand, if the job is simple and requires little effort, the payment should be a moderate one.

(ii) Nature of the product:

The remuneration plan of an organisation also depends on the nature and number of products. If the product offered for sale is a consumer product, it needs little selling effort on the part of the salesmen. Therefore, they are usually paid less compared to those who sell specialties, luxuries or technical goods which require sustained selling efforts. Similarly, salesmen who sell a variety of goods are expected to earn more than those who handle a single product.

(iii) Class of salesman:

Some kind of salesmen like travelling salesmen, creative salesmen are highly paid because their job is time-consuming and requires more selling efforts. On the other hand, counter salesmen, who perform routine type of activities, are comparatively paid less.

(iv) Financial capacity:

Firms which have limited financial capacity, plan the remuneration plan in such a manner so that it does not become a burden for them. In other words, the payment of the sales force should be justifiable. They can follow a remuneration plan entirely based on commission basis. On the other hand, financially sound companies are free to adopt any remuneration policy.

(v) Advertising activities:

Advertising and sales promotion measures undertaken by the organisation generally make the salesman's job comparatively easier. Firms spending heavily on advertising and other sales promotion activities necessarily make the salesman's job comparatively easier. Therefore, the remuneration package of the sales force of such firms can be kept low as their jobs are made easy and simple. On the other hand, salesmen making selling efforts on their own, without any background support made available through advertising and sales promotion activities have to be handsomely paid.

(vi) Channel of distribution

The channel of distribution also plays an important role in remuneration plan and ultimately influences the income of the sales force. The longer the channel, the easier in the job of the salesman since middleman take a lot of burden from the shoulders of the salesmen. In such cases, where little personal salesmanship is required, the salesmen usually get a moderate remuneration. On the other hand, firms using shorter channels of distribution have to undertake a lot of personal selling efforts. Therefore, the salesmen have to make lots of selling efforts and thus, need to be paid handsomely.

SALESMAN RECRUITMENT

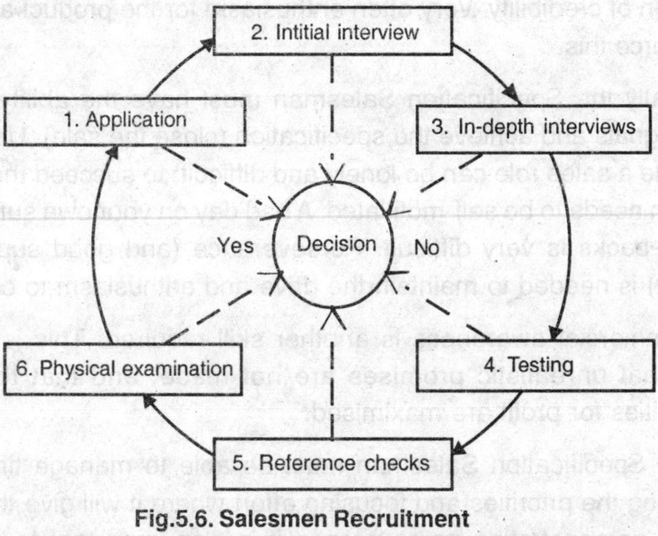

Fig.5.6. Salesmen Recruitment

Many Specification Salesmen start their career in non-sales roles and progress into sales. They might start in an architect's practice, working with a contractor or in a technical department with a manufacturer. This early experience gives them relevant technical and industry knowledge, which they can use to good effect when selling.

The specification sales role is one of business development first, selling second. The specifier will be looking for advice and support, and will involve the Specification Salesman if he can provide timely and accurate information.

Yet to be successful he, or she, must also understand the relationships within the project team. They should know who the decision makers are and be able to influence decisions.

There are a variety of skills required in a Specification Salesman, many of which can be developed with training. Skills can be grouped into three broad categories; Interpersonal, self-management and technical knowledge.

People buy from people and a salesman has to be able to create a strong relationship with his customers. Most important he needs to have credibility, which is achieved through demonstrating honesty and reliability to secure trust.

Fact finding using questioning and listening skills to identify opportunities is important. With a complex project it is necessary to identify the issues that will influence product selection for the client, designer and contractor and present only the product features which represent real benefits. The Specification Salesman must be able to influence by identifying doubts and concerns and addressing these to overcome objections.

To present these benefits effectively requires good communication skills, both on a one-to-one basis and in group presentations (i.e., a technical seminar). The ability to present effectively contributes to the customer's perception of credibility. Very often enthusiasm for the product and its benefits will reinforce this.

Finally the Specification Salesman must have the ability to recognise buying signals and achieve the specification (close the sale). Unlike an office-based role a sales role can be lonely and difficult; to succeed the specification salesman needs to be self-motivated. A bad day on your own suffering a series of knock-backs is very difficult. Perseverance (and good support from the company) is needed to maintain the drive and enthusiasm to continue.

Commercial awareness is another skill required. This is necessary to ensure that unrealistic promises are not made, and that the company's opportunities for profit are maximised.

The Specification Salesman must be able to manage time effectively, recognising the priorities and focusing effort where it will give the best return. Although demonstrating perseverance it is also important to recognise lost causes and move onto better opportunities.

Specification selling is a complex process and can take 18 months or more to progress from initial enquiry to order. There is a need to monitor and follow-up projects regularly over that time and with many projects running in parallel there is a lot of information to process. This requires strong organisational skills and as contact management or CRM systems are increasingly used, good IT skills.

IT skills must include the ability to create and present PowerPoint presentations, as well as managing email and the company's other reporting processes in a timely way.

Although a good Specification Salesman will have an impressive list of projects secured, he will also have lost some projects. Often for reasons beyond his control. If he is good he will have learnt from the experience of losing projects, using this to improve his performance. When recruiting asks for examples of projects lost, why they were lost and what was learnt from the experience.

Specifiers want technical advice and will only deal with a salesman who can provide it. Good product knowledge is thus a very important sales skill. Of almost equal importance is an understanding of the construction industry, including contractual relationships, the roles of the different members of the construction team and knowledge of the legislation.

If a Specification Salesman is to effectively deal with objections and present strong benefits they also need to know about their competitors' products, their strengths and weaknesses. But demonstrate professionalism by not openly criticizing competitors in front of customers.

When recruiting an established Specification Salesman you will expect him to have a network of specifier contacts. Be aware that if he has been working with a different category of product these contacts may not be relevant to your company.

Recruiting someone with all of these skills will not be easy. Candidates should be asked to provide examples of projects secured, volume of product, profitability, who they dealt with and the tactics used to secure projects.

One way to identify suitable candidates is to ask architects or contractors if they can suggest any good Specification Salesman that they deal with from other manufacturers. These can then be headhunted.

There is still a leap of faith to be made in recruiting and because of the long duration of a project poor selection may take time to become apparent. You can use an occupational assessment service. There are a variety of techniques which can help with your selection process.

A Personality Assessment can be used to reduce the reliance on subjective interpretation of CVs and increase the reliability of interviews by adding objectivity. It can help you to assess whether a candidate has the right skills and personality to do the job and decide if they will fit into your organisation.

Ability testing measures a person's potential to learn new skills and Aptitude testing measures their ability to perform job related tasks. This can be job specific, measuring an individual's sales performance potential.

SOLUTION SELLING: THE CHALLENGE — CASE STUDY-X

A global telecommunications leader faced the prospect of losing market share amid stiff competition in the rapidly expanding area of telecommunications. The client needed to improve its win/loss ratio to maintain and expand its position in the market. Its sales teams excelled in aggressiveness and work ethic but lacked key strategic skills to penetrate major accounts.

Solution

The client needed a new approach to develop highly inncvative and successful strategies to win new business from the competition and to protect existing business from competitive loss. SMG's sales consultants worked with the client to target specific accounts and customize the Strategic Selling program.

Each two-day Strategic Selling session began by analyzing the target account's business needs, challenges, goals, objectives, and strategies, as well as the key players involved in the decision-making process. The group then divided into teams, where they assessed competitor's vulnerabilities and strengths, and began planning their attack. Then, the teams developed successful response strategies to what-if scenarios as well as a detailed action plan to pursue the sale.

The Strategic Selling program was successful in identifying new strategies for the client's sales professionals when approaching customers. In one case, the client tried to win a large automobile company's business from its competitor.

During the Strategic Selling session, the client discovered that the automobile company was looking for a suitable business to co-sponsor its racing team. The account manager contacted the automobile company's advertising agency and won their support. Together, they met with the VP of Marketing and then the President of the automobile company. With the resulting marketing agreement, the company also agreed to purchase all of their telecommunications services from the client. This deal resulted in $50 million dollars of new revenue.

In another session, the client focused on trying to win a multi-year information technology contract from a large government agency. The requirements of the Request for Proposal seemed unnecessarily complex and very different from commercial requirements. The client used to build costly administrative systems from scratch to support these requirements. This elevated their costs to the point where they could not compete with the incumbent supplier, which already had their systems in place.

As a result of the Strategic Selling program, the client developed a new strategy: to bid as close to the requirements as possible without increasing cost. Simultaneously, the client lobbied that the procurement requirements artificially raised costs and was anti-competitive. The government agency ultimately awarded the contract to the client.

Question:

(i) Do you think that strategic selling programme is really successful?

(ii) "Sales teams excelled in aggressiveness and work ethic but lacked key strategic skills to penetrate major accounts" – Explain the statement and give your opinion.

CHECK YOUR PROGRESS

(A) True or False

(i) Missionary salesmen are appointed by distributors.

(ii) Travelling salesmen are appointed by manufacturers.

(iii) There is no concept called manufacturer's salesmen.

LET US SUM UP

A widely held view about a salesman is that he simply remains present at the counter and sells goods to the customers. But in reality, the job of the salesman is not that narrow and limited. In the modern business world, there are numerous types of selling jobs in any organisation. The duties and responsibilities are numerous and vary from salesman to salesman.

LESSON END ACTIVITY

Contact a manufacturer's rep for any type of product. (Such reps are usually listed in the yellow pages for most major cities). Find out what criteria reps use to select the manufacturers they are willing to represent. Also determine what types of assistance the various manufacturers they represent provide to the manufacturer's rep. There are several methods of classifying salesmen's job. They may be classified on the basis of: (a) organisation, (b) goods they sell, and, (c) services offered.

KEY WORDS

Missionary Salesmen:

There are certain kinds of salesmen who are appointed by the manufacturers to the merits of their goods. These salesmen are responsible for promoting sales creating additional demand, thereby developing new sales territories.

Staple Salesmen :

These kinds of salesmen specialize in selling necessities like food, clothes, stationery, grocery, etc. These goods are usually sold in many shops and similar types of goods are produced by many manufacturers. Consumers of these articles are free to compare the quality, price and utility of various products available, and choose the best one which suits their needs.

Travelling Salesmen:

Travelling salesmen are usually employed to contact prospective customers scattered in different areas of a country. Generally, these salesmen are required to sell high unit value and speciality goods.

REVIEW QUESTIONS

1. Explain different types of selling jobs.
2. Classify salesmen into different categories and write short notes on each category.
3. Write short notes on (i) Missionary salesman (ii) Travelling salesman (iii) Exporter's salesman (iv) Retailer's salesman.
4. Explain different motivation theory which has impact on performance of salesman.
5. Discuss different methods of compensation.

CHECK YOUR PROGRESS: MODEL ANSWER

(A)

(i) False
(ii) False
(iii) False

SUGGESTED READINGS

P.K. Sahu & K.C. Raut: *Salesmanship and Sales Management,* Vikas Publishing House Pvt Ltd, New Delhi, 2003.

S. A. Chunawalla: *Sales Management,* Himalaya Publishing House, Mumbai, 2005.

Spiro, Stanton, Rich: *Management of a Sales Force,* Tata McGraw Hill, New Delhi, 2008.

☒☒☒

Chapter 6
Relationship Marketing and Sales Force Automation

> "Marketing today is not a function; it is a way of doing business"
>
> *– Regis McKenna*

Relationship Marketing

Introduction – Levels of relationship marketing – Consultative selling-Different types of consultative roles, Customer Relationship Management, Meaning and Significance of CRM - Types of CRM (Operational, Collaborative, Analytical) - Strategies for building relationship marketing - CRM Vs Customer retention - CRM Process-Benefits - CRM process for marketing organisations - brand switching behaviour - e-CRM – Meaning - Importance of e-CRM - Difference Between CRM and e-CRM Sales Force Automation (SFA) Introduction – Definition – Advantages and promises of SFA – SFA Tools.

OBJECTIVES

At the conclusion of this lesson you should be able to understand :-

- The concept of relationship marketing
- Different levels of relationship marketing
- Consultative selling
- Understanding customer relationship management
- Different types of CRM
- Process of CRM
- Customer Brand switching behaviour
- E-CRM
- Understanding SFA
- SFA Tools

MARITZ TRAVEL: BUSINESS PROCESS MANAGEMENT HELPS MANAGE CONSTANT CHANGE - CASE STUDY IX

Maritz Travel is a global leader in incentive travel management — the 110-year-old firm provides companies with meeting facilitation, special events and incentive travel programs. It's a $1 Billion-plus operation with about 900 employees, part of marketing firm Maritz Inc., both based in St. Louis. If you know a top salesperson who's been rewarded with a special all-expenses-paid trip to Hawaii, say, that's an example of the sort of product that Maritz offers.

Early in 2006, Maritz began actively seeking a BPM solution to better control its processes. Problems included a lack of consistency in processes and the flow of information, areas where the same information was entered into the system over and over by different departments, and lots of repetition. "We're a very successful company and the largest of our kind," says Mike Tenholder, senior project director for Maritz Travel, who has spent 25 years in the travel industry and has an IT as well as a business background. "But we had a lot of room for improvement. We said, 'We really need… consistency in our business process, so everyone can work off the same page.'"

That first became clear late in 2005 when Maritz decided to conduct a value stream analysis — a basic assessment of business processes that helps gauge where value is added and where waste accumulates. Part of the assessment involved talking to a wide range of employees, Tenholder says, "each of [whom] came back loud and clear and said, 'We need a better way of managing our processes.'"

One challenge in the travel incentive business is variation. Unlike a manufacturing concern, Maritz is not producing widgets — it's booking airlines, negotiating hotel rooms, and accommodating groups of people. The variations from project to project are tremendous, Tenholder says. "We can not eliminate variation in our business, [but] we can manage it more effectively."

The travel industry also changes rapidly. "Things change in our travel industry so fast, that we can not be hard and fast connected to a client/server application," Tenholder explains. "We thought, maybe a business process management solution is where we need to go."

Enter Lombardi Software with TeamWorks Enterprise Edition. Lombardi's BPM suite offers the ability to create process-centric applications that work with a company's existing architecture to give visibility into data and processes. It also offers an "in-process" feature that yields real-time data on process performance.

Timing is Everything

Critical to the speed of Maritz's selection and rollout of a BPM solution was executive sponsorship. Chief Operating Officer Rich Phillips saw the value of a BPM solution early on and was the top executive sponsor who signed off on the project. "As a result of our value stream analysis work," Tenholder explains, "we came to him with a number of recommendations to improve processes... We [said], 'We cannot build a technology solution to address these issues. [We need] a consistent process flow, a central repository of client data, and we can not build them fast enough to solve our problems. We have to go out and buy something.' It did not take much convincing."

Once the decision was made, things moved quickly. The company studied ratings of BPM vendors from analyst groups Gartner Inc. and Forrester Research to select five top contenders. Maritz issued an RFP in late January, entertained presentations from the five finalists in mid-March, signed the deal with Lombardi at the end of March, and began implementation the second week of April. "Our company is ready for change," Tenholder says with a small laugh. "They are hungry for it."

The five systems Maritz evaluated were Oracle's BPEL Process Manager; FileNet's Business Process Management suite; FuegoBPM, a solution from Fuego, which was in the process of being purchased by BEA Systems; Savvion BusinessManager; and Lombardi's offering. It ended in a close contest between Savvion and Lombardi, Tenholder says. "It came down to people, and an understanding of what we wanted to accomplish. Lombardi just seemed to grasp it right away."

INTRODUCTION

In the past, the focus of marketing was on finding new customers to make the sale. Organizations have begun to realize that it is a lot cheaper to retain current customers than to attract new ones. This has led to a focus on relationship marketing that involves working closely with customers to build lasting relationships over time. Theodore Levitt says, "One of the surest signs of a bad or declining relationship is the absence of complaints from the customer."

Relationship marketing is establishing, developing, and maintaining successful relational long-term exchanges between organizations and ultimate customers. Understanding relationship marketing requires distinguishing between the discrete transaction (distinct beginning, short duration, and distinct ending) and the relational exchange, which traces to previous agreements and is longer in duration, reflecting an ongoing process. The goal of the discrete transaction is to get customers (short-term goal-oriented), whereas the goal of relationship marketing is to get and keep customers (long–term goal-oriented).

Relationship marketing has gained increased status in recent years in part because research has shown that it costs up to five times as much to acquire a new customer as it does to service an existing one.

In addition, studies have shown that fewer than 10% of dissatisfied customers repurchase a product, while these individuals relate their dissatisfaction to others at a rate five times that of satisfied customers.

The unit of value in business today is relationships. Clearly, marketers have an incentive to keep existing customers satisfied. The key to successful customer retention is superior customer satisfaction. Focused marketing means building relationships with the right people. Organizations have determined that even the loss of a sale in the short run may mean greater profits in a long-term relationship. It is not uncommon for an organization engaged in relationship marketing to recommend a competitor's product if they feel that the competing product would better satisfy the unique needs of the customer. Such a focus on satisfying customer needs helps build the trust that can result in a mutually beneficial and satisfying long-term relationship.

Relationships are built on value and service. Value for the customer is a result of increased global competition that acts as an unyielding pressure on prices. The consumer receives value from manufacturers operating huge factories and from retailers providing an infinite variety of goods. Yet, service has suffered as individual production facilities and stores have been replaced in this industry trend toward mergers with multiple factories and distribution sites. Service is part of a corporate culture and is the other characteristic of global competition. It is exercised for every transaction, large or small, to every customer. Those who render it will find they keep their customers.

THREE LEVELS OF RELATIONSHIP MARKETING

- Transaction selling
- Relationship selling
- Partnering

Transaction selling: customers are sold to and not contacted again

Relationship selling: the seller contacts customers after the purchase to determine if they are satisfied and have future needs

Partnering: the seller works continually to improve its customers' operations, sales, and profits

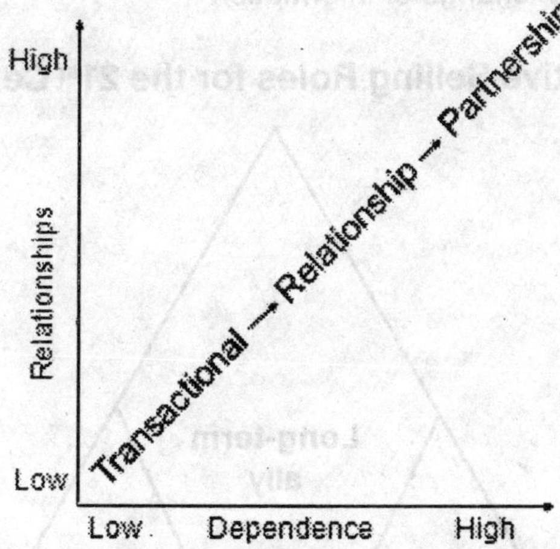

Fig.6.1.Dependence Increases as Relationships become More Important

Partnering with Customers

Exhibit.6.2. Different types of partnering

1. ***Individual excellence:*** Both partners add value, and their motives are positive (to pursue opportunity) rather than negative (to mask weakness).
2. ***Importance:*** Both partners want relationship to work because it helps them meet long-term stralegic objectives.
3. ***Interdependence:*** The partners need each other; each helps the other reach its goal.
4. ***Investment:*** The partners devote financial and other resources to the relationship.
5. ***Information:*** The partners communicate openly about goals, technical data, problems, and changing situations.
6. ***Integration:*** The partners develop shared ways of oprating: they teach each other and learn from each other.
7. ***Integrity:*** Both partners are trustworthy and honorable

CONSULTATIVE SELLING

The process of helping the customer achieve strategic short and long-term goals through the use of the seller's goods and/or services

- A highly interactive dialogue between a salesperson and a customer
- A balanced exchange of information

Three Consultative Selling Roles for the 21st Century

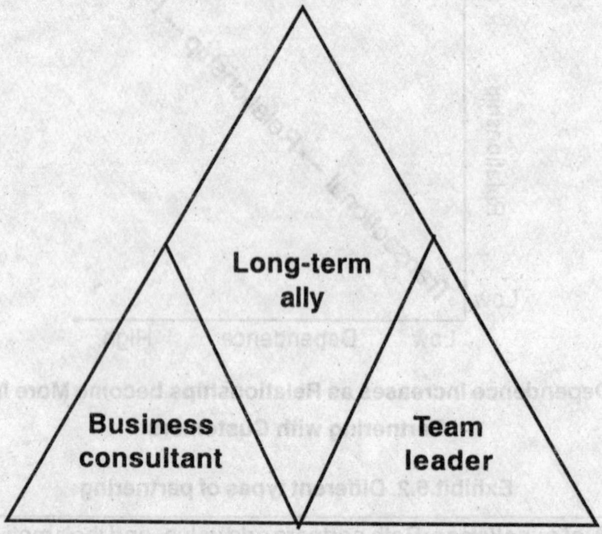

Fig.6.2. Three Roles of Consultative Selling

The Team Leader

Coordinates all of the information, resources, and activities needed to support customers before, during, and after the sale

The Business Consultant

Gives advice and service. Uses internal and external resources to gain an understanding of the customer's business and marketplace

The Long-Term Ally

Creates a "win–win" situation. As the customer's sales and profits grow, so do the salesperson's The ability of a salesperson to fulfill the role of long-term ally is a pivotal factor in determining whether a sales transaction is just a ***transaction*** or the beginning of a ***relationship***

The Customer-Seller Relationship Gap

- May occur when the salesperson's interest in the customer declines
- Usually after the sale
- Yet the customer's interest increases after the sale
- This is one reason why service after the sales is so important

CUSTOMER RELATIONSHIP MANAGEMENT

INTRODUCTION

The approaches in marketing functions are constantly changing in tune with the changing challenges that are faced at the market fronts. Today, marketers consider retaining of customers as a much more challenging job than acquiring customers in the context of growing competitive forces. Thus, the traditional transactional approach of marketing became insufficient to achieve the marketing goals and necessitated the emergence of a new approach namely Relationship Marketing.

TRADITIONAL TRANSACTION APPRAOCH

The focus on this type of approach is on individual transaction and does not concern continuous relationship with customers. It does not contain a strategic long term perspective. The customers are viewed as outsiders to the business. Very little attention is paid to the customer services and customer commitments.

RELATIONSHIP MARKETING

This focuses on continuous multiple transactions rather than isolated individual transactions. The customers are viewed as insiders to the business and aims to build a long -term and never -ending relationship with them. It focuses on developing a hard core loyal customer with the idea of retaining them forever. The relationship Marketing approach has gradually taken the shape of Customer Relationship Management. Customer Relationship Management focuses more widely on customers and on the entire functions connected.

DEFINITION OF CUSTOMER RELATIONSHIP MANAGEMENT

There have been a number of studies in the recent times on how customer retention can contribute significantly to profitability. In the times of Internet, it is worthwhile to analyse how this low-cost reach can lead to profitability. Some companies like Siebel, Oracle and Broadvision have created useful CRM products, which can track a number of dimensions of consumer behaviour. There is a basic need on the part of any organisation to have a good internal coordination before a CRM package can be used effectively. The impact of consumer behaviour dimensions on CRM is equally important to firms conducting business on the Net. A study indicated that though the acquisition costs of consumers can be high on the Net, they spend more over a period of time if they develop loyalty towards an online store. Even so, McKinsey study in 1999, proved that among customer attraction, customer conversion and customer retention, the greatest profitability comes from the investments made in customer retention rather than customer attraction or conversion.

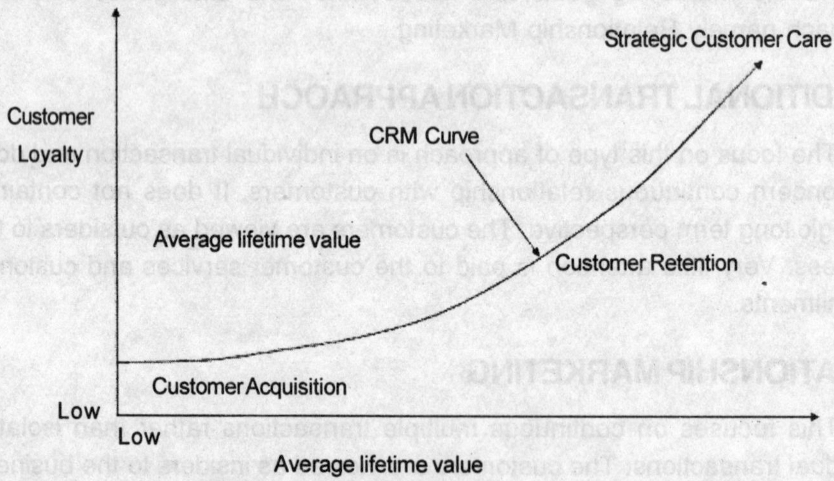

Fig. 6.3. CRM & Customer Lifetime Value

Peter Drucker said, "The purpose of a business is to create customers." Implied in his words and his work is the importance of keeping those same customers and of growing the depth of their relationship with you. Initially, new customers cost you money-money spent on advertising and marketing and money spent learning what they want and teaching them how best to do business with you. CRM can be the single strongest weapon you have as a manager to ensure that customers become and remain loyal.

CRM is a comprehensive approach for creating, maintaining and expanding customer relationships.

The relationship marketing approach has great significance from the organisations' point of view due to the following:

- ❖ Reduction in customer recruitment cost
- ❖ Generation of more and more loyal customers
- ❖ Expansion of customer base
- ❖ Reduction in advertisement and other sales promotion expenses
- ❖ Benefiting customer selectivity approach
- ❖ Increase in the number of profitable customers
- ❖ Easy introduction of new products
- ❖ Easy business expansion possibilities
- ❖ Increase in customer partnering, etc.

CRM can be defined as:

"A management process of acquiring customers by understanding their requirements, retaining customers by fulfilling their requirements more than their expectations and attracting new customers through customer specific strategic marketing approaches. The process invites total commitment on the part of the entire organisation in evolving and implementing relationship strategies that would be rewarding to all concerned."

SIGNIFICANCE OF CRM

The following are some of the points that gives an overview about the importance of Customer

- ❖ Relationship management
- ❖ Reduction in customer recruitment cost.
- ❖ Generation of more and more loyal customers.
- ❖ Expansion of customer base.
- ❖ Reduction in advertisement and other sales promotion expenses.
- ❖ Increase in the number of profitable customers.
- ❖ Easy introduction of new products.
- ❖ Easy business expansion possibilities.

EMERGING CONCEPTS OF CRM

1. Conceptual Framework of Customer Relationship Management
2. CRM: A Research Agenda
3. Implications of Globalization on Customer Relationship Management
4. Effective Customer Relation Management Through Customer Knowledge Management
5. A Generalized Model for the Structure of Business Relationships: A Meta-analysis of Relationship Literature
6. Regain Management: Issues and Strategies
7. Winning Markets through Effective Customer Relationship Management

BENEFITS FOR CRM

❖ Reduction in customer recruitment cost

❖ Generation of more and more royal customer

❖ Expansion of customer base

❖ Reduction in advertisement and other sales promotion expenses

❖ Benefiting customer selectivity approach

❖ Increase in number of profitable customers

❖ Easy introduction of new products

❖ Easy business expansion possibilities

❖ Increase in customer partnering

CRM APPLICATIONS

The CRM applications are a convergence of

1. Functional Components
2. Channels

And the functional components include:

❖ Sales Applications

❖ Marketing Applications

❖ Customer Service and Support Application

SALES APPLICATIONS

- ❖ Sales Forecasting
- ❖ Proposal Generation and Management
- ❖ Compensation
- ❖ Pricing
- ❖ Territory Assignment and Management
- ❖ Expense Reporting

MARKETING APPLICATIONS

- ❖ Marketing Campaign Planning, Execution and Analysis.
- ❖ Budgeting and Forecasting
- ❖ A Marketing Encyclopedia

CUSTOMER SERVICE AND SUPPORT APPLICATIONS

- ❖ Customer care
- ❖ Field Service
- ❖ Problem and Solution Database
- ❖ Service agreements and Contracts

TYPES/VARIATIONS OF CRM

There are several different approaches to CRM, with different software packages focusing on different aspects. In general, Customer Service, Campaign Management and Sales Force Automation (SFA) form the core of the system.

OPERATIONAL CRM

Operational CRM provides support to "front office" business processes, e.g., to sales, marketing and service staff. Interactions with customers are generally stored in customers' contact histories, and staff can retrieve customer information as necessary.

Analytical CRM analyzes customer data for a variety of purposes:

- Designing and executing targeted marketing campaigns
- Designing and executing campaigns, e.g., customer acquisition, cross-selling, up-selling, add-on-selling
- Analyzing customer behaviour in order to make decisions relating to products and services (e.g., pricing, product development)
- Management information system (e.g. ,financial forecasting and customer profitability analysis)

Analytical CRM generally makes heavy use of data mining and other techniques to produce useful results for decision-making. It is at the analytical stage that the importance of fully integrated CRM software becomes most apparent. Logically speaking, the more information that the analytical software has available for analysis, the better its predictions and recommendations will be.

SALES INTELLIGENCE CRM

Sales Intelligence CRM is similar to Analytical CRM, but is intended as a more direct sales tool. Features include alerts sent to sales staff regarding:

- Cross-selling/Up-selling/Switch-selling opportunities
- Customer drift
- Sales performance
- Customer trends
- Customer margins
- Customer alignment
- Campaign Management
- Campaign management combines elements of Operational and Analytical CRM.

Campaign management functions include:

- Target groups formed from the client base according to selected criteria
- Sending campaign-related material (e.g. on special offers) to selected recipients using various channels (e.g. e-mail, telephone, SMS, post)
- Tracking, storing, and analyzing campaign statistics, including tracking responses and analyzing trends

COLLABORATIVE CRM

Collaborative CRM covers aspects of a company's dealings with customers that are handled by various departments within a company, such as sales, technical support and marketing. Staff members from different departments can share information collected when interacting with customers. For example, feedback received by customer support agents can provide other staff members with information on the services and features requested by customers. Collaborative CRM's ultimate goal is to use information collected by all departments to improve the quality of services provided by the company. CRM also plays a role of data distributor within customers, producers and partners. Producers can use CRM information to develop products or find new market. CRM facilitates communication between customers, suppliers and partner by using new information system such e-mail, link and data bank.

CONSUMER RELATIONSHIP CRM

Consumer Relationship System (CRS) covers aspects of a company's dealing with customers handled by the Consumer Affairs and Customer Relations contact centers within a company. Representatives handle in-bound contact from anonymous consumers and customers. Early warnings can be issued regarding product issues (e.g., item recalls) and current consumer sentiment can be tracked (voice of the customer).

SIMPLE CRM

A relatively new spin-off of the traditional CRM model first appearing in 2006. At their core, CRM tools are designed to manage customer relationships. As described above there are countless supplemental features and capabilities. Simple CRM systems breakdown the traditional CRM system to focus on the core values—managing contacts and activities with customers and prospects. These systems are designed to create the most value for the immediate end user rather than the organization as a whole. Many times they focus on satisfying the needs of a particular marketplace niche, organizational unit, or type of user rather than an entire organization.

SOCIAL CRM

Beginning in 2007, the rapid growth in social media and social networking forced CRM product companies to integrate "social" features into their traditional CRM systems. Some of the first features added are social network monitoring feeds (i.c. Twitter timeline), typically built into the system dashboard. Other emerging capabilities include messaging, sentiment analysis, and other analytics. Many industry experts contend that Social CRM is the way of the future, but there are still many skeptics. Top CRM minds agree that online social communities and conversations carry heavy consequences for companies. They must be monitored for real-time marketplace feedback and trends.

EFFECTS OF CRM

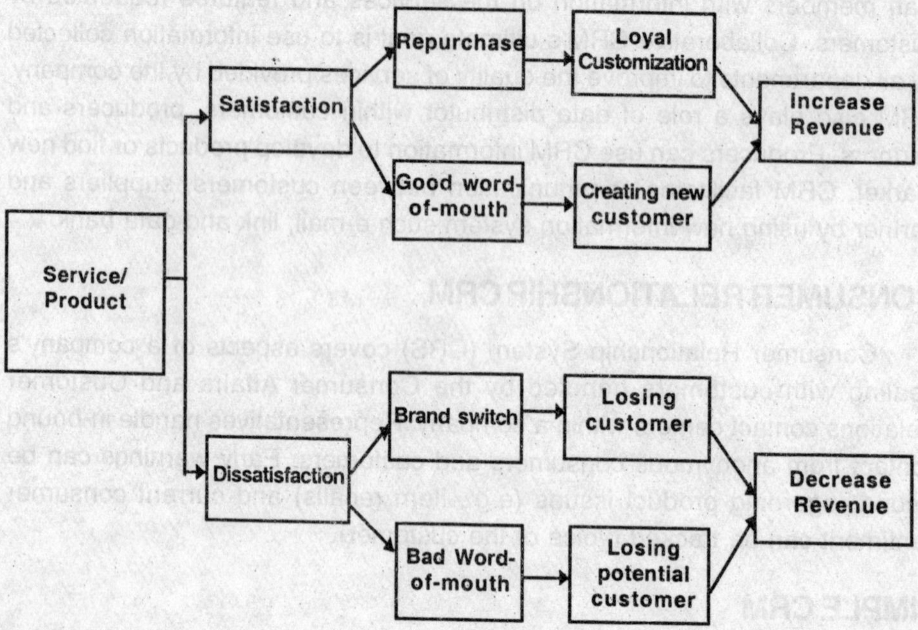

Fig. 6.4. Effects of CRM

CRM STRATEGIES

Customer Acquisition

- Gain the greatest number of new "Best" customers as early in their lifespan" as possible.

Customer Retention

- Retain and expand your business and relationships with your customers through up-selling, cross-selling and servicing.

Customer Loyalty

- Offer programs to ensure that your customers happily buy what you offer only from you.

Customer Evangelism

❖ Enable loyal customers to become a volunteer sales force.

Cost Reduction

❖ Reduce costs related to marketing, sales, customer service and support.

Improve Productivity

❖ Enhance your e-business strategies.

BUILDING CUSTOMER RELATIONSHIP MANAGEMENT:

Step 1: Acquisition: It is a vital stage in building customer relationship. The acquisition process constitutes the following stages.

❖ Enquiry

❖ Interaction

❖ Exchange

❖ Co-ordination

❖ Adoption

Each one of the above stages assumes a significant role in the acquisition process. In the enquiry stage, the prospective buyer undertakes a detailed enquiry with regard to several aspects pertaining to the organisation, product, nature of transaction and all other related aspects. Having stored the information he passes on to the interaction stage, where the customer interacts with the organisation and obtains additional information, clarifies and ensures already collected information.

Terms of exchange, mode of delivery and other things related to exchange, are settled at the exchange stage. Further coordinated effort on either side would lead the customers moving to adoption of the product or service concerned, and that completes the acquisition process.

Step 2: Customer Interaction Management (CIM): Interaction plays a lead role in building customer relationships. CIM constitutes the customer relationship technologies with additions of technology-based interactive solutions. The interactive channels that are currently available enable very effective customer interactive communications, which leads to CIM, which further leads to relationship building.

In view of technology growth, the interaction management is facilitated by communication in terms of media, message, speed, accuracy, distance, content, reach, repetition etc. The customer interaction management stands for intensive interaction between customers and the organisation, which is supported by technology-enabled mechanisms such as Internet

CIM can assume the following routes:

- Online routes- e-mails, web communities, chat rooms.
- Offline routes- telephone, fax, mails, interactive television network.
- Outsourcing

Step 3: Customer Retention: The focus of the organisations is more on customer retention than simply on customer acquisition. Customer retention is the process of keeping customers in the customer inventory for an unending period by meeting the needs and exceeding the expectations of those customers. It is the approach of converting a casual customer into a committed loyal customer.

CRM is a complete system with a number of inter-linkages- beginning with what type of consumers should be targeted to finally obtaining efficiency in it. Unless an organisation has a holistic view of CRM, it may begin to concentrate on those aspects of CRM may not have critical linkages with the other important dimensions of marketing. Online processing or customer call-centres alone cannot lead to a successful CRM. A CRM has to start with a good database of consumers and it should have a historical perspective on them. For example, it should be possible for a CRM programme to have specific strategies for prospects, first-time buyers, repeat buyers and advocates. CRM strategies have to take into consideration these differences to qualify consumers for a CRM programme. This is important because a CRM programme has to be beneficial both to the company and its consumers and holds true in the case of both consumer and industrial products.

CRM HIERARCHY

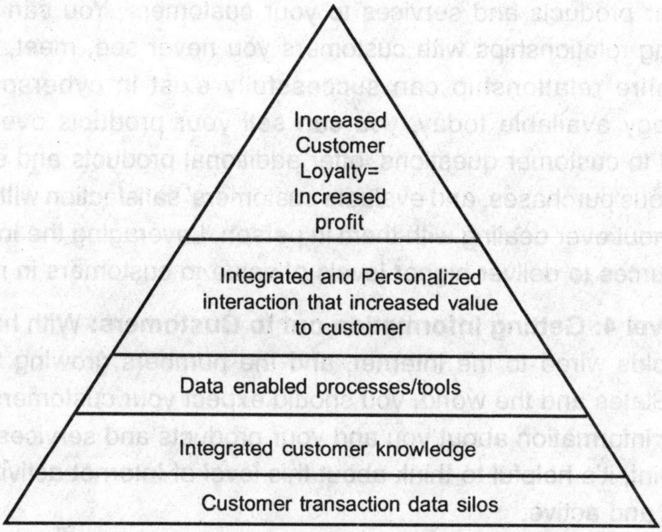

Fig. 6.5. CRM Hierarchy

E-CRM:

E-commerce really is not a new game. It's an extension of the game we have been playing since the dawn of commerce- the game of creating, maintaining, and expanding customer relationships. To play the game of business in this century, it's important to know what e-commerce can do for you and how it's changing customer expectations. Working with the touchstone of your CRM strategy, you will be able to use new rules and the new tools offered by e-commerce to satisfy your customers.

The Internet can enable your CRM strategy in three ways:

Level 1: Getting information out to customer: The Internet can provide an avenue for getting information about your business and your products and services to your current and potential customers. At its most basic level, this means letting them know you are there and how to reach you in the "real world". It can be as simple as a Web-based brochure that describes your products and services and tells customers where you are located and how to reach you by phone.

Level 2: Getting information back from customers: The next level of sophistication means you not only provide information to your customers, but also learn more about them and from them. The Internet allows you to collect all sorts of useful – and sometimes not so useful – data about your customers. Sometimes this means customers respond to questions and provide you useful information. In other cases you may be able to collect information that's very useful to your business without interfering at all with the customer experience.

Level 3: E-commerce sales: At its highest level, you can use the Internet to deliver products and services to your customers. You can have mutually rewarding relationships with customers you never see, meet, or speak with! Your entire relationship can successfully exist in cyberspace. With the technology available today, you can sell your products over the Internet, respond to customer questions, offer additional products and services based on previous purchases, and evaluate customers' satisfaction with your offerings – all without ever dealing with them in person. Leveraging the Internet can free up resources to deliver higher levels of value to customers in new ways.

Level 4: Getting Information out to Customers: With half of American households wired to the internet, and the numbers growing throughout the United States and the world, you should expect your customers to search the Web for information about you and your products and services. From a CRM standpoint, it's helpful to think about this level of Internet activity in two ways, passive and active.

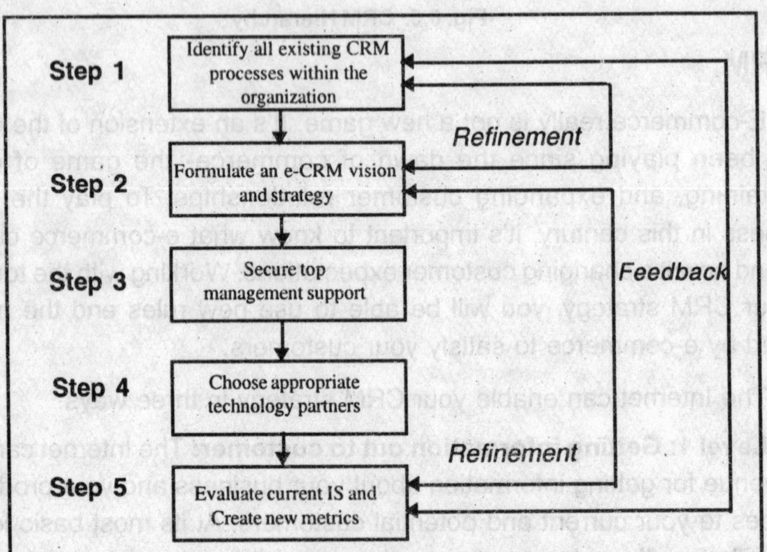

Fig. 6.6. e-CRM Implementation Steps

As the internet is becoming more and more important in business life, many companies consider it as an opportunity to reduce customer-service costs, tighten customer relationships and most important, further personalize marketing messages and enable mass customization. Together with the creation of Sales Force Automation (SFA), where electronic methods were used to gather data and analyze customer information, the trend of the upcoming Internet can be seen as the foundation of what we know as e-CRM today. We can define e-CRM as activities to manage customer relationships by using the

Internet, web browsers or other electronic touch points. The challenge hereby is to offer communication and information on the right topic, in the right amount, and at the right time that fits the customer's specific needs.

Channels, through which companies can communicate with its customers, are growing by the day, and as a result, getting their time and attention has turned into a major challenge. One of the reasons e-CRM is so popular nowadays is that digital channels can create unique and positive experiences – not just transactions – for customers. An extreme, but ever growing in popularism, example of the creation of experiences in order to establish customer service is the use of Virtual Worlds, such as Second Life. Through this so-called e-CRM, companies are able to create synergies between virtual and physical channels and reaching a very wide consumer base. However, given the newness of the technology, most companies are still struggling to identify effective entries in Virtual Worlds. Its highly interactive character, which allows companies to respond directly to any customer's requests or problems, is another feature of e-CRM that helps companies establish and sustain long-term customer relationships.

Furthermore, Information Technology has helped companies to even further differentiate between customers and address a personal message or service. Some examples of tools used in eCRM:

- Personalized Web Pages where customers are recognized and their preferences are shown.
- Customized products or services (Dell).

CRM programs should be directed towards customer value that competitors cannot match. However, in a world where almost every company is connected to the Internet, e-CRM has become a requirement for survival, not just a competitive advantage.

DIFFERENT LEVELS OF ECRM

In defining the scope of e-CRM, three different levels can be distinguished:

Foundational services:

This includes the minimum necessary services such as web site effectiveness and responsiveness as well as order fulfillment.

Customer-centered services:

These services include order tracking, product configuration and customization as well as security/trust.

Value-added services:

These are extra services such as online auctions and online training and education.Self-services are becoming increasingly important in CRM activities. The rise of the Internet and e-CRM has boosted the options for self-service activities. A critical success factor is the integration of such activities into traditional channels. An example was Ford's plan to sell cars directly to customers via its Web Site, which provoked an outcry among its dealers network. CRM activities are mainly of two different types. Reactive service is where the customer has a problem and contacts the company. Proactive service is where the manager has decided not to wait for the customer to contact the firm, but to be aggressive a contact the customer himself in order to establish a dialogue and solve problems.

BENEFITS OF e-CRM

- Convenience
- Improvement in overall quality of customer experience
- Increased profitability

PITFALLS

- Huge money is required to implement e-CRM.
- Results are not according to expectations.
- Results are not according to expectations.
- Sales and Marketing are reluctant to adopt new automated CRM System

CRM AND e-CRM: THE DIFFERENCE

Being able to take care of your customer via the internet, or, customers being able to take care of themselves online: that's the difference between CRM and e-CRM. It implies a myriad of issues, questions, approaches, technologies, and architecture that are different from client/server-based CRM. Many of them are issues general to the Internet. Others are issues related to the certain of applications for the Internet. The third group is related directly to e-CRM and its actual value to business.

MOBILE CRM

One subset of Electronic CRM is Mobile CRM (m-CRM). This is defined as "services that aim at nurturing customer relationships, acquiring or maintaining customers, support marketing, sales or services processes, and use wireless networks as the medium of delivery to the customers. However, since communications is the central aspect of customer relations activities, many opt for the following definition of m-CRM: "communication, either one-way or interactive, which is related to sales, marketing and customer service activities conducted through mobile medium for the purpose of building and maintaining customer relationships between a company and its customer(s).

e-CRM allows customers to access company services from more and more places, since the Internet access points are increasing by the day. m-CRM however, takes this one step further and allows customers or managers to access the systems for instance from a mobile phone or PDA with internet access, resulting in high flexibility. An example of a company that implemented m-CRM is Finnair, who made it possible for their customers to check in for their flights by SMS.[Since m-CRM is not able to provide a complete range of customer relationship activities it should be integrated in the complete CRM system.

IMPLEMENTING AND INTEGRATING CRM SOLUTIONS

Several CRM software packages exist that can help companies in deploying CRM activities. Besides choosing one of these packages, companies can also choose to design and build their own solutions. In order to implement CRM in an effective way, one needs to consider the following factors:

- ❖ Create a customer-based culture in the organization.
- ❖ Adopt customer-based managers to assess satisfaction.
- ❖ Develop an end-to-end process to serve customers.
- ❖ Recommend questions to be asked to help a customer solve a problem.
- ❖ Track all aspects of selling to customers, as well as prospects.

Furthermore, CRM solutions are more effective once they are being implemented in other information systems used by the company. Examples are Transaction Processing System (TPS) to process data real-time, which can than be send to the sales and finance departments in order to recalculate inventory and financial position quick and accurate. Once this information is transferred back to the CRM software and services it could prevent customers from placing an order in the belief that an item is in stock while it is not.

FAILURES

Designing, creating and implementing IT projects has always been risky. Not only because of the amount of money that is involved, but also because of the high chances of failure. However, a positive trend can be seen, indicating that CRM failures dropped from a failure rate of 80% in 1998, to about 40% in 2003.Some of the major issues relating to CRM failure are the following:

- Difficulty in measuring and valuing intangible benefits.
- Failure to identify and focus on specific business problems.
- Lack of active senior management sponsorship.
- Poor user acceptance.
- Trying to automate a poorly defined process.

PRIVACY

The effective and efficient employment of CRM activities cannot go without the remarks of safety and privacy. CRM systems depend on databases in which all kinds of customer data is stored. In general, the following rule applies: the more data, the better the service companies can deliver to individual customers. Some known examples of these problems are conducting credit-card transaction online of the phenomenon known as 'cookies' used on the Internet in order to track someone's information and behavior. The design and the quality of the website are two very important aspects that influence the level of trust customers experience and their willingness of reluctance to do a transaction or leave personal information. As the use of the Internet, electronic CRM solution and even the existence of e-business is rising, so are the efforts in order to further develop the systems used and increase their safety for customers in order to further reap the benefits of their use.

THE CRM PROCESS

The final objective of the CRM process is to originate a powerful new tool for customer retention. The focus of any process is to achieve something we have always wanted, but didn't have the proper resources. The CRM implementation and success rate purely depend upon the process, which includes the future, revenue, customer value, customer retention, customer acquisition and profitability.

A Closed-loop CRM Process:

- **Gathering information:** Initially, gather information about customers. Customer data comes from sources both internal and external to organisation.
- **Perform data aggregation:** It is here that the data is merged and compressed into a complete view of the customer. A large customer data repository is produced.
- **Create "exploration warehouses":** These are extracts of the customer data needed to support specific analyses, such as customer profitability and predictive modelling. Exploration warehouses are the engines for analytical applications that support identification of opportunities and developing strategies.
- **Execution of strategies:** Execute these strategies by developing and launching marketing campaigns across targeted segments of customers. Campaign execution inevitably results in an interaction with customers.

Finally, once a customer interaction takes place and the customer responds, capture that response and "recycle" it to use in the on-going learning, analysis, and refinement process.

Each time the process loop is completed, more is learned about the needs and wants of customers. Marketing improves as understanding of customers is enhanced and the ability to anticipate their needs increases.

CRM IMPLEMENTATION

If you attempt to implement a CRM package without knowing how implementation work, it is likely that you will face problems throughout the project and you could be in for a fall-and a big one at that, it could even be a job termination. The statement of work and the change management processes have to be clear prior to starting the installation.

Forget about planning it in the course of customisation. Figure it out this way. The industry thumb rule is that the implementation services will cost you at least double to triple the price of the software itself. This definitely needs your attention.

It is definitely necessary to have a formal steering committee that consists of the stake holders, program managers, project managers, and so on who would review the project as it moves through the implementation stages.

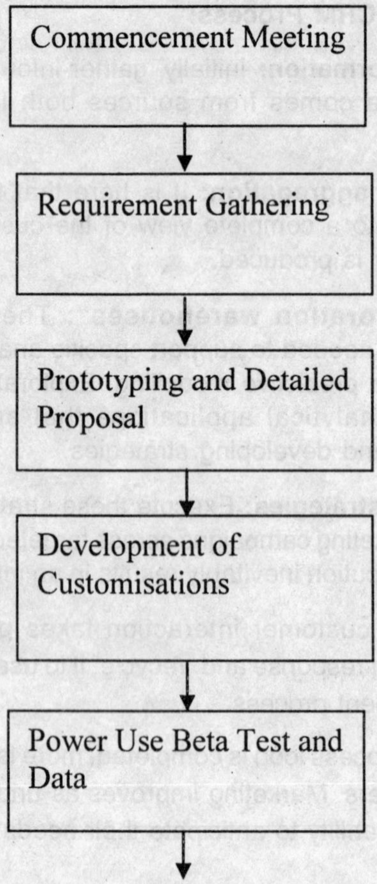

Fig. 6.7. CRM Implementation Steps

MYTHS OF CRM

- ❖ CRM is Primarily about Technology
- ❖ Successful CRM projects are managed by IT
- ❖ "Executive buy-in is the key"
- ❖ "We need to roll this out across the enterprise ASAP"
- ❖ "CRM systems are intuitive?. Users will only need some initial hand holding."

CRM: NOT A PANACEA

- ❖ Not feasible for every market and customers
- ❖ Customers don't want to be committed to every brand/relationship
- ❖ Not feasible for low-involvement, habitual purchasing in

- B2B or B2C
- Some markets/customers may have low "personalization potential".
- The organizational capability to produce a seamless/personalized experience is more difficult to master than a transactional approach.

CRM AND CUSTOMER LOYALTY

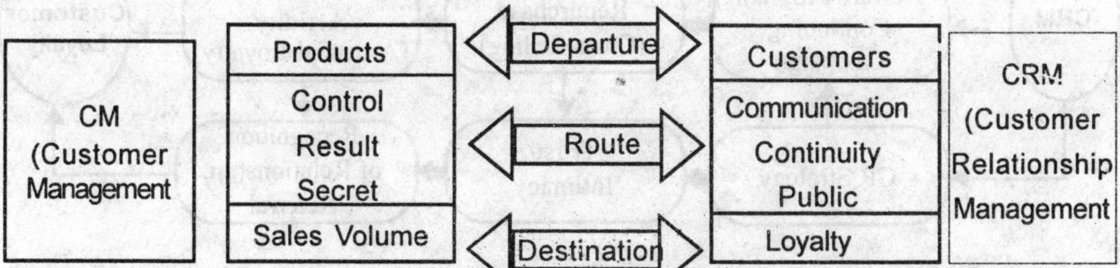

Fig.6.8. CRM and Customer Loyalty

The key to the successful adoption of relationship marketing lies in the building of client loyalty in dynamic business environments. (Morris, 1999)

In a business context loyalty has come to describe a customer's commitmentto do business with a particular organization, purchasing their goods and services , and services and products to friends and associates. (Barnett,2000)

Loyal Customer can mean a consistent source of revenue over a period of many years. However, this loyalty cannot be taken for granted. It will continue only as long as the customer feels they are receiving better value than they would obtain from another supplier.

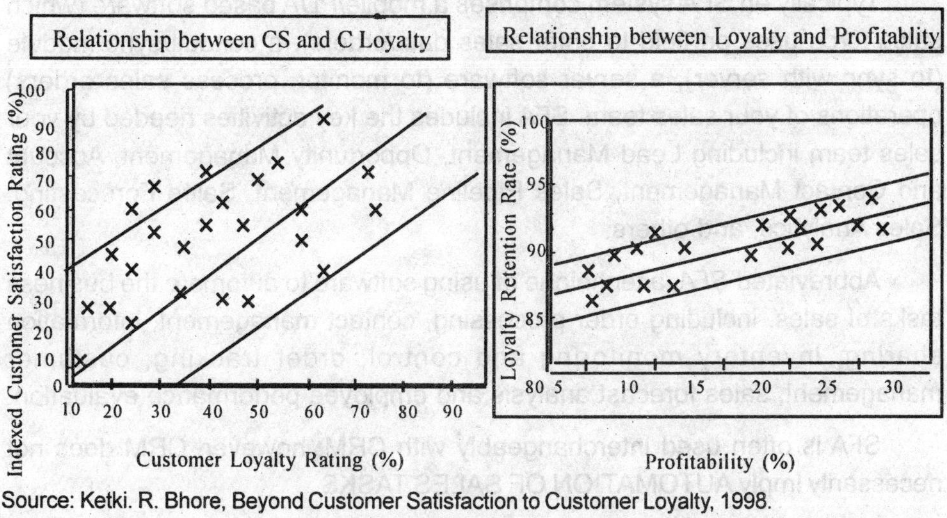

Source: Ketki. R. Bhore, Beyond Customer Satisfaction to Customer Loyalty, 1998.

Fig.6.9. Relationship between CS and CL

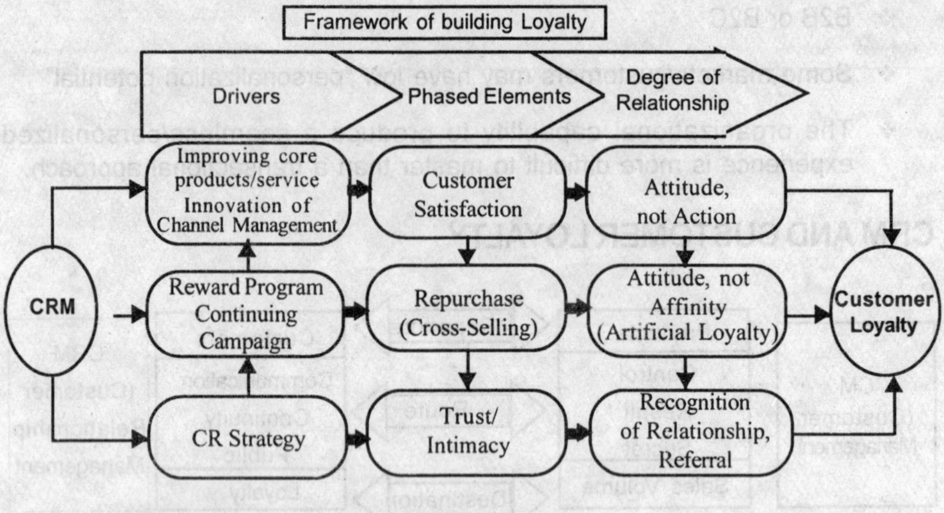

Fig.6.10. CRM AND CL

SALES FORCE AUTOMATION (SFA)

Sales force automation (SFA) makes use of enterprise technologies, such as web access to data, to increase productivity, reduce costs and improve customer service levels. It also allows members of a sales force to have direct access to up-to-date information about all customers, both current and potential.

True SFA automates work flow, like click to call, sales stage duration alerts. Auto routing and updating of sales leads using business rules. It is not just access to data. It is automation of sales processes that eliminate manual work. Just like it says: Automation. Many sales tool vendors use SFA as a feature and this is terribly misleading due to No SFA being inherent in their products.

Typically an SFA system comprises a mobile/PDA based software (which sales force uses on field to enter sales data/orders), a conduit/sync module (to sync with server), a server software (to monitor, process sales orders) operations of your sales team. SFA includes the key activities needed by your sales team including Lead Management, Opportunity Management, Account and Contact Management, Sales Pipeline Management, Sales Forecasting, Sales Analytics, and others.

Abbreviated *SFA*, a technique of using software to automate the business tasks of sales, including order processing, contact management, information sharing, inventory monitoring and control, order tracking, customer management, sales forecast analysis and employee performance evaluation.

SFA is often used interchangeably with CRM; however, CRM does not necessarily imply AUTOMATION OF SALES TASKS.

THE EVER-EVOLVING SFA

- Early 1990's companies with field sales forces were faced with tremendous amounts of customer information.
- Software vendors realized this unmet and unrecognized need.
- Info about customers was kept in "little black books" that left with the sales reps.

THE PROMISE OF SFA

❖ Putting account information directly in the hands of field sales staff.

❖ Making them responsible for it with the promise of.....

❖ Making them more productive.

❖ Synchronize information with the corporate client/server database.

SALES FORCE AUTOMATION TOOL

Sales Process/Activity Management

- Include a sequence of sales activities
- Guide sales reps through each discrete steps in the sales force

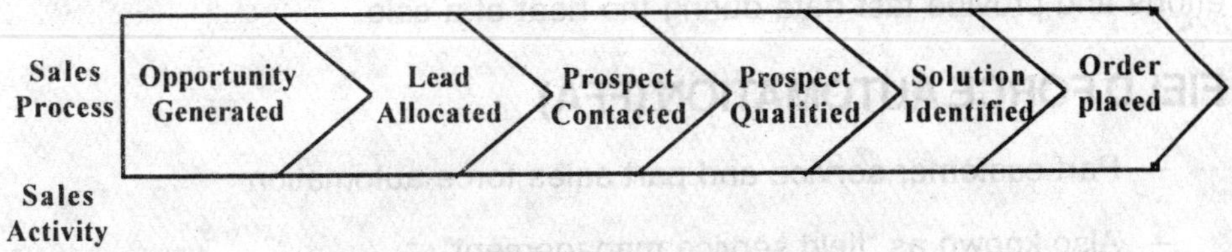

Fig.6.11. Sales process and Sales activity

Offer calendars to assist in the planning of key customer events

❖ Proposal presentations

❖ Product demonstrations

❖ Alarm Reminders

❖ Signal important tasks

❖ Generate documents as they are needed

❖ Make decisions based on the user's input

Lead Management: Also known as "opportunity management" and

"pipeline management"

- ❖ Track customer account history
- ❖ Monitor leads
- ❖ Generate next steps and
- ❖ Refine selling efforts online
- ❖ Allows sales management to automatically distribute client leads to a field or telemarketing rep based on the area's product knowledge or territory

Configuration Support: Automatically factors in complex customer attributes and requirements to build a solution from scratch among the companies who may use such tools

- Computer technology vendors
- Appliance manufacturers
- Telephone companies

KNOWLEDGE MANAGEMENT

Many CRM tools geared to SFA include functions specific to accessing and conversing on a range of corporate documentation to supplement sales efforts and provide fast data during the heat of a sale.

FIELD FORCE AUTOMATION (FFA)

- Part customer service and part sales force automation
- Also known as "field service management"
- Field technicians receive dispatch orders via their PDAs, pagers, and cell phones
- Making use of these same devices during the actual repair.

AN SFA CHECKLIST FOR SUCCESS

- ❖ Understand how SFA will help, and enlist salesperson stakeholder ship at the beginning
  - Initial requirements gathering
  - Rollout tool
- ❖ Communicate the value to the sales force up Front

– Invest in-and enforce-training.

❖ Beware of inherent sales processes packaged into SFA tools

– Customize YOUR sales process

❖ Understand the infrastructure necessary to support wireless technologies

❖ Let SFA use affect sales compensation.

❖ Change hiring practices and job role descriptions to include use of CRM

ELBEE TO GO EXPRESS WITH SFA - CASE STUDY-X

Elbee Express services, a Mumbai based Express Courier company has operations in about eleven thousand six hundred locations in India with one hundred forty five offices. The company has tied up with various partners internationally to cater the foreign customers

With the increasing scale of business, Elbee has deployed IT applications to cater to the demand. The implementation of e-TABS in 2006 was to track the consignment during transit through the consignment number. The same service was subsequently made available through SMS.

Following on the same lines of improving customer service through IT, Elbee has signed up with Airtel Enterprise Services to roll out SFA (Sales Force Automation Application) for Pick-up and Delivery Processes. The SFA will be implemented in about a month and a half. It is under the POC stage. "The SFA application will enhance delivery information by four to five hours," said Shirish Gariba, VP, IT and e-Commerce. Going by the present practice, the consignment delivery information is available to the customer only after the delivery employee files the information by the end of the day".

"Why should we let the customer wait for that extra four to five hours", stresses Gariba. The companies delivering consignments to their customers' demands payment on the basis of the time interval between getting the order and the date of delivery. The SFA will help our commercial customers in this regard.

"Elbee wants to create a niche for the distribution of securitized products like Debit Cards, Credit Cards, Bank Cheque books etc. Since SFA will float real time information about consignment delivery, it will help us focus on the same."

QUESTIONS

1. How SFA will change the way a delivery employee works
2. How Elbee Express can integrate its operations globally through SFA

(Adapted from the source: www.biztec2.in.com)

CHECK YOUR PROGRESS

(A) Fill in the Blanks

(i) SFA stands for..................................

(ii) CRS stands for ....

(iii) CIM atands for ....

LET US SUM UP

Relationships are built on value and service. Value for the customer is a result of increased global competition that acts as an unyielding pressure on prices. The consumer receives value from manufacturers operating huge factories and from retailers providing an infinite variety of goods. Yet, service has suffered as individual production facilities and stores have been replaced in this industry trend toward mergers with multiple factories and distribution sites. Service is part of a corporate culture and is the other characteristic of global competition. It is exercised for every transaction, large or small, to every customer. Those who render it will find they keep their customers.

CRM is a comprehensive approach for creating, maintaining and expanding customer relationships.

Consumer Relationship System (CRS) covers aspects of a company's dealing with customers handled by the Consumer Affairs and Customer Relations contact centers within a company. Representatives handle in-bound contact from anonymous consumers and customers. Early warnings can be issued regarding product issues (e.g. item recalls) and current consumer sentiment can be tracked (voice of the customer).

Sales force automation (SFA) makes use of enterprise technologies, such as web access to data, to increase productivity, reduce costs and improve customer service levels. It also allows members of a sales force to have direct access to up to date information about all customers, both current and potential.

True SFA automates work flow, like click to call, sales stage duration alerts. Auto routing and updating of sales leads using business rules. It is not just access to data. It is automation of sales processes that eliminate manual work. Just like it says: Automation. Many sales tool vendors use SFA as a feature and this is terribly misleading due to NO SFA being inherent in their products.

Typically an SFA system comprises a mobile/PDA based software (which sales force uses on field to enter sales data/orders), a conduit/sync module (to sync with server), a server software (to monitor, process sales orders) operations of your sales team. SFA includes the key activities needed by your sales team including Lead Management, Opportunity Management, Account and Contact Management, Sales Pipeline Management, Sales Forecasting, Sales Analytics, and others.

LESSON END ACTIVITY

Find out an Indian company which implemented SFA system and track the performance of that company because of SFA.

KEY WORDS

Relationship marketing

It is establishing, developing, and maintaining successful relational long-term exchanges between organizations and ultimate customers.

Transaction selling

Customers are sold to and not contacted again

Relationship selling

The seller contacts customers after the purchase to determine if they are satisfied and have future need

Partnering

The seller works continually to improve its customers' operations, sales, and profits

Consultative Selling

The process of helping the customer achieve strategic short and long-term goals through the use of the seller's goods and/or services

CRM

It is a comprehensive approach for creating, maintaining and expanding customer relationships.

Mobile CRM

One subset of Electronic CRM is Mobile CRM (m-CRM). This is defined as "services that aim at nurturing customer relationships, acquiring or maintaining customers, support marketing, sales or services processes, and use wireless networks as the medium of delivery to the customers.

Customer Interaction Management (CIM)

Interaction plays a lead role in building customer relationships. CIM constitutes the customer relationship technologies with additions of technology-based interactive solutions. The interactive channels that are currently available enable very effective customer interactive communications, which leads to CIM, which further leads to relationship building.

Sales Force Automation (SFA)

A technique of using softwareto automate the business tasks of sales, including order processing, contact management, information sharing, inventory monitoring and control, order tracking, customer management, sales forecast analysis and employee performance evaluation.

REVIEW QUESTIONS

1. Write short note on "Relationship Marketing".
2. Define CRM.
3. List out the importance of CRM.
4. What are the marketing applications of CRM?
5. Define Operational CRM.
6. Define Analytical CRM.
7. Define Collaborative CRM.
8. What is sales intelligence CRM?
9. What do you understand by Social CRM?
10. Explain briefly the concept of CIM.

11. Differentiate between customer retention and CRM.
12. What do you understand by e-CRM?
13. Explain the benefits of e-CRM?
14. What are the pitfalls of e-CRM?
15. List out the difference between CRM and e-CRM.
16. What is Mobile CRM?
17. What are the Myths of CRM?
18. Write a short note on Online decision making.
19. Explain the different approaches to CRM.
20. Elaborate the relationship between CLV & CRM.
21. What are the emerging concepts of CRM? Explain.
22. Explain the various applications of CRM.
23. Describe the different types of CRM.
24. Explain the process of building CRM.
25. Elucidate different strategies of CRM.
26. Explain the concept of e-CRM and different strategies.
27. Explain CRM process and its implementation.
28. Explain in detail online decision making process.
29. What do you understand by SFA. Explain various SFA tools.
30. How SFA can enhance sales rep efficiency? Explain.

CHECK YOUR PROGRESS: MODEL ANSWER

(A)

(i) Sales Force Automation

(ii) Customer Relationship System

(iii) Customer Interaction Management

SUGGESTED READINGS

1. Bholanath Dutta: *Marketing Management*, 2nd Edition, Parshva Publisher, New Delhi, 2010.

2. Bholanath Dutta: *Consumer Behaviour*, Ist Edition, Kalyani Publisher, 2010.

☒ ☒ ☒